Yearbook of Chinese Theology 2018

Yearbook of Chinese Theology

Editor-in-Chief

Paulos Z. Huang (*School of Philosophy at Beijing Normal University and International Journal of Sino-Western Studies*)

Editorial Board

Abraham Chen (*Nanjing Theological Seminary, China*)
Lauren Pfister (*Baptist University of Hong Kong*)
Xiangchen Sun (*Fudan University, Shanghai, China*)
Philip L. Wickeri (*Graduate Theological Union, Berkely, CA, USA*)
Huilin Yang (*Renmin University of China*)
Zhigang Zhang (*Peking University, Beijing, China*)
Xinping Zhuo (*Chinese Academy of Social Sciences, Beijing, China*)
Johanna Kettunen-Huang (*Helsinki, Finland*)

VOLUME 4

The titles published in this series are listed at *brill.com/yct*

Yearbook of Chinese Theology 2018

Edited by

Paulos Z. Huang

Guest Editors for This Volume

Xiaofeng Tang
Donghua Zhu

BRILL

LEIDEN | BOSTON

The yearbook has been indexed in Book Citation Index (BCI)

Typeface for the Latin, Greek, and Cyrillic scripts: "Brill". See and download: brill.com/brill-typeface.

ISSN 2352-7684
ISBN 978-90-04-38374-6 (hardback)
ISBN 978-90-04-38497-2 (e-book)

Copyright 2019 by Koninklijke Brill NV, Leiden, The Netherlands.
Koninklijke Brill NV incorporates the imprints Brill, Brill Hes & De Graaf, Brill Nijhoff, Brill Rodopi, Brill Sense, Hotei Publishing, mentis Verlag, Verlag Ferdinand Schöningh and Wilhelm Fink Verlag.
All rights reserved. No part of this publication may be reproduced, translated, stored in a retrieval system, or transmitted in any form or by any means, electronic, mechanical, photocopying, recording or otherwise, without prior written permission from the publisher.
Authorization to photocopy items for internal or personal use is granted by Koninklijke Brill NV provided that the appropriate fees are paid directly to The Copyright Clearance Center, 222 Rosewood Drive, Suite 910, Danvers, MA 01923, USA. Fees are subject to change.

This book is printed on acid-free paper and produced in a sustainable manner.

Contents

Editorial   VII
   Paulos Huang and Donghua Zhu
List of Contributors   XXII

PART 1
Systematic Theology and Chinese Humanities

1. The Names of God in the Tang Jingjiao Document *Yishen Lun* (*A Discourse on God*)   3
   David Tam

2. The Unique Features of Chanting in Jingjiao Liturgy, as Revealed in Unearthed Jingjiao Documents   22
   Chengyong Ge, translated by D. Tam

PART 2
Practical Theology in Chinese Context

3. The Multiple Identities of the Nestorian Monk Mar Alopen: A Discussion on Diplomacy and Politics   37
   Daniel H.N. Yeung

4. The Ethic of Love in Ancient Judaism and Early *Jingjiao* and Its Impact on Ancient China's Religious Narrative   50
   Melville Y. Stewart

PART 3
Church History in China

5. The Church of the East in China (Jingjiao)   71
   Mar Aprem Metropolitan

6   Fangshan Cross Temple (房山十字寺) in China: Overview, Analysis and Hypotheses   82
    Xiaofeng Tang and Yingying Zhang

PART 4
Biblical and Scriptural Studies

7   Yishu (Jesu) Worship in Xiapu Manichaean Manuscripts   97
    Fuxue Yang and Wengjing Xue

8   Spirit in *Atrahasis*   113
    Donald Wang

PART 5
Comparative Religious and Cultural Studies

9   A Comparative Perspective on Two Yelikewen Official Families in the Yuan Dynasty   125
    Xiaoping Yin

10 From "Shiyuan 十願" (Ten Vows) to "Shijie 十誡" (Ten Commandments): Importance of Absent Elements in Translation as Case Study of Inculturation of Christianity during the early Tang Dynasty (7th century)   143
    Zhu Li-Layec

PART 6
A Review and Academic Report

11 Review of the Studies on the Research History of Authenticity of *The Discourse on Monotheism* and *The Jesus Messiah Sutra* in Kyou-shooku   155
    Lanping Wang and Qiaosui Zhang

Index   163

EDITORIAL

Was Nestorius Really a Heretic? An Exploration of Luther's Comments on Nestorius

Paulos Huang and Donghua Zhu

For a very long time, Jingjiao (the Church of the East) in Tang Dynasty China has been considered as a heresy derived from Nestorius of Syria (d. *ca.* 451). However, recent research has raised two challenges to the above conclusion. On the one hand, Nestorius' theology was not so important for the discussions of Jingjiao, although he was honored by the Church of the East as a teacher and saint. On the other hand, Nestorius was not perhaps as heretic as believed by later people, for he was regarded as the founder of the "Nestorian heresy" that insisted Christ consisted of two completely separate persons, one human and one divine.[1] In the present article we are going to explore the second issue whether Nestorius really was a heretic or not, based on Martin Luther's comments.

The basic opinion of Luther on Nestorius is that Nestorius held a correct faith in Jesus Christ as one person (not two persons) in two natures (true man and true God), but that he made mistakes in expressing himself. For Nestorius' belief was a correct doctrine of Christology following Christian orthodoxy from ancient times until today. Luther says, "Nestorius holds to no more than one Christ, so he could not have taken Christ to be two persons; otherwise, he would indeed have had to say both yes and no against himself in the same article."[2]

However, Nestorius was condemned as heretic. Why? Luther says,

> What was it that was condemned about Nestorius and why was this third principal council convoked against him if he did not teach otherwise than that Christ is true God and true man, and one single Christ, not two Christs, that is, one person in two natures – as we all believe and as all Christendom has believed from the beginning?[3]

---

[1] LW (*Luther Works*, American Edition, published by Concordia Publishing House and Fortress Press in 55 volumes) 41, 94, footnote 264.

[2] LW 41, 97.

[3] LW 41, 97.

Whether the accusers' arguments were unintentional mistakes, or intentionally framed confusions, Nestorius had problems and the question was which real errors could be ascribed to him. Luther believed that the situation arose due to Nestorius' own faults and the errors of his accuser. He felt Nestorius was condemned mainly on the following issues.

1 Nestorius was Condemned because of His and His Accusers' Personalities

Based on the *Historia Triparita*, Book XII, chapter 4,[4] Luther tried to find the reason of Nestorius' and his accusers' problems within their personalities. After important church fathers and bishops were gone, e.g., St. Ambrose, St. Martin, St. Jerome, St. Augustine, St. Hilary, and St. Eusebius, the emperor Theodosius II did not want to choose a bishop from the priests or clergy of the city Constantinople. The main reason seems to have been that the people there were considered proud, ambitious, and unruly, causing nothing but trouble. Even St. John Chrysostom was such a person. Thus, Nestorius from Antioch was appointed patriarch and bishop of Constantinople, and the emperor sent him to participate in the Ephesus Council (431). Luther says, Nestorius was not only a man of strict and chaste life, with a pleasing voice, eloquent, and outspoken foe of all heretics;[5] but also "a proud and unlearned man, and when he became such a great bishop and patriarch he supposed that he should be looked upon as the most learned man on earth, needing neither to read the books of his predecessors and of other people, nor to learn their way of speaking about these things. Instead, since he was eloquent and endowed with a good voice, he wanted to be a self-made doctor or master, and no matter how he expressed it or pronounced something, it should be accounted correct."[6] It is clear that for Luther Nestorius had so many problems in his personality to annoy other people.

Contrary to Augustine or Ambrose, the accusers of Nestorius tried their best to put words in Nestorius' mouth so that they could punish such a proud and unlearned man whom they displeased.[7] For example, Nestorius "encountered

---

4 MPL 69, 1204-1207; PNF2 (*The Nicene and Post-Nicene Fathers of the Christian Church*, First Series: edited by Philipp Schaff. Second Series: edited by Philip Schaff and H. Wace, New York, 1886-1900) 2, 169-172.
5 LW 41, 94.
6 LW 41, 97-98.
7 LW 41, 97: "Thus, the pope and his followers put the words into Nestorius' mouth that he viewed Christ as a mere man and not also as God, and that he took Christ to be two per-

other proud bishops, whom his pride displeased, especially Cyril of Alexandria; for there was no Augustine or Ambrose at hand."[8] It is a pity Nestorius encountered these accusers, one can only imagine the fate of Nestorius.

The accusers of Nestorius, as according to papal decretals and papal writers, believed Nestorius denied the divinity of Christ and regarded Christ as no more than a mere man. That Nestorius taught that Christ was first born of Mary as mere man and then led such a holy life that the Godhead merged with him, and Jesus Christ thus became God.[9] Luther says, such accusations were not in accordance with Nestorius' actual teachings, and that Nestorius taught Christ was one person in two natures (true God and true man), which is accordance with the doctrine that all Christendom believed from the beginning.[10] It was therefore a pity that Nestorius had been discredited by these accusations and punished for words he did not say or mean

Luther saw Nestorius as a proud and unlearned man, who pretended to be the most learned on earth and acting as a great bishop and patriarch needing neither to read nor to learn from his predecessors and other people. And the current pope and his followers were not so good as those church fathers who had already passed away. Thus, intentional confusions or unintentional mistakes happened between Nestorius and his accusers. In Luther's words, "the proud, unlearned bishop [Nestorius] instigated a bad Greek quarrel, or as the Roman Cicero said of the Greeks, 'A controversy has long disturbed the little Greeks, who are fonder of argument that of truth.'"[11] The personalities of Nestorius and his accusers played an important role in condemning him.[12]

---

sons or two Christs." LW 41, 98. This was not only from the histories, but also from the very words and documents of the popes and their writers, such as *Decreti Secunda Pars*, causa XXIV, ques. 3, C. XXXIX. CIC 1, 1005.

8   LW 41, 98.
9   See, *Decreti Tertia Pars, De Consecratione,* dist. V. C. XXXIX. CIC (*Corpus Iuris Canonici*, edited by E. Friedberg, Graz, 1955) 1, 1423; MPL (*Patrologia, Series Latina,* 221 vols. in 222, edited by J. P. Migne, Paris, 1844-1904) 187, 957. See also Crabbe (quoted in WA 50, 583, n.c.). LW 41, 96.
10 LW 41, 96-97.
11 In *De Oratione*, I, 11: "*Iam diu torquet controversia verbi homines graeculos contentionis cupidiores quam veritatis.*" See E. W. Sutton and H. Rackham (trans.), *Cicero: De Oratione, Book I and II* ("The Loeb Classical Library" [2 vols.; Cambridge: Harvard University Press, 1942], I, 36.)
12 LW 41, 99-100.

2 Nestorius was Condemned because of His Language, Speech and Expression

Nestorius did not consider Jesus Christ to be two persons, but Cyril of Alexandria and other bishops, who were displeased with Nestorius, could speak with persuading rhetoric. Finally, they succeeded in making church leaders and other common Christians believe that Nestorius was a heretic even though he was not. In fact, Luther says, "Nestorius had learned in the church of Antioch that Christ was true God born of the Father in eternity, as the Nicene council had defended, and afterward born a true man of the Virgin Mary. Nestorius did not question these two items; he himself had preached them for a long time. Indeed, he had even persecuted the Arians at the Council of Nicaea, condemning them so vehemently that he had also instigated many murders and much bloodshed, so staunchly did he regard Christ as true God and man."[13]

For example, Nestorius did not intend to regard Christ only as a mere man, but his words gave this impression to ordinary Christians. Luther said that Nestorius was a very peculiar saint and an injudicious man, "for after he concedes that God and man are united and fused into one person, he can in no way deny that the *idiomata*[14] of the two natures should also be united and fused."[15] Nestorius' meaning "was that Christ, in his divinity, was immortal; but he lacked the intelligence to express this thought properly."[16]

Nestorius "adheres faithfully to Christ as one person in two natures, but his ignorance does not know what and how he is speaking, like one who does not quite know how to speak of such things, but still wants to speak as an expert."[17]

Thus, Nestorius' skill of expression and rhetoric, or lack thereof, caused him much trouble.

3 Nestorius was Condemned because of Logic Problem

Nestorius' folly is also thought to lie in his logic of expression. Nestorius said 'yes' and 'no' to the same thing at the same time. He accepts the premise, but he denied the conclusion. Luther says,

---

13 LW 41, 98.
14 *Idioma* means property, attribute, features, characteristics, nature, etc.
15 LW 41, 101.
16 LW 41, 102.
17 LW 41, 98.

"Thus his folly is exactly that against which one teaches in the schools, 'One who admits the premise of a good conclusion cannot deny the conclusion'.[18] In German we would say, 'If the one is true, the other must also be true; if the second is not true, then the first is not true either.'"[19]

"Here you see Nestorius' logic which admits a 'premise' and denies the 'conclusion' and thus also be true in any real conclusion or consequence. On the other hand, if the last is false, the first must also be false. They not only admit but absolutely insist that good works atone for sin; yet they condemn that which follows, that such works are not good, indeed, are nothing and no works, just as this conclusion is irrefutably: *Qui docet id quod non est, docet nihil*, 'He who teaches what is not, teaches as much as nothing.' One may likewise say of faith, 'He who teaches a faith that does not justify alone and without good works teaches as much as no faith at all.' For a faith that justifies with or by good works is nothing at all."[20]

Thus, for Luther, it is clear that Nestorius held the correct doctrine concerning Jesus Christ as one person with two natures, but he had made mistakes in expressions of logic.

4   Nestorius was Condemned because of the Problem of Mary as the Mother of God (*Theotokos*)

Nestorius did not correctly express himself concerning the problem of *Theotokos*, bearer of God,[21] *i.e.*, Mary as the Mother of God. In fact, Nestorius began to defend his priest Anastasius,[22] who had preached that one should not call the holy Virgin the mother of God, for she was human and she could therefore not give birth to God.[23]

As a basis, Nestorius said that Jesus Christ receives his divine *idioma* from Godhead the Father, and his human *idioma* from Mary. Such an expressions should have been in accordance with the traditional Christian orthodoxy gen-

---

18   "*Qui concedit antecedens bonae consequentiae, non potest negare consequens*," a proposition that appears in various Roman works; see *De Oratione*, II, 53, in Sutton and Rackham (trans.), *op. cit.*, II, 357. Cf. also *C.R.* (*Corpus Reformatorum*, edited by C.G. Bretschneider and H. F. Bindseil, Halle/Saale, 1834-1860) 13, 617, 627.

19   *Ist eines war, so muss das ander aruch war sein, ist das andere nicht war, soi st das erst auch nicht war*. LW 41, 101-102.

20   LW 41, 112.

21   *Historia Tripartita*, XII, 5. *MPL* 69, 1208a; *PNF2* 2, 172.

22   Anastasius was a presbyter in Constantinople, and he was sympathetic to Nestorius' cause. He is mentioned only by Socrates in the *Historia Tripartita*, VII, 2.

23   LW 41, 95.

erally. But in his detailed analysis, according to Luther, Nestorius did not express himself correctly.

Nestorius denied Mary as the Mother of God, and only called Mary the Mother of Christ, when he tried to make a distinction between God and Christ. Luther says,

> Moreover, he [Nestorius] also conceded that Christ, God's Son, was born of the Virgin Mary into his humanity, not into his divinity, which we and all Christians also say. But here is where the problem arose: he did not want Mary to be called the mother of God because of this, since Christ did not derive his divinity, or, to express it plainly, since Christ did not derive his divinity from her as he did his humanity. There we have the entire bone of contention: God cannot be born of a human being or have his divine nature from one [man]; and a human being cannot bear God or impart the divine nature to God.[24]

Since Nestorius "insisted on the literal meaning of the words, 'God born of Mary,' and he interpreted 'born' according to grammar or philosophy, as though it meant to obtain divine nature from the one who bore him, and the *Tripartita* also says that he viewed these words as an abomination – as we, and all Christians (if that were to be the sense of these words), do too."[25]

Of course, within the Trinity the Godhead Father differs from the Son Christ, and logically Mary as a person with flesh body is only the mother of the Son Jesus Christ. But as a true man and true God, Jesus the man cannot be separated from Christ the God. Within the nature of Jesus Christ, the divine and human natures are united rather than separated. Thus, if Mary was considered only as the mother of Jesus rather than the mother of God, the two natures of Jesus Christ would be separated rather than united. In fact, the Reformed Protestants believe quite similarly to Nestorians on this issue of Mary as the Mother of God.[26]

Nestorius was condemned at the Ephesus council (431), because he failed to see what he was denying or what he was saying. Although Nestorius admitted Christ is God and man in one person, he did not call the Virgin Mary God's mother, because Christ's divinity does not come from his mother Mary. Luther says, "This was rightly condemned in the council, and ought to be condemned.

---

24 LW 41, 98.
25 LW 41, 98.
26 Luther offers also many biblical textual evidences to prove that the Virgin Mary should be called as the mother of God, e.g., Luke 1:32, 1:43, 2:11, Galatians 4:4, I Corinthians 2:8, Acts 20:28, Philippians 2:6-7, etc., Cf. LW 41, 105-106.

And although Nestorius has a correct view on one point of the principal matter, that Christ is God and man, one should nevertheless not tolerate the other point or mode of expression, that God was not born of Mary and was not crucified by Jews just as one should not tolerate the sophists (who declares very correctly that a mother cannot bear or impart a child's soul) when he says that a child is not the mother's natural child and a mother is not the child's natural mother."[27] "For whoever admits that a mother bore a child who has body and soul should admit and believe that the mother has borne the whole child and is the child's true mother, even though she is not the mother of the soul; otherwise, it would follow that no woman is the mother of any child, and the fourth commandment, 'Honor thy father and thy mother,' would have to be abolished. Thus, it should also be said that Mary is the true natural mother of the child called Jesus Christ, and that she is the true mother of God and bearer of God, and whatever else can be said of children's mothers, such as sucking, bathing, feeding – that Mary suckled God, rocked God to sleep, prepared broth and soup for God, etc. For God and man are one person, one Christ, one Son, one Jesus, not two Christs, not two Sons, not two Jesuses; just as your son is not two sons, two Johns, two cobblers, even though he has two natures, body and soul, the body from you, the soul from God alone."[28]

Furthermore, it is interesting to compare Nestorius' understanding of Virgin Mary with theRoman Catholic Church and Reformed Protestants. For Roman Catholics, Mary is the Mother of God, and she has no original sin. As an opinion, this has become the extreme opposite of Nestorius, in that the human nature of Mary is ignored. Such an understanding is in fact also heretic to Luther and Lutheran tradition. Luther considers Mary as the Mother of God, but she was a human with original sin. This opinion holds in the middle ground between of Nestorius and Roman Catholics.

In summary, we find that in his comments to *Ephesus Council* of 431 (1539), Martin Luther has made a quite detailed analysis on Nestorius' doctrine through an analysis on the following three issues: 1) When the doctrine of Nestorius was condemned at the Ephesus Council as a heresy, this was because one of the main accusers Cyril of Alexander declared that Nestorius viewed Jesus Christ as two persons. This was not in line with Nestorius' own words. 2) Nestorius did not correctly express himself in speech and in logic when he dealt with the problem of Mary as the Mother of God. 3) For Luther, Nestorius'

---

27 LW 41, 99.
28 LW 41, 100.

error was that he did not admit a *communatio idiomatum*,²⁹ and this issue was discussed again from many angles.

5 The Aforementioned Issues Derive from Nestorius' Error Not to Admit a *Communatio Idiomatum*

Luther stated that Nestorius' error did not lie in believing that Christ was a pure man, or that he considered him as two separate persons. On the contrary, Nestorius did confess to the divine and human natures within the one person of Jesus Christ. Nestorius' main error, according to Luther was that he did not admit a *communicatio idomatum*, i.e., "communication of the properties". This was "a doctrine propounded by scholastic theology, which states that while the two natures were separated in Christ, the attributes of the one may be predicated by the other, in view of their union in Christ."³⁰ Luther interpreted this doctrine in the context of his own theology.³¹

For Luther, *idioma* could be similar to properties and "means that which is inherent in a nature or is its attribute", and "for *idioma* in Greek, *proprium* in Latin, is a thing – let us for the time being, call it an attribute."³²

Nestorius also made a distinction between human and divine *idioma*. Luther defines that *idiomata naturae humane* (attributes of human nature) "such as dying, suffering, weeping, speaking, laughing, eating, drinking, sleeping, sorrowing, rejoicing, being born, having a mother, suckling the breast, walking, standing, working, sitting, lying down, and other things of that kind, which are called *idiomata naturae humane*, that is, qualities that belong to man by nature, which he can and must do or even suffer."³³ And an *idioma deitatis* is "an attribute of divine nature", and "it is immortal, omnipotent, infinite, not born, does not eat, drink, sleep, stand, walk, sorrow, weep."³⁴

For Nestorius, to be God is an immeasurably different thing than to be man, and this means that the *idiomata* of the two natures cannot coincide.³⁵ Luther offers an imagined dialogue Nestorius could have had.

---

29 This means "communication of the properties".
30 LW 41, 100, footnote 277.
31 Cf. Paul Althaus, *Die Theologie Martin Luthers* (Gütersloh, 1962), 160-174.
32 LW 41, 100.
33 LW 41, 100.
34 LW 41, 101.
35 LW 41, 101.

> Now if I were to preach, 'Jesus, the carpenter of Nazareth (for the gospels call him 'carpenter's son' [Matt. 13:55]) is walking over there down the street, fetching his mother a jug of water and a penny's worth of bread so that he might eat and drink with his mother, and the same carpenter, Jesus, is the very true God in one person,' Nestorius would grant me that and say that this is true. But if I were to say, 'There goes God down the street, fetching water and bread so that he might eat and drink with his mother,' Nestorius would not grant me this, but says, 'To fetch water, to buy bread, to have a mother, to eat and drink with here, are *idiomata* or attributes of human and not of divine nature.' And again, if I say, 'God was crucified by Jews,' he says, 'No! For crucifixion and death are *idiomata* or attributes not of divine but of human nature.'[36]

Such a speech could give Christians the impression that Nestorius considered Christ as a mere man and separated the persons, although Nestorius did not intend to do so. But Nestorius "simultaneously seriously took Christ to be God and man in one person and yet declined to ascribe the *idiomata* of the natures to the same person of Christ. He wants to hold to the truth of the first, but what follows from the first should not be true."[37]

Although Luther did not make a clear definition of *communication*, it seems that human *idiomata* and divine *idiomata* are united rather than separated within one person of Jesus Christ. Luther says,

> We Christians must ascribe all the *idiomata* of the two natures of Christ, both persons, equally to him. Consequently Christ is God and man in one person because whatever is said of him as Christ must also be said of him as God, namely, Christ has died, and Christ is God; therefore God died – not the separated God, but God united with humanity. For about the separated God both statements, namely, that Christ is God and that God died, are false; both are false, for then God is not man. If it seems strange to Nestorius that God dies, he should think it equally strange that God becomes man; for thereby the immortal God becomes that which must die, suffer, and have all human *idiomata*. Otherwise, what would that human *idiomata*? It would be a phantom, as the Manichaeans had taught earlier. On the other hand, whatever is said of God must also be ascribed to the man, namely, God created the world and is almighty: the man Christ is God, therefore the man Christ created the world and is almighty.

---

36 LW 41, 101.
37 LW 41, 102-103.

> The reason for this is that since God and man have become one person, it follows that this person bears the *idiomata* of both natures.[38]

If only a man rather than God died for us, we are lost; "but if God's death and a dead God lie in the balance, his side goes down and ours goes up like a light and empty scale."[39] In fact, "God in his own nature cannot die; but now that God and man are united in one person, it is called God's death when the man dies who is one substance or one person with God."[40]

Luther says, "He who denies the *idiomata* or attributes of a nature can be said to deny the substance or nature itself."[41] Thus, the verdict should have been: "Although Nestorius confesses that Christ, true God and true man, is one person, but does not ascribe the *idiomata* of human nature to the same divine person of Christ, he is in error, just as much as if he denied the nature itself."[42]

Thus, the Ephesus council (431) did not establish any new aspect of faith, it only defended the old faith against the new notion by Nestorius.

It is necessary to mention another extreme opposite of Eutyches (*ca.* 378-454), who was archimandrite of a large monastery at Constantinople and was condemned in the Fourth Principal Chalcedon council (451) for teaching a contradictory heresy similar to Nestorius. They taught that "Christ is two yet one person or nature, and again, that there are two natures and yet only one nature in Christ, surely do contradict each other; indeed, each one contradicts himself."[43] Nestorius does not want to give the *idiomata* of humanity to the divinity of Christ, even though he maintains that Christ is God and man. Eutyches, on the other hand, does not want to give the *idiomata* of divinity to humanity, though he also maintains that Christ is true God and true man.[44]

Luther sums up as follows: "whoever confesses the two natures in Christ, God and man, must also ascribe the *idiomata* of both to the person; for to be God and man means nothing if they do not share their *idiomata*. That is why both Nestorius and Eutyches were rightfully condemned because of their error and reason."[45]

---

38 LW 41, 103.
39 LW 41, 103.
40 LW 41, 104.
41 LW 41, 104.
42 LW 41, 104.
43 LW 41, 108.
44 LW 41, 109.
45 LW 41, 109.

6 Luther and Nestorius in Retrospect

In order to clarify the middle ground Luther took between Nestorius and the Roman Catholics, it is necessary to include parenthetical reference to modern studies, to reflect on precisely how Luther's sympathetic criticism provided a basis for the rediscovery of Nestorius' contribution to the two-nature Christology. In his comprehensive and instructive historical treatment of church history, Philip Schaff pointed out that Luther helped to establish a new attitude toward Nestorius: "For his sad fate and his upright character, Nestorius, after having been long abhorred, has in modern times, since Luther, found much sympathy; while Cyril by his violent conduct has incurred much censure."[46] According to Luther, Nestorius held the correct faith in Jesus Christ as one person in two natures (true man and true God). Nestorius really did not teach more than one Christ, hence he could not regard Christ as two persons; otherwise he would have contradicted himself in the same article.

So from the perspective of another modern historian Friedrich Loofs, Luther really did justice to Nestorius to a very high degree. In scholarship, Nestorius' doctrine has been considered more favourable even before the discovery of his *Bazaar of Heraclides*. Loofs was even able to say boldly that "if Nestorius had lived in the time of the council of Chalcedon, he would possibly have become a pillar of orthodoxy."[47]

With the discovery of the Syriac MS of *Bazaar of Heraclides*[48] at the end of 19th century, Scholars such as Friedrich Loofs, R. Seeberg, R.V. Sellers, E. Schwarz and J. F. Bethune-Baker re-examined the teaching of Nestorius, and tried to show that Nestorius was not "Nestorian." It must surely be true that Nestorius was never fully a "Nestorian," because, just as Bethune-Baker pointed out, Nestorius persistently maintained that there are two natures in the one Christ, and forcibly refuted the idea that there are two persons.[49]

> It is right for us to say," Nestorius said in his defense in *Bazaar of Heraclides*, "that the two natures unconfused I confess to be one Christ. In one

---

[46] Philip Schaff, *History of the Christian Church, Volume III: Nicene and Post-Nicene Christianity, AD 311-600* (New York: Charles Scribner's Sons, 1908), 729.

[47] Friedrich Loofs, *Nestorius and his place in the history of Christian doctrine* (Kessinger Publishing, 2004), 21.

[48] The title of the Greek version may have been *Treatise of Heraclides* while the Syriac version was *Bazaar of Heraclides*.

[49] James Bethune-Baker, *Nestorius and His Teaching: A Fresh Examination of the Evidence* (Cambridge University Press, 1908), 83-84.

nature, i.e., the Godhead, He was born of God the Father, and in the other, i.e. the manhood, of the holy Virgin.⁵⁰

Given the primary concern of Nestorius to emphasize both complete natures of Christ, the divine and the human, we have good reason to think that Luther really did do justice to Nestorius in his accurate evaluation of what Nestorius tried to say. Almost everything that is known about Nestorius came through the medium of those hostile to Nestorius at the time, or those concerned to maintain the ecclesiastical tradition in later times, without any attempt to form an independent judgement until Luther's re-evaluation. In other words, it is Luther who initiated a renewal of the evaluation of Nestorianism which continues until today.

We can even regard "the Common Christological Declaration between the Catholic Church and the Assyrian Church of the East" as a sophisticated regression to the middle ground provided by Luther:

> As heirs and guardians of the faith received from the Apostles as formulated by our common Fathers in the Nicene Creed, we confess one Lord Jesus Christ ... His divinity and his humanity are united in one person, without confusion or change, without division or separation. In him has been preserved the difference of the natures of divinity and humanity, with all their properties, faculties and operations. But far from constituting 'one and another', the divinity and humanity are united in the person of the same and unique Son of God and Lord Jesus Christ, who is the object of a single adoration.... The controversies of the past led to anathemas, bearing on persons and on formulas. The Lord's Spirit permits us to understand better today that the divisions brought about in this way were due in large part to misunderstandings.⁵¹

Already in the Tome of Leo the Great that formed the basis of Chalcedon, it had been laid down that there is a *communicatio idiomatum* of the two natures

---

50   Nestorius, *Bazaar of Heraclides* (Oxford: Clarendon Press, 1925), 299.
51   The starting point to a common affirmation could be the Council of Nicea of 325 AD. On November 11, 1994, Pope John Paul II and Mar Dinkha, Catholicos of the Assyrian Church of the East, signed a Christological declaration in Rome: "As heirs and guardians of the faith received from the apostles as formulated by our common Fathers in the Nicene Creed." In that statement, the Assyrian Church is described as using the phrase, "the Mother of Christ our God and Saviour", and the Roman Catholic as using the phrase, "the Mother of God" and also as "the Mother of Christ." They conclude both respect the preference of the other. See <http://www.vatican.va/roman_curia/pontifical_councils/chrstuni/documents/rc_pc_chrstuni_doc_11111994_assyrian-church_en.html>.

of Jesus Christ. As mentioned above, Luther stated that Nestorius' error was not that he believed Christ to be two persons. The radix of the problem is that Nestorius did not allow for the *communicatio idiomatum* of the two natures. According to Luther, the mutual exchange of properties serves the meaning of salvific economy with a resulting deification of Jesus' humanity. Luther said, "Just as the Word of God became flesh, so it is certainly also necessary that the flesh became Word. For the Word became flesh precisely so that the flesh may become Word. In other words: God becomes man so that man may become God."[52]

It is easy to see that Luther presented here, following Athanasius and Irenaeus, the idea of deification (*theosis*) as a union of Word and man. This is also the reason why Tuomo Mannermaa, one of the most influential Finnish scholars of Luther studies, could associate Luther's view of *inhabitatio dei* with the Eastern Orthodox concept of "*theosis*."[53] Mannermaa notably endeavoured to excavate the underlying meaning of *communicatio idiomatum* and to achieve a more clearly defined concept of *theosis* which still remained undeveloped with Luther and absent with Nestorius. From Mannermaa's point of view, "the *theosis* of the believer is initiated when God bestows on the believer God's essential properties; that is, what God gives of himself to humans is nothing separate from God himself."[54] Although he is correct in thinking that there is an ontological aspect in the so-called "axle" and "motor" of Luther's theology,[55] Mannermaa radicalized it even further toward the high-pitched idea of *theosis*.[56]

---

52   *Luthers Werke*, section 1, vol. 1, 25-32. Cf. Paul M. Collins, *Partaking in Divine Nature: Deification and Communion* (London: T & T Clark International, 2010), 148.

53   For Mannermaa, the Lutheran idea of justification includes an indwelling of the person of Christ. "In faith, the person of Christ and that of the believer are made one, and this oneness must not be divided." "Christ is both the favor and the donum." "Christ is the true agent of good works in the Christians." See Tuomo Mannermaa, *Christ Present in Faith: Luther's View of Justification* (Fortress Press, 2005), 5, 42, 50.

54   Mannermaa, "Why is Luther So Fascinating?" in Carl Edward Braate & Robert W. Jenson (eds), *Union with Christ: The New Finnish Interpretation of Luther* (Grand Rapids: W.B. Eerdmans, 1998), 10.

55   According to Steiger, Luther carried his doctrine of the *communicatio idiomatum* to its peak and "radicalized it as he makes it the hermeneutical motor of his whole theology, or an axle around which many other theological themes now begin to turn." Cf. Johan Anselm Steiger, "The *communicatio idiomatum* as the Axle and Motor of Luther's Theology," *Lutheran Quarterly* 14, no. 2 (2000): 125-58.

56   Three representative works of Tuomo Mannermaa have been translated by Paulos Huang from the original Finnish into Chinese language. Cf., Man Duoma, translated by Paulos Huang 2018: *The Works of Tuomo Mannermaa as the Father of Finnish School for New Interpretation of Martin Luther* (Shanghai, Sanlian shudian).

Barth once interpreted the major implication of Luther's *communicatio idiomatum* as leading theology directly to a "high-pitched" anthropology.[57] If what Barth meant by the word "high-pitched" is its emphasis on the *inhabitatio dei* and the salvific role of Christ's Humanity, we can say, indeed, that Nestorian Christology is also a kind of "high-pitched" anthropology.[58] However, if the "high-pitched" Christology means the doctrine of a humanity which is not only capable of deification, but already deified; if the supreme achievement of Christology is the apotheosised flesh of Jesus Christ, which is merely a "hard shell" concealing the "sweet kernel" of the divinity of humanity as a whole and as such, "a shell which we can confidently discard and throw away once it has performed [its] service,"[59] then we should say, it is not only Mannermaa but also Luther who showed a tendency to collapse the humanity into the deity of Christ in the doctrine of *communicatio idiomatum* and *theosis*. It is not surprising that in this connection G. C. Berkouwer proceeds to consider that Lutheranism has some monophysite tendencies.[60]

Without doubt, it is no less important to Luther's criticism of Nestorian ignorance of *communicatio idiomatum* than is his sympathetic understanding of Nestorian two-nature Christology. Luther's sympathetic criticism did draw attention back to the Chalcedon's stipulation, by which a middle ground is provided: on the one hand, the Nestorian temptation represents a "division" Christology, refuted by the stipulation "without division;" on the other hand, Luther himself did put at risk Chalcedon's "without confusion" in his radical interpretation of *communicatio idiomatum*. Scholars such as Philip Schaff, Friedrich Loofs, R. Seeberg and J. F. Bethune-Baker had shown clearly that Luther really did justice to Nestorius in the two-nature Christology, while theologians such as Karl Barth and G. C. Berkouwer had warned correctly of the tendency to collapse the humanity into the deity of Christ in its own way just as problematic. The above references to modern studies are of great significance in clarifying misunderstanding of Nestorism, and in cultivating a healthy Middle Way attitude toward this controversial historical case.

---

57   Karl Barth, *Church Dogmatics* (London: T & T Clark International, 2004), IV/2:81-82.
58   Theodore of Mopsuestia (350-428) contributed substantially to the elaboration and dissemination of the Antiochene Christology and stood as the classic representative of the theology of the East Syriac church. Nestorius is a student of Theodore of Mopsuestia. Cf. Frederick G McLeod, *The Roles of Christ's Humanity in Salvation: Insights from Theodore of Mopsuestia* (Washington, DC: Catholic University of America Press, 2005), chapters 3, 6 and 7.
59   Cf. Karl Barth, *Church Dogmatics*, IV/2:81.
60   G. C. Berkouwer, *The Person of Christ* (Wm. B. Eerdmans Publishing Co., 1954), 43.

Editor-in-chief is Dr. Paulos Huang (Visiting Scholar in Collaborative Innovation Center of Confucian Civilization at Shandong University, *International Journal of Sino-Western Studies*, University of Helsinki, Finland), and Acquisition Editor from Brill is Ms. Tessel Jonquière and Assistant Editor Ingrid Heijckers-Velt. Prof. Xiaofeng Tang (China Academy of Social Sciences) and Donghua Zhu (Tsinghua University) have been invited as guest editors for this special volume of Jingjiao. As part of the cooperation between Brill Publishers and the International Journal of Sino-Western Studies (ISSN 1977-8204), the former will grant permission to the latter to publish the Chinese translation/version of the articles in the volumes of this yearbook series.

Most essays in this special volume of Jingjiao are based on the papers presented originally at the 1st Beijing International Symposium of Jingjiao Studies, entitled, *The Practice of Faith: A Way of Life for Jingjiao Followers in China*, which held as a part of the CASS Annual Conference on the Study of Christianity in November 2017. The contributors are a diverse group of scholars from Europe, Asia and North America who came together to discuss how the cross-cultural and cross-religious dialogues impacted the practice of faith among the Jingjiao followers in China, and how the multiple cultural backgrounds impacted interpretation within the context of theological, literary, and historical research. As the cast of contributors shows, this Symposium was a gathering of pioneering scholars and a marvelous occasion at which to absorb something of Chinese Jingjiao research at its leading edge. There are many people who deserve grateful acknowledgement as this volume goes to press. Special thanks are due to Ms. Zhang Yingying, Ms. Yin Han and Mr. Zheng Junhao for their devoted service.

(May 4th, 2018, Helsinki & Beijing)

List of Contributors

Mar Aprem Metropolitan
Dr., B.D., M.Th., S.T.M., D. Th., Ph.D. Thrissur, Kerala, India. Email: john_thachil@yahoo.com

Chengyong Ge
Professor, Chinese Academy of Cultural Heritage, Beijing, China. Email: gechengyong00@163.com

Paulos Huang
Visiting scholar, Collaborative Innovation Center of Confucian Civilization at Shandong University, Chief Editor for International Journal of Sino-Western Studies, University of Helsinki. Email: paulos.z.huang@gmail.com

Zhu Li-Layec
Ph.D. University of Constance, Germany. Email: zhulilayec@gmail.com

Melville Y. Stewart
Professor, Bethel University, USA. Email: stemel03@yahoo.com

David Tam
Ph.D. Tsinghua University, Beijing, China. Email: dtwtam@hotmail.com

Xiaofeng Tang
Professor, Institute of World Religions, Chinese Academy of Social Sciences, Beijing, China. Email: tangxf@cass.org.cn

Donald Wang
Ph. D. Candidate, Trinity International University, USA. wuagedon@gmail.com

Lanping Wang
Professor, Institute for Dunhuang Studies, Lanzhou University, Gansu Province, China. Email: wanglanp@163.com

Fuxue Yang
Professor, Dunhuang Academy, Gansu Province, China. Email: 1584322834@qq.com

Daniel H.N. Yeung
Academic director, Institute of Sino-Christian Studies, Hong Kong, China, Email: daniel_yeung@iscs.org.hk

Xiaoping Yin
Associate professor, School of Humanities, South China Agricultural University, Guangdong Province. Email: arena_yin@hotmail.com

Qiaosui Zhang
Lecturer, Ningbo University of Technology, China. Email: hgwc@qq.com

Yingying Zhang
Lecturer, Shanghai Lixin University of Accounting and Finance, Shanghai, China. Email: l: vinessazy@163.com

Donghua Zhu
Professor, Department of Philosophy, Tsinghua University, Beijing, China. Email: zhudonghua@tsinghua.edu.cn

PART 1

Systematic Theology and Chinese Humanities

∵

CHAPTER 1

The Names of God in the Tang Jingjiao Document *Yishen Lun* (*A Discourse on God*)

David Tam

1 Introduction

The first time it was revealed that the Jingjiao document *Yishen Lun* (一神論, *A Discourse on God*; hereto *"Discourse"*) existed was by Toru Haneda in his 1918 article "景教經典一神論解說" ("An Interpretation of Jingjiao Document *Discourse on God*"), in the magazine *Geimon*.[1] With respect to its origin, he said, "The original manuscript, like the many other priceless manuscripts obtained by the Britain Marc Aurel Stein and the Frenchman Paul Pelliot, came from the Mogao Caves. Prof. Tomeoka bought it, and dozens of other manuscripts, from a book seller."[2] Haneda regards it as a Jingjiao document because a part of it corresponds (in general) with the Sermon on the Mount. This view is widely accepted in subsequent scholarship, and it therefore forms one of the eight documents of Jingjiao Christianity sanctioned by decrees in China from 638 to 845. The entire text, in the form of photographs, was published in 1931.

There are very few studies specifically on *Discourse*. General studies on Jingjiao usually would give it some introduction, for examples, P.Y. Saeki's *The Nestorian Documents and Relics in China* (1951),[3] Weng Shaojun's *Chinese Annotations on Jingjiao Manuscripts* (1995),[4] Tang Li's *A Study of the History of Nestorian Christianity in China and its Literature in Chinese: Together with a New English Translation of the Dunhuang Nestorian Documents* (2002),[5] Ceng Yangqing's *A Study of Tang Jingjiao Chinese Documents*) (2005),[6] Nie Zhijun's *Study*

---

1 The article was reprinted in 羽 田, et al. 《羽田博士史学論文集 下卷 (言語・宗教篇)》(京都: 東洋史研究会, 1958), pp. 235-239.
2 Based on Lin Wushu's (林悟殊) Chinese translation in his 《敦煌文書與夷教研究》(上海: 上海古籍出版社, 2011), p. 324.
3 P.Y. Saeki, *The Nestorian Documents and Relics in China* (Tokyo: Toho Bunkwa Gakuin: Academy of Oriental Culture, Tokyo Institute, 1951)
4 翁紹軍,《漢語景教文典詮釋》(香港: 漢語基督教文化研究所, 1995)
5 Tang Li, *A Study of the History of Nestorian Christianity in China and its Literature in Chinese: Together with a New English Translation of the Dunhuang Nestorian Documents* (Frankfurt am Main: Peter Lang, 2002)
6 曾陽晴,《唐朝漢語景教文獻研究》(臺北: 花木蘭文化工作坊, 2005)

of Terms in Tang Jingjiao Manuscripts (2010),[7] and Wu Changxin's *Annotations on the Xian Stele and Da Qin Jingjiao Documents*) (2015).[8] Amongst these works, P.Y. Saeki and Tang Li's provide translation (in English) for all the Jingjiao documents discovered in (or attributed to) Dunhuang, and scholars writing in Chinese, such as Weng Shaojun and Wu Changxin, provide only interpretation and remarks on selected terms. Apart from these general works, there are essays by F.S. Drake (1935)[9] on the structure and outline of *Discourse*, and Liu Weimin (1962)[10] on philosophical and theological observations. Lin Wushu wrote on the authenticity of the document, which is discussed in a later section.

The next section of the paper will present the aim and approach of this article; following that, Section III will address the date, authorship, and authenticity of the document; Section IV provides a summary of the text highlighting the use of *Yishen* and *Tianzun* in the document; Section V compares the pair of names *Yishen* and *Tianzun* in *Discourse* with the pair *Allaha* and *Marya* in *the Peshitta*, the Syriac Bible; Section VI determines which is equivalent to which between these two pairs of names; Section VII discusses the considerations the author might have put into deriving these two names; and Section VIII concludes the article, with some additional comments.

II   Aim and Approach of the Study

The purpose of this paper is to study the names of God in *Discourse*, the 7th Century Chinese manuscript of Jingjiao, Christianity in the Tang Dynasty. Whilst, in the document, God is also called *Fu* (父, the Father) once in the Trinitarian formula,[11] and three times as Christ's Father,[12] the principal names for God in the document are *Yishen* (used 78 times) and *Tianzun* (16 times). This article therefore studies how *Yishen* and *Tianzun* are used in the document, and how they correspond to the names of God in the Bible.

---

7   聶志軍, 《唐代景教文獻詞語研究》(湖南: 人民出版社, 2010)
8   吳昶興, 《大秦景教流行中國碑－大秦景教文獻釋義》(臺北: 橄欖出版社, 2015)
9   F.S. Drake, "The Nestorian Literature of the Tang Dynasty" in *The Chinese Recorder*, 66 (1935), pp. 681-687
10 劉偉民, 〈唐代景教之傳入及其思想之研究〉, 載《聯合書院學報》第一期, 1962 年6 月, 頁 1-64
11 Line 308: "人來向, 水字於父、子、淨風, 處分具足。"
12 Lines 326-327: "誰是汝父, 來向天下, 亦作聖化。"; Lines 333-334: 禮拜世尊者, 於彌師訶父處, 將向天堂。"; Lines 335-336: "彼彌師訶處, 無行不具足, 受處凡世尊, 喻如自父。"

Literally, the two words in *Yishen* mean "one" and "god" respectively, and the two words in *Tianzun* mean "that which is the highest"[13] and "that which is supremely honored."[14] In the translation and annotation works cited in the above, these two terms are treated as appellations for God. For examples, Saeki translates "万物見一神" in Line 1[15] as "All things manifest the one God";[16] "所以一神乞願必得" in Line 234 as "For everyone that asks the one God will surely be given what he asks";[17] and "弥師訶與一神，天分明見" in Line 394 as "the Messiah together with the one God sees (us all) distinctly and clearly from Heaven."[18] Tang slightly alters Saeki's wording of "the one God" to "the One-God", but otherwise she treats *Yishen* the same way as Saeki. Wu, in his remark on "一神神妙之力" of Line 9, notes that it means "一神不可思議，特別高超的能力" ("the unimaginable, out-of-this-world kind of power of Yi Shen"),[19] thus treating *Yishen* as a proper noun. For the term *Tianzun*, scholarship is also in consensus that it is used in the document as a name for God. Hence Saeki's translation of "天下無者天尊作" in Line 50 as "All things ... in the universe are also created by the Lord of Heaven";[20] and "天尊處天下" in Line 51 as "And they are all to be disposed by the Lord of Heaven."[21] Tang Li again slightly alters Saeki's term to "heavenly Lord," but otherwise treats *Tianzun* the same way Saeki does. Wu annotates, with respect to *Tianzun*: "傳統對天的尊崇，指上帝" ("the reverence to the highest in Chinese tradition, meaning Shangdi.")[22]

While it is clear that *Yishen* and *Tianzun* are proper nouns or names of God in *Discourse*, much yet needs to be asked and studied: why does the author use two names for God? Are they interchangeable? Does each have a special meaning? How is this nomenclature for God in *Discourse* compared to those in the biblical and church traditions? This paper intends to address these questions. The study will approach *Yishen* and *Tianzun* as they appear in the text, used by the author. We will track the usage by way of a summary of the document highlighting these two names, compare this nomenclature with that in the Bible

---

13 "天", 《康熙字典》：《說文》"顛也 。至高在上 ，從一大也 。" 《漢典》 <http://www.zdic.net/> viewed on 19 Sep. 2017.
14 "尊" ，《說文》高稱也。《廣韻》重也，貴也，君父之稱也。《漢典》 <http://www.zdic.net/> viewed on 19 Sep. 2017.
15 For the text of *Discourse on God* and the line numbers, this article follows those appended in 林悟殊, 《唐代景教再研究》 (北京: 中國社會科學出版社, 2003), pp. 350-380.
16 Saeki (1951), p. 161.
17 Ibid, p. 209
18 Ibid, p. 229
19 吳昶興 (2015), 頁 78. This author's translation.
20 Saeki (1951), p. 167
21 Ibid.
22 吳昶興 (2015), 頁 87. This author's translation.

(Syriac and Hebrew), determine the equivalency of names, and draw some observations on how these two names are derived.

III   Date, Authorship and Authenticity

It is commonly held in scholarship that *Discourse* was written in 641 AD, because Line 365 says that "弥師訶向天下見, 也向五音身六百四十一年不過, 已於一切處。" ("Therefore, it is clear that from the time when Mishihe appeared to the world, and took on the *wuyin* body,[23] it has not been more than 641 years, but [the gospel] is already everywhere.") Haneda, according to Saeki, first pointed out this passage and said that based on it, the authorship date should be 641 AD Saeki, and subsequent scholarship, adopts the same view.[24] Hidemi Takahashi of the University of Tokyo, in a recent personal communication with this author, advised that Syriac authors often gave different dates for the birth of Jesus,[25] and Bishop Īshō'dād of Merv (mid-9th Century), in eastern Persia, placed Jesus' birth date in 6 BC (or 307 A.Gr.). If the author of *Discourse* followed Īshō'dād[26] in this regard, this would mean that the document could have been composed in 636/7 AD.

---

23   "五音身人" should read "五蔭身人". The term "五蔭" ("*wuyin*") is the Chinese translation for the Five *Skandhas*, which refers to the Buddhist concept of a complete person consisting of the five transitory personal elements of 色、受、想、行、识 (body, perception, conception, volition, and consciousness.) The term is used 26 times in *Yishenlun*, either standalone or as in "五蔭身" (the *wuyin* body), in a straightforward way with no elaboration. Nowhere else in the text addresses the five transitory personal elements, in part or in whole, directly or indirectly. Therefore there is no indication that the writer subscribes to the full philosophy of the Five *Skandhas*. That said, however, it is also obvious that he chooses not to use other more ordinary terms for the physical body such as "身軀" or "軀體". The least one can ascertain from the Narrator's use of "*wuyin*" is that when he wants to speak of the body, he does not mean just the physical flesh-and-bone body, but a full person, with all its natures and attributes.

24   Saeki, pp. 115, 116, 117, etc., Drake, p. 686; Li, p. 109; Wu, p. 77)

25   Takahashi, Hidemi. "Re: *Yishen*lun and year 641." Message to David Tam. 30 November 2017. E-mail. Takahashi quotes the following sources for his information: (1) Bernhard, L., *Die Chronologie der Syrer* (Vienna, 1969); (2) Īšō'dād of Merv, *Commentary on the Gospels*: ed. & trans. M.D. Gibson, *The Commentaries of Isho'dad of Merv,* Bishop of Ḥadatha (c. 850 AD), 3 vols. (Cambridge, 1911); (3) Bīrūnī, *Kitāb al-Āṯār al-bāqiya 'an al-qurūn al-ḫāliya*: ed. E. Sachau, *Chronologie orientalischer Völker von Albêrûnî* (Leipzig, 1878); trans. E. Sachau, *The Chronology of the Ancient Nations* (London, 1879).

26   Merv was an important ecclesiastical and missionary centre for the Persian Church. Erica Hunter writes "In AD 7C, a process of amalgamation seems to have taken place with suffragan bishops being under the umbrella of the metropolitans of Herat and Merw. Furthermore, the importance of Merw, as the headquarters for missions east of the Oxus

In 635 AD, according to the *Monument Commemorating the Propagation of Daqin Jingjiao in the Central Territory* ("大秦景教流行中國碑", often called "the Xian Stele; hereto "the Monument"), Alouben and his delegation arrived Chan-gan.[27] In 638 AD, an imperial decree was issued, saying: "The truth does not have a fixed name, and attainment of it does not require a fixed entity. The teachings take the local circumstances into consideration, bringing great benefits to the people. A Persian monk, named Aluoben, brought a faith based on Scriptures to the Capital. Having examined its main tenets, we find that it is purely excellent and natural, aimed for attaining the basic truths, and beneficial to all mankind. Let it be published throughout the Empire, and let the proper authority build a monastery in the Yining Precinct for the accommodation of twenty-one monks."[28] According to the Monument, in this initial period, under the auspices of the Tang emperor Taizong, they did not only build temples, but also translated (and perhaps also composed) texts and documents ("翻經書殿",[29] "翻經建寺"[30]).

Against this background, P.Y. Saeki calls this document an "Aluoben document," and he says that "for convenience's sake," he would call the author "Aluoben or his men".[31] From then on this has been the standard way to term the authorship of this document, and given its all-inclusiveness, there can hardly be any objection.

Based on the timeframe (636/7 AD) and the content of the Monument, we know that the author was from the Church of the East (ܥܕܬܐ ܕܡܕܢܚܐ *edta d'madenha*). According to Baum and Winkler, "in the European Middle Ages, it [the "Church of the East"] was geographically far larger than any Western church, with followers along the Silk Road, in Central Asia, China, and of

---

River, may be suggested since in AD 644 the metropolitan converted a large number of Turkic people." (Hunter, Erica C. D. "Syriac Christianity in Central Asia." Zeitschrift Für Religions- Und Geistesgeschichte, vol. 44, no. 4, 1992, pp. 365)

27   It should be noted that the 638 imperial decree does not give a date to Aluoben's arrival.
28   "道無常名，聖無常體，隨方設教，密濟群生。大秦國大德阿羅本，遠將經像來獻上京，詳其教旨，玄妙無為；觀其元宗，生成立要，詞無繁說，理有忘筌，濟物利人，宜行天下。"Volume 49, 唐會要 (*Tang Hui Yao*) in 中國哲學書電子化計劃 Website (<http://ctext.org/wiki.pl?if=gb&chapter=677933>, viewed on 19 Sep. 2017).
29   "帝使宰臣房公玄齡，總仗西郊，賓迎入內。翻經書殿，問道禁闈，深知正真，特令傳授。"《大秦景教流行中國碑》("The Monument"). 吳昶興 (2015), 頁 21.
30   "赫赫文皇，道冠前王。乘時撥亂，乾廓坤張。明明景教，言歸我唐。翻經建寺，存歿舟航。百福偕作，萬邦之康。" ("The Monument"). 吳昶興 (2015), 頁 37.
31   Saeki (1951), p. 8.

course in India."³² Erica C.D. Hunter, in her article "Persian contribution to Christianity in China: Reflections in the Xi'an Fu Syriac inscriptions", examines the Monument, particularly the Syriac names and wordings on it, and comes to the conclusion that the inscriptions substantiate the direct link of the Church of the East with the patriarchate in Mesopotamia, because, for examples, it affirms the authority of the Patriarchate of Henanisho based in Seleucia-Ctesiphon, and the names of the clerics and monks were, in one form or another, used throughout the Sassanid territories.³³

Like many ancient manuscripts, *Discourse* is not immune to an authenticity issue. Scholars including Lin Wushu (林悟殊)³⁴ and Wang Lanping (王蘭平),³⁵ etc., have written about it. Lin suggests that the document is a forged copy of an original one, which has since been lost. His suspicion is mainly due to, in his view, there was a lack of clarity in how the document came about, the manuscript appearing too perfect with no markings of correction, titles apparently having been misplaced and some words having been accidentally rendered in modern forms, etc. Nevertheless, Lin remarks that his suspicion is only a hypothesis (猜想) that would require further proof.³⁶ This article, due to length, cannot give a comprehensive review of the authenticity issue, although it would note Wu Changxin's comment that Lin speaks mostly on factors external to the document, less on the content itself,³⁷ and Wang Lanping finds that the variations in the form of a word are not uncommon for Dunhuang manuscripts, and should not be regarded as a sign of forgery.³⁸ While the debate on

---

32 Baum, Wilhelm, Dietmar W. Winkler. *The Church of the East: A Concise History.* London: Routledge Curzon, 2003), p. xi.

33 Erica C.D. Hunter, "Persian contribution to Christianity in China: Reflections in the Xi'an Fu Syriac inscriptions", Winkler, Dietmar W., and Li Tang. *Hidden Treasures and Intercultural Encounters: Studies on East Syriac Christianity in China and Central Asia.* vol. 1.1, Lit. Wien, Piscataway. NJ, 2009, p. 80.

34 林悟殊,《唐代景教再研究》(北京: 中國社會科學出版社, 2003) 頁 186-207. The same article was reprinted in his 《敦煌文書與夷教研究》(上海: 上海古籍出版社, 2011), 頁343-351; and 《中古三夷教辨證》(中華書局, 2005), 頁183-188 。

35 王蘭平,〈日本杏雨書屋藏富岡文書高楠文書真偽再研究〉, 載《敦煌學輯刊:》(1): 10 2016, 頁10-19

36 林悟殊,《敦煌文書與夷教研究》, 頁 344

37 吳昶興,《大秦景教流行中國碑》, 頁 lxix

38 王蘭平,〈日本杏雨書屋藏富岡文書高楠文書真偽再研究〉, 頁 10: "近十多年來, 日本杏雨書屋藏 "富岡文書", 《一神論》和 "高楠文書", 《序聽迷詩所經》之真實性受到林悟殊, 榮新江先生質疑, 認為其或為近人編造之贗品。其中林先生質疑證據之一是《一神論》存在 "肉"、"宍"、"因"、"回"、"與"、"与"、"作" 和 "㑅" 等並寫現象, 然而上述同字不同形寫法並用的現象亦存在于諸多公認敦煌藏經洞寫本真跡, 因此不能將同一件寫本存在以上字體並行現象視為贗品之證據。相反依據以上兩件寫本影印件, 從字形角度作了進一步分析, 結果表明《序聽迷詩所經》,《一神論》未顯示出作偽痕跡。"

the authenticity of the Tomioka document would continue, we note that Lin, despite his concern, has also remarked that: "the current manuscript is still a valuable reference material for the study of early Christianity in China, and it is still unique in terms of the information it provides."[39] He quotes Luo Xianglin (羅香林) that *Discourse* "is deep in theology, the deepest amongst all Jingjiao documents," and cites Weng Shaojun (翁紹軍)'s remark that *Discourse* "is extremely rich in its theology and philosophy."[40]

In summary of the above, the Jingjiao document *Discourse* was commonly held as written in 641, but considering that the Syriac Christians often had Jesus' birth date a few years before 1 AD, and that Īshōʻdād of Merv had it in 6 BC, (307 A.Gr.), the document therefore could be written around 636/7 AD (948 A.Gr.). The author of the document would be Aluoben or his companions, and he was from the Church of the East, of the Syriac Christian tradition. Lin has raised an authenticity issue of the current manuscript, but recent studies show that some of the concerns might not be necessary, and Lin himself holds that even the current copy is forged, he believes that it still serves as a valuable source for Jingjiao study.

IV A Summary of the Text

As mentioned in earlier, the approach taken in the study is to track *Yishen* and *Tianzun* in *Discourse* to find out how the author uses them, and what we can learn from the usage. The following is a summary of the text highlighting the use of these names:

Lines 1 to 50

There is one and only One God (*Yi Shen*). All things, whether they are visible or invisible, manifest *Yishen*, because they are created by *Yishen*. For example, the sky is not supported by columns and beams, but it does not collapse, and this shows the power of *Yishen*, and in turn the existence of *Yishen*. When we see an arrow flying across the sky, we know that there is an archer. When we see the universe being so stable, we know that there is *Yishen*. There is only one and only One God (*Yishen*) in the universe: a house, if more than one master, would not be in good order; a man, if more than one soul, would not be in good shape. *Yishen* fills the world, like the soul filling the body, but He is not restricted to any one place or

---

39 林悟殊,《敦煌文書與夷教研究》, 頁 343-344. This writer's translation.
40 Ibid, pp. 327-329. This writer's translation.

any one time. *Yishen* is holy, always sanctified and glorified, and He never changes.

Lines 50 to 78

What the world does not originally have, *Tianzun* has created. *Tianzun* is in the world, both visible and invisible. *Yishen* sustains the world with His divine power, and all things are properly and abundantly established. *Yishen* is not flesh, nor spirit, and the human eye cannot see Him even a little. People should pray to *Yishen*, and their prayers will be answered. If people have knowledge, they know who *Yishen* is. If not, they cannot separate "gods" and *Yishen*, and will conjure all sorts of images of gods.

Lines 78 to 164

Man comprises the body (五蔭身), soul (魂魄) and spirit (神識). The soul, together with the spirit, allows the body to see, to hear, to speak and to move. Man should not worship ghosts and devils, but should obey the governance of *Yishen*. Man should, in all earnest, worship *Tianzun*, so that their sins will be forgiven. They should serve *Yishen Tianzun* (一神天尊), worship *Yishen*, so that their sins will be forgiven. Man should cleanse their heart and body, and observe the holy feasts and liturgies sanctioned by *Tianzun*. All these should be done in this world, for there will be no such opportunities in the next.

Lines 164 to 205

The Demon was once the same kind as the angels in Heaven, serving *Yishen*, but it became arrogant and contemptuous, and for some evil reasons it departed from its abode in Heaven. It then bewitched and confused people, bringing them to dwell in evils, in the sinful places, worshipping their master Satan. On the other hand, in this world, the one who reminds us of the good, and wants the best of things for us, is *Yishen*. From beginning to end, He wants us to be with Him, to be holy.

Lines 206 to 249

When one worships, he needs not make people notice. He only needs to let *Yishen* see. When one wants to be close to *Tianzun*, he should learn to be worry-free, because the food and clothes that people need, *Yishen* has them all ready. If Man prays to *Yishen*, the door will be opened, and the prayers will be answered.

Lines 249-304

People should listen closely to the Gospel of *Mishihe* (弥師訶, Christ), about His suffering, death, burial, and resurrection, as well as His instruction that the Gospel should be spread to all people near and far. *Mishihe* was accused of acknowledging to be *Shizun* (世尊), and was arrested, tortured and crucified. Three days later he arose from death and, in his appearance to disciples, instructed them to bring the gospel to all peoples, and for those who believed, to baptize them in the name of the Father, Son and *Jingfeng* (淨風, the Holy Spirit).

Lines 304 to 366

Mishihe ascended to heaven, and the disciples were filled with *Jingfeng*, and were under the governance of *Tianzun*. The disciples praised *Mishihe*, saying: "For my sins, you let your own body encounter death. Your body was raised from death in three days, and by the power and might of *Tianzun*, you ascended to Heaven." Now, the author says, 641 years after *Mishihe* coming to the world, people in Rome and Persia are worshiping *Shizun Yishu Mishihe* (世尊翳數弥師訶, Lord Jesus Christ), although some in Persia still worship the Devil.

Lines 367 to 405

This new faith, the author says, is made possible by the power of *Tianzun*. He says that the governance of *Yishen* is adequate for our salvation, and we should take this path, because there is no other path. People should go to Heaven, but there is a judgment by *Tianzun*. He says that people are going to be judged by *Yishen*, and for those who worship the sun, moon, stars, fire, and gods, etc., they will be cast to the lake of fire in Hell. For those not practicing the faith, they are subject to *Tianzun*'s judgment. All those who accept the salvation belong to *Yishen*, and for those who do not, they should know that *Yishen* will judge people. Those who believe and practice the faith will go to heaven, to the place of eternal happiness. Those who follow the Devil will go to hell, to the place of eternal fire.

v   The Two Names of God

From the summary above, it should be apparent that *Yishen* and *Tianzun* are often used in an interchangeable way, as names (or titles) for God. In fact, the phrase *Yishen Tianzun* in Line 146 shows that the two names can form one single appellation. Other examples that show the interchangeability of the two terms are: (1) whereas Lines 3-4 says that 一切萬物，並是一神所作，可見者不可見者，並是一神所造 ("All Things are put together by *Yishen*. Those that are visible and those are invisible are all made by *Yishen*"), Line 50 says 天下無者天尊作 (What the world did not originally have, they have since been put together by *Tianzun*); (2) whereas Line 37-38 says 天下有一神 (There is *Yishen* in the world), Line 51 says 天尊處天下 (*Tianzun* is in the world); (3) people are advised to 禮拜一神 (worship *Yishen*) in Lines 146, 151, and 161, and they are also counselled to 禮拜天尊 (worship *Tianzun*) in Line 139; (4) the divine power is characterized as 一神之力 (*Yishen's* power) for over 25 times in the document, while it is also called 天尊神力 (*Tianzun's* power) in Lines 106 and 368, as well as 天尊氣力 in Line 328.

The author was a Syriac Christian, and he was likely using the Syriac version of the Bible, the *Peshitta*, because, according to *The Concise Oxford Dictionary of the Christian Church*, the *Peshitta* became the official text of the Bible in Syriac-speaking Christian lands in the early 5th century.[41] In both the Old and New Testaments (OT and NT) of the *Peshitta*, God is called *Allaha,* meaning "God", and *Marya,* meaning "Lord". These two names are used in an interchangeable way, and in fact, the compound name "the Lord God", or *Marya Allaha* (ܐܠܗܐ ܡܪܝܐ) in Syriac, appears in the Bible for over 350 times. In terms of interchangeability of *Allaha* and *Marya*, we have the following examples in the OT: (1) Ex. 13:9 has the phrase ܠܢܡܘܣܐ ܕܡܪܝܐ (*lamoseh d'Marya*), meaning "the law of the Lord", and Joshua 24:26 has ܠܢܡܘܣܐ ܕܐܠܗܐ (*lamoseh d'Allaha*) meaning "the law of God"; (2) Daniel 2:18 says ܐܠܗܐ ܕܫܡܝܐ (*Allaha d'sarya*) meaning "God of Heaven", whereas Daniel 5:23 says ܡܪܝܐ ܕܫܡܝܐ (*Marya d'sarya*) meaning "Lord of Heaven"; (3) I Chronicles 16:6 says ܩܒܘܬܐ ܕܩܝܡܗ ܕܐܠܗܐ (*obata d'qoleh d'Allaha*), meaning "the ark of the covenant of God", whereas 1 Chronicles 15:25 says ܩܒܘܬܐ ܕܩܝܡܗ ܕܡܪܝܐ (*obata d'qoleh d'Marya*), meaning "the ark of the covenant of the Lord". In the NT, we have (4) Acts 10:3 saying ܡܠܐܟܐ ܕܐܠܗܐ (*malaka d'Allaha*) meaning "angel of God", whereas Acts 8:26 ܡܠܐܟܐ ܕܡܪܝܐ (*malaka d'Marya*) meaning "angel of the Lord"; (5) Revelation 19:15 ܐܠܗܐ ܕܟܠ ܐܚܝܕ (*Allaha d'kal ahayad*) meaning "God Almighty", whereas II Corinthians 6:18 ܡܪܝܐ ܕܟܠ ܐܚܝܕ (*Marya d'kal ahayad*), meaning "Lord Almighty".

Where did this two-name usage for God in the *Peshitta* come from? It ultimately came from the Hebrew Bible. The Syriac name *Allaha* corresponds with the Hebrew name *Elohim* (אֱלֹהִים), and *Marya* with *Adonai* (אֲדֹנָי), which is a

---

41   "Peshitta", *The Concise Oxford Dictionary of the Christian Church* (3 ed.) Edited by E.A. Livingstone Oxford University Press, 2013.

substitute for *Yahweh* (יְהֹוָה *YHWH*).⁴² According to literary and source criticism, the two-name usage arose because the Hebrew Bible was compiled over an extended period of time, and materials from two separate earlier traditions about God were merged (the J, or "Yahwist" strand and the E, or "Elohist," strand.)⁴³ This two-source hypothesis, which has been the prevailing theory in OT studies since the 18th Century, has in recent years been challenged by OT scholars such as Herbert C. Brichto and Seely J. Beggiani. Brichto finds arguments of the source criticism problematic because, in part, it pretends that the biblical passages assigned under J-source or E-source only use *Yahweh* and *Elohim* exclusively, with no hints (nuance, intention, and extension) of the other name.⁴⁴ If in fact the J source (Yahwist strand) has elements of *Elohim*, and the E source (Elohist strand) has elements of *Yahweh*, the two-source theory is not that clear-cut and sound. As an alternative, Brichto advocates a poetical approach that would take the OT (or more particularly, the Genesis) as a self-contained document, so that the overall narrative, as a coherent account, can be understood and appreciated.⁴⁵ Seely J. Beggiani explains that the two-name usage is not due to sources, but to "a heightened sense of the sanctity of the deity and of the sacredness of its own proper name led to the avoidance of a too frequent employment of the name *Yahweh* which gradually became ineffable, and to its replacement by a synonymous substitute."⁴⁶

This two-name usage in the OT, naturally, is transmitted into the daily life of church communities, including that in the Syriac tradition. For example, *Allaha* and *Marya* are both used in the liturgies in an interchangeable way. In the

---

42   "Tetragrammaton", *The Concise Oxford Dictionary of the Christian Church* (Oxford University Press, 3rd ed., 2013): "The technical term for the four-lettered Hebrew name of God יהוה (i.e. YHWH or JHVH). Because of its sacred character, from c.300 BC the Jews tended to avoid uttering it when reading Scripture and substituted 'Adonai' (i.e. the Hebrew word for 'Lord'), whence the rendering Κύριος of the LXX, Dominus of the Vulgate, and 'the LORD' in most English Bibles. When vowel points were put into Hebrew MSS those of 'Adonai' were inserted into the letters of the Tetragrammaton, and since the 16th cent. the bastard word 'Jehovah', obtained by fusing the vowels of the one word with the consonants of the other, has become established. The original pronunciation is commonly thought to have been 'Yahweh' or 'Jahveh'; both these forms (nowadays mostly the former) are found in scholarly works."

43   "Yahwist source", in *Encyclopædia Britannica* (<https://www.britannica.com/topic/Yahwist-source>, accessed on 18 October 2017); "Elohist source", in *Encyclopædia Britannica* (<https://www.britannica.com/topic/Yahwist-source>, accessed on 18 October 2017).

44   Brichto, Herbert C., and MyiLibrary. *The Names of God: Poetic Readings in Biblical Beginnings*. Oxford University Press, New York, 1998. p. 8-9.

45   Ibid., p. 7.

46   Beggiani, Seely, J. *Early Syriac Theology*. Catholic University of America Press, Washington, 2014. p. 100.

Eucharist liturgy "*The Order of the Hallowing of the Apostles*" composed by, according to church tradition, Mar Addai and Mar Mari, *Marya* is used 21 times and *Allaha* 15 times, and the combined form *Marya Allaha* three times. To the author of *Discourse*, perhaps due to habit and perhaps due to what Beggiani calls "the heightened sense of the sanctity of the deity and of the sacredness," he would not find it appropriate to use only one name for God, thus these two names in *Discourse*, *Yishen* and *Tianzun*.

VI   Which is Which

The question then is: between *Yishen* and *Tianzun*, which one corresponds to *Allaha* and which one to *Marya*. Although *Allaha* and *Marya* are used interchangeably, it does not mean that they cannot be differentiated at all. Umberto Cassuto, in studying the emergence of the two names in the book of Genesis, holds the view that the use of *Yahweh* and *Elohim* in the Book of Genesis is subject to certain rules.[47]

> (a) The Tetragrammaton [i.e., יְהֹוָה (YHWH)] occurs when Scripture reflects the concept of God, especially in His ethical aspect, that belongs specifically to the people of Israel; אֱלֹהִים (*Elohim*) appears when the Bible refers to the abstract conception of God that was current in the international circles of the Sages, the idea of God conceived in a general sense as the Creator of the material world, as the Ruler of nature, and as Source of life;

> (b) The name יְהֹוָה (YHWH) is used when Scripture wishes to express that direct and intuitive notion of God that is characteristic of the unsophisticated faith of the multitude, but אֱלֹהִים (*Elohim*) is employed when it is intended to convey the concept of the philosophically minded who study the abstruse problems connected with the world and humanity;

> (c) יְהֹוָה (YHWH) appears when the Bible presents the Deity to us in His personal character and in direct relationships to human beings or to nature; whereas אֱלֹהִים (*Elohim*) occurs when Holy Writ speaks of God as a Transcendental Being, who stands entirely outside nature, and above it.

---

47   Cassuto, Umberto. *The Documentary Hypothesis and the Composition of the Pentateuch: Eight Lectures.* 4th ed. ed., Jerusalem, Magnes Press, Hebrew University, 1965.

Herbert C. Brichto essentially agrees with Cassuto, but he finds Cassuto's rules overly precise, "and the reading of these two names as dichotomous categories when they may in many or most cases overlap in nuance, intention, and extension.⁴⁸ He observes:⁴⁹

> ... in the name יְהֹוָה (YHWH) as essentially personal, relating in particular intimacy with Israelite forebears or pre-Abrahamitic exemplars of His beloved, though oft erring, human creations; this in contrast with אֱלֹהִים (Elohim) as often less than personal, sometimes almost an abstraction, the Cause of all phenomena – nature and the animate denizens of earth – and in dialogue with humans outside the Abrahamitic continuum or within that continuum.

In reference to Cassuto and Brichto's above analysis, we read again the beginning section of *Discourse*, and it is not hard to conclude that *Yishen* represents an abstract conception of God and the cause of all phenomena, as it says all things visible and invisible are created by *Yishen*, and that just like when we see a flying arrow and we know that there is an archer, when we see the harmony of the sky we know *Yishen* exists. It says that *Yishen* is in the world, and while He is invisible, He fills *Tiandi* (天地, the cosmos), like the soul filling the body. The first 50 lines of *Discourse* is about God's existence and attributes, manifested by the nature. In this theological/philosophical account, only *Yishen* is used. When *Tianzun* first appears in Lines 50/51, He is said to be engaging Himself in this world ("天尊處天下"). He respects everything in the world (Line 107: "天尊敬重一切"), and he counsels and judges on Man's piety and virtues (Line 156: "如功德無天尊證，即不成就"). *Tianzun*, as portrayed, indeed reflects the ethical aspect of God, and the personal relationship God has with the creation and Man. Therefore, we can conclude, while there are indeed much overlap in their usage, *Yishen* corresponds with *Allaha* (or its Hebrew counterpart *Elohim*) and *Tianzun* with *Marya* (*Adonai*), or what *Marya*/*Adonai* signifies, Yahweh (YHWH).

To sum up, *Yishen* and *Tianzun* are used in a highly interchangeable way as names for God in *Discourse*, and are even combined to form one appellation, such as *Yishen Tianzun* in Line 146. This follows the pattern of *Allaha* and *Marya* in the *Peshitta* (the Syriac Bible) and *Elohim* and *Yahweh* in the Hebrew Bible. As *Yishen* represents an abstract conception of God and the cause of all phenomena, and *Tianzun* is used in a more personal/ethical way, it can be

---

48 Brichto (1998), p. 11
49 Ibid., p. 10

determined that *Yishen* represents *Allaha/Elohim* and *Tianzun* represents *Marya/Adonai/Yahweh*.

VII The Formulation of *Yishen* and *Tianzun*

This section explores what the factors could be in the formulation of these two names for God in *Discourse*.

Yishen

As mentioned above, the two words in *Yi-shen* literally means "one" and "god" respectively, and it is used as a proper noun for God in the document. In this name, *yi* (一, one) is used an adjective, qualifying the noun *shen* (神, God), but it is not used in the numerical sense, but in the sense of "one and only one", as in the expression "神唯獨一神" ("God is the one only one God") in Line 23. When the word *Shen* appears in the document without *yi*, it often refers to the "various gods", as in "眾人先自緣善神" ("Then people start to search out for their own indulging various gods") in Line 167, and "在於木石之上，著神名字" ("to carve names of various gods on trees and rocks") in Lines 176-177.

Elohim is the plural form of *El* (אֵל), meaning gods. However, in the OT, it is used as a proper noun for God through conjugation of the verbs and adjectives associated with it into singular form. Brichto, in considering the morphology of *Elohim*, says that in that name, there is a "transformation of a common noun into a proper name expressive of the idea that, the common noun having but one member, that noun is more a particular than a genus."[50] The same can be said about *Yishen*, for *shen* is a common noun, and if not qualified, it carries a plural sense, as in 祭神如神在 ("Make sacrifice to the gods, as if the gods were present") and 山川神祇 ("gods of hills and rivers") from the 論語 (The Analects) and 禮記 (The Book of the Rites). As there is no grammatical conjugation in Chinese language, the device used by our author is to add the word *yi* in the front to transform the common noun *shen* into a proper name, and in so doing, the common noun *shen* now has but one member, and it becomes more a particular than a genus.

Therefore, in devising the name *Yishen*, the author seems to have more the Hebrew name *Elohim* in mind, than the Syriac *Allaha*. It is worth noting here that in all the Jingjiao documents, the name *Yishen* appears only in *Discourse*. In later Jingjiao documents, which are commonly attributed to Jingjing (景淨) of the mid-8th Century, *Aluohe* (阿羅訶) is used to transliterate *Allaha*.

---

50 Ibid., p. 19

Tianzun

As mentioned above, *Tianzun* literally means "that which is the highest" and "that which is supremely honored", and it is an epithet for God. Tang Li is of the view that the common word *zun* (尊) in *Tianzun* and *Shizun* (世尊) suggests that both of these two names have a Buddhist origin.[51] However, although the author would most likely have obtained the term *Shizun* from Buddhist sources (as it was how the Buddha was commonly called), he might have found *Tianzun* more generic, used in various classical traditions including Taoism and Buddhism. The term probably begins in "天尊地卑，乾坤以定" ("heaven is lofty and honorable; earth is low") of *I-Ching* (易經, *Book of Changes*), dated to 西周 (the Western Zhou Dynasty) of 11th to 8th Centuries BC. Here, *tian-zun* ("天尊") is not a noun, but a phrase, literally meaning "heaven is lofty and honorable". The phrase is in parallel formation with *di-bei* ("地卑"), which literally means "earth is low", also not a noun. In subsequent eras, we see that *tian-zun* start to be used as an epithet for the Buddha, such as in the *Sutra of Infinite Life* ("佛說無量壽經") of the 3rd Century: "今日天尊行如来之德" ("Today the Buddha practices the virtue of with neither origin nor destination"), as well as in Taoism, such as in *Suishu Jingji Zhi* ("隋書 經籍志") of the 6-7th Centuries: "元始天尊" ("*Tianzun* from the Beginning").[52]

In the NT of the *Peshitta*, *Marya* is a direct translation of κύριος (*kyrios*), as they both mean "the Lord." In *Discourse*, this NT sense of *Marya* is represented by *Shizun* (世尊), and we know this through the expression "世尊翳數弥師訶" ("*Shizun Yishu Mishihe*") in Line 365, which is equivalent to the "Lord Jesus Christ" ("Κύριος Ιησούς Χριστός"). Furthermore, *Tianzun* is never used in the NT sense of *Marya* in *Discourse*. Therefore, *Tianzun* is used exclusively in the OT sense of *Marya*, addressing God (not Jesus), equivalent to *Adonai/Yahweh*.

Marya in the OT is a direct translation of *Adonai*, and they both mean "the Lord." As mentioned above, *Adonai* is not an original name for God, but a substitute for *Yahweh*, because the pronunciation of the latter was long lost (see Footnote 42 above). Was the author using *Tianzun* for the substitute *Marya*, or the original *Yahweh*? Since the author was devising a new nomenclature in addressing God in a new language, he should have felt free from the historical entanglement of the "God" language in the Bible, and had an opportunity to

---

51 Tang (2002), p. 132
52 欽偉剛（譯），福永光司[日]. "中國宗教思想史（上）." 宗教學研究, no. 4, 2008, pp. 122-137. "天尊" 指天界的尊神, 也是前出 《隋書》〈經籍志〉 稱呼道教最高神 (元始天尊) 的詞語。只是, 三世紀曹魏時代的康僧鎧等所譯 《佛說無量壽經》 卷上見有 "今日天尊行如來德" 的表現。六世紀, 中國北朝後期, "天尊" 一詞與秦漢時代的古語 "元始" 結合, 構成了 "元始天尊" 一詞, 被用來稱呼道教的最高神。

make it direct and simple. In this sense, we would believe that he would want to use *Tianzun* on the original, i.e., on *Yahweh*.

VIII Conclusion

In this paper, we have established that the author of *Discourse* addresses God on a two-name basis, i.e., *Yishen* and *Tianzun*. Since the author was from the Syriac tradition, we examine the Syriac Bible (*the Peshitta*), and we find that God is also called by two names: *Allaha* and *Marya*, and they are used interchangeably. Based on Cassuto and Brichto's rules to differentiate the Hebrew equivalences of *Allaha* and *Marya*, i.e., *Elohim* and *Yahweh*, we have established that *Yishen* corresponds with *Allaha,* and *Tianzun* with *Marya*.

We then further note that there is a parallel between *Yishen* and *Elohim* in the ways they are formulated, in that some literary device is employed to turn a common noun into a proper name. We could therefore infer that *Yishen* is derived from *Elohim* directly,[53] not from *Allaha*. With respect to *Tianzun*, it does not represent the NT sense of *Marya*, for that is represented by Jesus' title *Shizun*. For the OT sense of *Marya*, i.e, *Adonai*, it is a substitute of original *Yahweh*, and in our view, the author of *Discourse* would want *Tianzun* to represent the original, i.e., Yahweh, for he had no reason not to, but bound by the substitute.

One more note: in later Jingjiao documents, we find neither *Yishen* nor *Tianzun* was used. Only *Aluohe*, which is a straight transliteration of *Allaha*, is used. This seems to represent a shift in language policy of the Jingjiao Church, to one that reflects more the Syriac usage than the biblical one. In this way, the more precise and clearer nomenclature for God in *Discourse* was lost. One would wonder what had caused this shift.

Bibliography

Primary

《一神論》(*Discourse on God*), a photo-copy of the manuscript, with line numbers, is included in 林悟殊(2003).
《大秦景教流行中國碑》(the *Monument Commemorating the Propagation of Daqin Jingjiao in the Central Territory*); text included in 吳昶興 (2015).

---

53   We also cannot resist to note how closely *yi* in Yishen and *e* in Elohim sound alike.

唐太宗貞觀十二年詔 (Decree of 638 AD), in 唐會要(Tang Hui Yao), online database for Chinese classical texts 中國哲學書電子化計劃(<http://ctext.org/wiki.pl?if=gb&chapter=677933>, viewed on 19 Sep. 2017).

Secondary

羽田,《羽田博士史学論文集: 下卷 (言語・宗教篇)》(京都: 東洋史研究会, 1958)

劉偉民,〈唐代景教之傳入及其思想之研究〉, 載《聯合書院學報》第一期, 1962 年6 月, 頁1-64

吳昶興,《大秦景教流行中國碑－大秦景教文獻釋義》(臺北：橄欖出版社, 2015)

摩普綏提亞的狄奧多若著, 朱東華譯《教理講授集 — 摩普綏提亞的狄奧多若》（香港：道風書社, 2015）

景天星,〈"五蘊" 概念釋論〉載《五臺山研究》no. 4, 2016, pp. 16-18。

曾陽晴,《唐朝漢語景教文獻研究》(臺北: 花木蘭文化工作坊, 2005)

朱謙之,《中國景教》(北京：人民出版社, 1993)

林悟殊,《中古三夷教辨證》(北京: 中華書局, 2005)

林悟殊,《唐代景教再研究》(北京: 中國社會科學出版社, 2003)

林悟殊,《敦煌文書與夷教研究》(上海: 上海古籍出版社, 2011),

欽偉剛（譯），福永光司[日]. "中國宗教思想史（上）." 宗教學研究, no. 4, 2008, pp. 122-137

江文漢,《中國古代基督教及開封猶太人》(上海知識出版社: 1982)

王蘭平,〈日本杏雨書屋藏富岡文書高楠文書真偽再研究〉, 載《敦煌學輯刊》1(2016), pp. 10-33

羅香林,《唐元兩代之景教》(香港: 中國學社, 1966)

翁紹軍,〈論漢語景教經文的傳述類型〉, 載《世界宗教研究》4(1996), 頁 110-118

翁紹軍,《漢語景教文典詮釋》(香港: 漢語基督教文化研究所, 1995)

聶志軍,《唐代景教文獻詞語研究》(湖南: 人民出版社, 2010)

馮承鈞,《景教碑考》(上海：商務印書館, 1931)

高永久,〈西域景教考述〉, 載《西利亞戈北史地》3(1994), 頁 64-70

《中國哲學書電子化計劃》(<http://ctext.org/dictionary.pl?if=gb&id=12632>)

《漢典》www.zdic.net

Baum, Wilhelm, Dietmar W. Winkler. *The Church of the East: A Concise History.* London: Routledge Curzon, 2003)

Beggiani, Seely, J. *Early Syriac Theology.* Catholic University of America Press, Washington, 2014. p. 100

Brichto, Herbert C., and MyiLibrary. *The Names of God: Poetic Readings in Biblical Beginnings.* Oxford University Press, New York, 1998

Cassuto, Umberto. *The Documentary Hypothesis and the Composition of the Pentateuch: Eight Lectures.* 4th ed. ed., Jerusalem, Magnes Press, Hebrew University, 1965.

Drake, F.S., "The Nestorian Literature of the Tang Dynasty", *the Chinese Recorder,* 66 (1935), pp. 681-687

Ferreira, Johan, *Early Chinese Christianity: The Tang Christian Monument and Other Documents* (Sydney: St Paul's Publications, 2014)

Hunter, Erica C. D. "Syriac Christianity in Central Asia." *Zeitschrift Für Religions- Und Geistesgeschichte,* vol. 44, no. 4, 1992, pp. 362-366

Hunter, Erica C. D., "Persian contribution to Christianity in China: Reflections in the Xi'an Fu Syriac inscriptions", Winkler, Dietmar W., and Li Tang. *Hidden Treasures and Intercultural Encounters: Studies on East Syriac Christianity in China and Central Asia.* vol. 1.1, Lit. Wien, Piscataway. NJ, 2009.

Legge, James, *The Nestorian Monument of Hsi-an Fu in Shen-hsi, China.* (London: Trubner & Co, 1888)

Saeki, P.Y., C.E. Couling, *The Luminous Religion: Nestorian Christianity in China.* (London: The Carey Press, 1925)

Saeki, P.Y., *The Nestorian Documents and Relics in China* (Tokyo: Toho Bunkwa Gakuin: Academy of Oriental Culture, Tokyo Institute, 1951)

Saeki, P.Y., *The Nestorian Documents and Relics in China* (Tokyo: Toho Bunkwa Gakuin: Academy of Oriental Culture, Tokyo Institute, 1951)

Saeki, P.Y., *The Nestorian Monument in China* (London: Society for Promoting Christian Knowledge, 1916)

Saeki, P. Y., *The Nestorian Documents and Relics in China* (Tokyo: the Maruzen Company Ltd, 1937)

Tang Li, *A Study of the History of Nestorian Christianity in China and its Literature in Chinese: Together with a New English Translation of the Dunhuang Nestorian Documents* (P. Lang, 2002)

The Concise Oxford Dictionary of the Christian Church (3 ed.) Edited by E.A. Livingstone Oxford University Press, 2013

Wigram, W.A., *An Introduction to the History of the Assyrian Church 100-640 AD.* (London: Society for Promoting Christian Knowledge, 1910)

Wilhelm, B. & Winkler, D.W., *The Church of the East: A Concise History* (Routledge; Reissue edition, 2010)

Winkler, Dietmar W. & Tang, Li eds. *From the Oxus River to the Chinese Shores: Studies on East Syriac Christianity in China and Central Asia (orientalia – patristica – oecumenica)* (Wien: Lit, 2013)

Winkler, Dietmar W. & Tang, Li eds. *Winds of Jingjiao: Studies on Syriac Christianity in China and Central Asia (orientalia – patristica – oecumenica)* (Wien: Lit, 2009)

Winkler, Dietmar W., and Li Tang. *Hidden Treasures and Intercultural Encounters: Studies on East Syriac Christianity in China and Central Asia.* vol. 1.;1;, Lit, Wien; Piscataway, NJ, 2009.

Wylie, Alexander, "The Nestorian Tablet of se-gan Foo." *Journal of the American Oriental Society*, 5 (1855), pp. 277-336

CHAPTER 2

The Unique Features of Chanting in Jingjiao Liturgy, as Revealed in Unearthed Jingjiao Documents

Chengyong Ge, translated by D. Tam

Jingjiao is a global system within Christianity that comprises faith, philosophy, governance, cultivation, discipleship, etc. Although Jingjiao was conveyed in the Chinese language through translated texts, inscriptions on monuments and pillars, building architecture, emphasis in filial piety, etc., it had not, in general, entirely deviated from the orthodox of the Nestorian tradition. The chanting during worship was one such feature inherited and maintained.

Zunjing, the Dunhuang manuscript (P. 3847), was a document used by the Jingjiao missionaries to lead the congregation into liturgical chants. Its end part represented some preacher's notes listing the sacred books to be commemorated. It is fascinating that in the Christian prayer books discovered in Turfan, the liturgical language of the Church of the East was kept, and at the same time the tones of liturgical chants, as well as other markings, were also recorded, providing some precious first-hand information about liturgical chants.

I

In 1904 to 1907, the "German Turfan Expedition" discovered at the monastery site of Shuipang near Bulayiq (about 10 km south of Turfan) a large number of Christian manuscripts, as well as Buddhist and Manichean manuscript fragments. Some other Christian manuscripts also surfaced in nearby areas such as Kuche. These manuscripts, kept in Germany after their discovery, were partially lost or damaged during World War II. The surviving parts include 1090 fragments of pamphlets, some two-page or single-page sheets, and some torn-outs papers. The languages and scripts appearing on these fragments are diverse, including Syriac, Sogdian written with Syriac and Sogdian alphabets, New Persian written with Syriac alphabets, Uyghur Türk tili written with old Uyghur alphabets, Pahlavi written with Pahlavi alphabets, etc.[1]

---

1 Mark Dickens: Scribal Practices in the Turfan Christian Community, Journal of the Canadian society for Syriac Studies. Volume 13, 2013.

Our interest is in the Christian manuscript fragments that are bilingual, such as the Syriac-Sogdian interlinear biblical texts, or unilingual but decorated with rubrics written in another language, providing instructions to clergy on details of the chant. Were the missionary pastors using Syriac for liturgical chants, or Sogdian, or Uyghur? We can tell from this type of fragments. If several languages were used interchangeably, the fragments should likely have been used by believers from several ethnic groups.

Christian manuscript fragments are mainly written in Syriac, Sogdian, or a combination of the two, indicating that the former was the one used in liturgy, and the latter was the one actually spoken (the mother tongue) of the Sogdians, one that was used for trade along the Silk Road, and was instrumental in the spread of religions including Christianity.

Since the beginning when the Nestorians of the Syriac Church of the East first celebrated liturgy, they integrated chants into liturgical celebration. Such chanting started as a vocal way to learn the scripture, allowing for an experience of the gospel through sound, and the beauty of the doctrines through practice. The purity, solemnity and love expressed in the chanting or singing echo, at the same time, people's state of mind. It is the low and thick voice of the men, and the soft and tender voice of the women, and sometimes the combination of the two, to bring comfort to people's heart.

Chanting was a mix of music and poetry recital that the ancients used. It embodies the religion's concerns for humanity and the eagerness to console. It transports rhythmic poetry to chanting, at the same time leaving room for the chanters to interpret and express grace. Nevertheless, chanting is not singing, and although there is a certain musical intonation in chanting, such tones are supposed to be simple or even monotonous. The importance is that the voice is articulated clearly to convey the scriptures without errors. If the intonation is too complex, or too musical, it becomes singing.[2] Chanting combines reciting, humming, praising and singing, and these techniques are used together and alternately in liturgical chanting and singing, training the believers to work on the lyrics and voice. The importance is for them to acquaint with the doctrines in the process, so that they could learn, devote themselves and assimilate.

According to the late German scholar 克里木凯特 (Hans-Joachim Klimkeit), the Sogdian manuscripts from Turfan were originally part of a large volume of translated Syriac scriptures, including parts of the Old Testament and New Testament, some edited documents, legends, and a substantial amount

---

2 Regarding the differences between chanting and singing, see p. 69 of Chen Xiaolu "History of Christian Music", Zongjiao Wenhua Chubanshe, 2006, with respect to the ways of singing and psalm tones.

martyrdom literature, such as Acts of the Persian Martyrs, the Apostolic Canons, etc.³

The Turfan Christian fragments vary in types, and various languages are alternately used in them, but at least more than half of them are fragments in Syriac language. This shows that in the liturgical texts, Syriac is the main language used. Some of them have rubrics written in Sogdian, indicating that Sogdian, or occasionally the Uighur language, was used in other faith documents (such as the Creed). The missionary priests used Syriac or Sogdian, mixed in with Old, Middle, or New Persian languages, etc., when they did Bible readings, from mainly the Book of Psalms.⁴ As the missionaries were far away from the headquarter of the Church of the East, they tended to translate texts from Syriac to Sogdian more often (or occasionally reciting in Uyghur). For the documents that people expected to read in the church, especially abstinent literature, annotations, commentaries and biographies of the saints, and frequent reference to the Desert Fathers, this would have required the Jingjiao clergy to provide instead a softer, more subtle tone, rhythms, intonation, thus using the voice of chant to bring echoes of God in the distance. Their mission is to use the language most familiar to the local people, anywhere in the world, to chant their "divine meeting" with Christ, to chant an understanding of the world of life and insights into their destiny.

When we realize that the prayer documents in Jingjiao liturgy are expressed in Syriac, Sogdian or Uyghur, and that it seems odd that no Christian literature is ever found in the land of Sogdia itself, we should not be too surprised, as Christians of various ethnic groups resided and traded along the Silk Road. They were accustomed to prayer booklets and prayer amulets. Since the miscellaneous or "secular" documents lacked a better description, they would not have been catchy and chanting on them would have been less pleasant. Therefore, if the Christian text was not with serious theology or church content, it was difficult to attract believers. When Turfan believers mostly used Sogdian, or a considerable part of them also used the Uyghur language, this undoubtedly reflected the fact that the latter was the mainstream language in Turfan and it did not matter what ethnic group this religious group consisted of. The texts used by Turfan Christians were more often works composed in the Uyghur language or translated into Uyghur. This reflected the steadfastness and

---

3 Hans-Joachim Klimkeit, Christianity in Central and Southern Asia before Vasco da Gama, trans. Lin Wushu, Taiwan Shuxin Chubanshe, 1995, p. 77.
4 Nicholas Sims-Williams: Sogdian and Turkish Christians in the Turfan and Tuh-huang Manuscripts", trans. Chen Huaiyu, Dunhuang Studies, vol 2, 1997.

determination of the Uyghur Christians to spread their faith in the mid-Ninth to the Twelfth centuries, in areas dominated by Buddhism.

With respect to punctuation and pronunciation, the markings used in the Turfan Christian texts include black or red single dots, full black and full red horizontal double dots or vertical double dots, as well as triple and quadruple dots on slant lines, etc. These are often used to provide marginal titles and annotations. They also are for marking the rhythm bars, and helping users to find the right pitch, ensuring that a pleasant and moving chant.[5] In particular, the lead singers among the pastors would have some primary notes on the texts to assist him making the correct pronunciation.

With respect to the red letters and the marginal notes, they appear on most of the fragments, for clearly indicating the titles or the beginning of a new text. In the Psalms, red characters are often used to label one or more numbers of hymns, headlines of hymns, or the main part of Mar Aba. In Biblical scriptures, red texts and characters are used to indicate dates and the references for the Bible readings; In the liturgical texts, they are used to mark liturgical parts or to guide the pastors or to help the deacons to find their respective parts of the liturgy.

In particular, the musical notes and other markings are most interesting. The pitch of the chant is designed for humming the text, and it is found in nearly 30 fragments, most of which are Bible verses in Syriac, Syriac-Sogdian or Sogdian languages (all spelled in Syrian letters). Although these tones had been discussed by Egon Wellesz as early as 1919,[6] different vowels are frequently marked to highlight the distinctive features.

It should be said that different people's accent would often change to suit the regions and ethnic groups they were in. The clergy lead singers would have acquired the basic skills such as timbre, pitch, rhythm, pingyi, and tuning. Simple Bible verses could turn into sophisticated composition of metrical poetry, but this need not bore the believers. The missionary carefully scrutinized various classics and tries various ways repeatedly to overcome any technical issues, so that the believers could experience the powerful appeal of language in the process of listening and speaking.

---

5 Yang Zhouhuai "Christian Music", Religion and Culture Press, 2001, p. 28. The 6th century "Neumes" recording method of Christian music is the earliest method of recording and propagating music. The adding of the Neumes symbols and lines to the lyrics by the church led to the three- and ten-line notation of the 10th century, and the five-line notation of the 13th century.

6 Wills, "A Chronicle of the History of Eastern Music – The Symbols in the Sogdian Text for Chanting Doctrines," in Journal of Musicology I, 1919, pp. 505-515.

Either liturgical chanting or singing, it was a way of people to convey their feelings, and it contained a deep-rooted trust relationship between people and a sense of common understanding about life. This is like hearing one's own mother tongue in a noisy crowd, in some foreign lands. Dissolving into the eternity of one's own nature,[7] and this is the realm of religious chanting.

II

There are differences between the Syriac Book of Psalms used by the Church of the East, and that appearing in the fragments in Turfan. In the Syriac documents, biblical texts account for 22%. Eighteen fragments of Psalms are in Syriac. Whether Gospels or other prayer documents, they all indicate that they have been substantially altered by the missionary pastor, so that they are of a form that could more easily be recited.[8]

Besides the many Syriac liturgical texts, there were also a small number of Sogdian and Uyghur language texts used in the church, including a Sogdian translation of the Gloria in excelsis Deo. Church calendars are also found in the fragments, which are important references for observing feasts such as the Easter and other moveable feasts, especially the Great-Lent and Pentecost. There are also calendars written with Syriac alphabets, many of which are marked in the back in Sogdian. The biography and legends of saints accounted for only a relatively small proportion (2%) in the Syriac literature; there is a two-page sheet from the legend of "Mar Barshabba", the founder of the legendary Merv Christianity. There are eight fragments from the Syriac "Saga of St. George", which has versions of Sogdian and Uyghur.[9] Admonition, annotations, and general abstinence literature often appear in the Sogdian Christian texts, but almost no Syriac language is used. This shows that local Christians observed

---

7 Min Min, "On the Expression of Emotion in Western Religious Music", Symphony – Journal of Xi'an Conservatory of Music, No. 2, 2002.
8 Barbati, Chiara:The Christian Sogdian Gospel Lectionary E5 in Context. (Veröffentlichungen zur Iranistik, Band: 81). P59-64,E5: language. Published by Wien: Verlag der österreichischen Akademie der Wissenschaften 2016. [The Study on the Turfan text in The Christian Sogdian Text of the Gospel.]. Preferred Citation. Nicholas Sims-Williams: The Christian Sogdian manuscript C2., Schriften zur Geschichte und Kultur des Alten Orients. Berlin Turfantexte, vol. 12 (Berlin, 1985). Preferred Citation. Nicholas Sims-Williams: The Christian Sogdian manuscript C2., Schriften zur Geschichte und Kultur des Alten Orients. Berlin Turfantexte, vol. 12 (Berlin, 1985).
9 Nicholas Sims-Williams, The Recent Research on the Sogdian Christian Literature, Chinese translation in Bibo, Journal of Xinjiang Normal University, (Philosophy and Social Science Edition), No. 4, 2014, pp. 77-83.

disciplines and their initial pledge at conversion. The literature on wisdom education, wedding wishes and medicine has within it believers' confession to God's grace and their submission to be God's lambs.

We believe that the missionaries of the monastery of Shuipang near Bulayiq may not be able to read and write Syriac, and the ascent might also have been a problem. Nevertheless, through the markings on the Selection of Bible Verses, the Psalms, the Daily Office, and the legend of "Mar Barshabba", they led a life of chanting. In terms of Christianity on the Silk Road, the Church of the East dominated the Silk Road from the Sasanian Empire in Persia to the Tang Dynasty in China. Along this entire Central Asian corridor, there were bishops in the cities of Samarkand, Bukhari, Tashkent, and Suyab. The Eastern Syriac Christian literature discovered in the temple site of Gaochang, Turfan has been fully authenticated through cross-referencing the contents of existing known texts, especially the worship literature, and the markings for east Syriac pronunciation. This is all related to chanting, especially when facing the noble women such as the wives of the Khan, the singing of the "Christian faith", "we believe in the one and only one God" and "Nicene Creed" had to be filled with sentiments. Reciting in a low, not strong, tone, the prayer had to be sincere and rich with moving tone. Not surprisingly, the priests would remember these marked texts, especially the Psalms, which were memorized countless times throughout their life in the missions. The missionaries relied on the texts they had memorized, giving God praise and adulation.

Chanting is a meticulous, creative, and reflective form of expression, with words, sounds, and affections, and is passed on by the missionaries from generation to generation. The purpose of chanting is not only to let others hear it, but also to allow your own soul and the soul of the scripture merge, through the sound of the chants to reach the deep and intimate exchange. If speech helped achieving evangelism, then evangelism helped sanctifying life.

The Turfan fragments of the Christian manuscripts help us understand the development of Jingjiao at a place far away from the Syriac-speaking homeland of the Church of the East. Despite being surrounded by distinctively different religious cultures such as Buddhism, Manichaeism, and Zoroastrianism, the missionaries were still committed to maintaining their own unique characteristics when copying Syriac texts, thus leaving behind the liturgical texts used in the church and in other settings, revealing the effects of variations in length and in pitch. Although the surviving texts are not complete, they nevertheless represent the earliest liturgical texts on paper written in Sogdian and Uighur, by the missionaries.

The discovery of the Jingjiao texts in Turfan has also brought up a series of questions. Were they written in Turfan or somewhere else, such as a diocese in

Central Asia, or in Syria proper? Can these texts be better identified with paleographical analysis? Can the original Syriac writing be restored by people speaking Syriac as mother tongue? Are the signs used by the calligrapher newly invented, or some original signs inherited? These questions have not yet all been answered, and without such knowledge we cannot gain further understanding of the daily life of the missionaries and the followers of Turfan through these text fragments.

III

The localization of Jingjiao in China ha been a major issue in the cultural exchanges between China and the West, and it has long attracted the attention of the international academic community. In the process of bringing in the Jingjiao scriptures, the missionaries had to sieve through the philosophy, spirit, and core beliefs in a large number of their classical literature and to confirm a set of liturgy and faith practice that could best fit the China's national conditions. They also had to adapt to the existing Buddhist and Taoist cultures, and at the same time to not lose their own unique features, maintaining characteristics and a spiritual outlook different than those of the Buddhists and Taoists.

At that time in China, the Tang dynasty was a kingdom filled with poetry, which had a wide reach in society. Most literati and people were addicted to metrical poetry that rhymed at the end of each line and carried artistic conception. From early childhood, they received education in poetry, and the training in how to compose poems in seven or five-character quatrains. Poetry represented the most sensitive tentacles in each ethnic language, and could best consciously assume the function of expanding and exploring the linguistic space of its times. The "Jingjiao monks in white robe" seem to be writing the rhythm of Chinese poetry, and they took up the burden of spreading the Bible, and on one hand they needed to have a wide vocal range, on the end being able to maintain a steady tone. They received training of Chinese poetry tirelessly when going through the learning process of transmission.[10]

Jingjiao missionaries insisted on reciting their own scriptures in ancient Syriac language, because they were concerned that translation into another language would violate the original meaning of the scriptures. They even thought that translating the scriptures into any other language could lead to deviation from the original meaning. Yet, how could they transmit if they did

---

10 Lin Wushu, "Review of the Jingjiao Manuscript P. 3847" in Further Study of the Dunhuang Jingjiao, see p. 134, China Social Sciences Press, 2003.

not translate? Therefore, in the bilingual or tri-lingual situation, translation between languages was a matter highly regarded.

The texts unearthed in Turfan led us to notice the apparently widespread imperfection in the classic Dunhuang Jingjiao literature, which were in fact an alternate use of languages. It was an experiment to switch from ancient Syriac to Chinese, while the Chinese were watching you how to speak and how to pronounce. The author wanted to feel the tremors and the impact that a word or a term could bring to the heart and soul, and to experience the biting power of words, to accumulate terms, to solemnly bind them up, and to reach directly to the hearts of the believers, and to sing in this noisy world, only to become quiet and peaceful in the humming during the chants.

From a start of poor communication with words to a more stable form at the end, Jingjiao literature had experienced over a century of historical development, during which the Jingjiao language did not stay unchanged, but instead had chosen to incorporate suitable Chinese expressions and terminology, to mark out the language reminders of God, and to feel the power of the voice of God in His calling. The language used by the Jingjiao missionaries on daily basis could not win the trust of the believers, and so they had to use the language of poetry to retell the nobility of the Bible, listening the realm of God in imagination, and converting the call of God to the call of resurrection, and turning the outcast son of God into the beloved son of God.

If we say that the physical body of poetry reflected the voice of its soul, the clear and distinct voice would have doubtless made the reciting of rhythmic verses full of the sense of natural beauty, through the passing on of vocal tradition – if in the parlance within the profession, it was because it was catchy and easy to become good in. This way of reciting really tested the vocal skills of the priest, because it required him to recite a hymn "without releasing air while maintaining the same facial expression", and although the recital itself sounded monotonous, it instantly made people feel the solemnity. While reading the same writing, the believers might perhaps be unable to feel the beauty of the hymn, but through the recital by the priest, they would have gained a different feeling while reading it only, obtaining the feeling of the flowing through of thought.[11]

All religions of all ages attached great importance to the power of reading and the charm of chanting. They were very familiar with the sound, pace, and

---

11   Chen Xiaolu, History of Christian Music, Religious Culture Press, 2006, p. 132. The manuscript of the Dunhuang Jingjiao hymnal manuscript Sanwei Mengdu Zan is the same in content and form as the Gloria in excelsis Deo of the Roman Church. It uses the form of seven-character rhyme poems and was therefore highly Sinicized. Its tune, however, cannot be determined.

rhythm of the Chinese characters in the texts. They were not only familiar with them, but also could chant them out like flowing water. Before the written text appeared, people memorized the entire scripture and all the words. The ancient Greek poetry singers, when they sang the historical epics for the people, they relied mainly on memorizing, not texts or writings. It can be said that a religion's memory is in its collective recital from memory.

In early Christianity, "words that could only serve memories" were even despised. What happened at the pulpit was a recitation of large amount of script, which was called "the ink book." Only those "living words" taught by the pope were regarded as authentic and well reflected "works". Besides the outstanding memory of some individual people, in order to ensure the accuracy of memory, "collective memory" by a group of people was relied upon.

In Zoroastrianism, for a long time the priests had not written down their own classic the Zend-Avesta. Instead the transmission relied on oral and memory tradition from ears to mouth, from generation to generation, and it was not until the sixth Century when Zend-Avesta appeared as a collection of text, with two parts, although regrettably, one part has been lost. The part that we can see today is the part surviving.

The "hymns" that the Manichaean priests recited were restructured from the "rhythmic texts", and they on one hand were pleasing to the ears, on the other they facilitated committing them to memory. It was because when faced with a poetical essay filled with rhymes and regular format, people could quickly remember them, and remember them very well. On the other hand, when faced with loose essays that hardly had any rhymes, the ease for memorization was greatly reduced – reciting poems and metrical poetry was definitely easier than reciting from dry memory the fragments of the rigid scriptures. Therefore, this is why within many religious classics, a large number of poetry and metrical works still exist.

Buddhist practitioners also like to stress on the importance of memorizing complete texts. It is said that this is the earliest source of Buddhist scriptures. In the Journey to the West, of the Tang Dynasty, the early Buddhist "memorization" is recorded: "Here the venerable Kasyapa with 999 great Arhats, after Tathagata's Nirvana, called a convocation (for the purpose of settling) the three Pitakas… On this Kasyapa rising, said "Consider well and listen. Let Ananda, who ever heard the words of Tathagata, collect by singing through the Sutra-pitaka." This passage is saying that when Tathagata died, his first disciple Kasyapa assembled a group of Arhats (the most distinguished elders in the community of faith). Amongst all the people, Kasyapa recited from memory the teaching of Buddha, and the other disciple Ananda was responsible for "praising" (checking with memory). This process lasted for two or three months before it ended. Buddhist practitioners have an amazing power of memory for their scriptures.

Many passages in Buddhist scriptures are actually written with rhymes, or the whole Buddhist scripture has a certain rhythm. The reason why we do not feel that rhythm is because of language barriers. Most people do not understand Sanskrit or Pali. However, the end of the Praina Sutra says: gate-gate-paragate-parasamgate-bodhisvaha. This is familiar to many Chinese Buddhists, because they are chanted with rhymes at the end of the sentences. However, in fact, if we use Sanskrit to recite a passage, we would experience the rhythms. It not only makes it easier for people to remember, but also make it more moving for the listeners.

In both Judaism and Christianity, there are requirements in chanting. In Judaism, there is an emphasis on the role of praise hymns and instrument music during religious ceremonies. For Christianity, when people ask how they should pray, Jesus teaches them "the Lord's Prayer", and the beginning line is "Our father in heaven!" If we combine the homophonic sounds before the chanting, to a certain extent, it can help us understand the feelings of both Jews and Christians towards God as the Father.[12]

In order to create an incomparably crystal-clear yet psychedelic tone, the missionaries, on the basis of the pitch, added overtones to make believers feel real and unreal at the same time, totally immerged in it, all the way until the final mixing of harmony. This made believers feel like they were part of the universe, and they could look out to see the galaxy, watching the stars going around their bodies. They thought of the missionary saints sent by God, and they could not help but burst into tears. In general, religions use the art of chanting to allow to comfort the suffering life of believers and to bring them to deeper reflections.

IV

Buddhism has traditionally used literary forms to propagate the traditions of their doctrines. Ji-song is the poetic expression of the Buddhist doctrines and sayings. If the starting point of lyrical poetry is a vivid image in the words, Ji-song promoting Buddhism and expounds the doctrine is religion. In the

---

12   Contributions of Early Church Music to Western Culture, see Edward Lippman: A History of Western Musical Aesthetics, University of Nebraska Press, 1992. (United States) Paul Henry Lang (Paul HenyLang), Gu Lianli et al. Translation of Music in Western Civilization, Guizhou People's Publishing House, 2001.

second volume of the Biographies of Eminent Monks, in the dialogue of Kumarajiva and Monk Rui, it says that: "In the customs of India, the observance of ritual is important, and they are good in string music. When in audience with the Emperor, there must be songs praising the Emperor's virtues. When in audience with the Buddha, the songs of admiration is important. Ji-songs in the scriptures reflect such formalities." This tradition of retrospective hymns to praise the Buddhist teachings originated from India. The word "Ji" is the abbreviation of the Sanskrit "Veda", which is translated as "Song", and when these Sanskrit and Chinese words are combined to form 'Ji-song'.

From the beginning of the Tang Dynasty, Ji-song put emphasis on the art of crafting rhythms and symmetry. With improvement of the literary accomplishment of the translators, Ji-song became more and more like songs, and the language of Buddhist doctrines became more and more like poetry, taking on certain regular forms. Although Ji-song was different from songs, but the poetization of Ji-song had created a kind of poetical Ji-song, and there was a trend that gave rise to a lot of "poetical monks" in the monasteries.

The Jingde Chuandeng Lu, in recording the Tang Buddhist monks' answers to the Buddhist basic tenets such as its ontological questions, they used poetics to express the secrets of Zen: "White clouds occasionally come to shroud the house, and no wind nor moon hover the four streams"; "The white monkeys carry their children into the green mountains, and the bees and butterflies kiss the green stamen among the flowers." In form and artistic articulation, these poems are typically seven or five-character quatrains. Therefore, the Buddhist sutras, in the form of Ji-song, had been translated into Chinese and appeared in large numbers in the vernacular language. From the Northern and Southern Dynasties to the Sui and Tang dynasties, a large number of vernacular poetical Ji's were preserved. Bai Juyi's Bajian Ji was his writing in commemoration of the eight words given to him by Ninggong: Vision, Perception, Steadiness, Wisdom, Enlightenment, Comprehension, Charity, and Relinquishing", and in his later years, he also wrote Liuzan Ji: Praising the Buddha, Praising the Doctrine, Praising the Monk, Concerning the Living, Concerning Repentance, Making Wishes, etc., and he even recomposed the translated Buddhist verses into poems to convey the Buddhist thoughts.

From the emergence of the poetical literature in the Tianbao Era, such as Dunhuang's Jiangmo Bianwen and Chanshi Weishi Yufeng Yinyuan, it can be seen that the monks were good in using vernacular language to persuade believers to return to the spiritual path. Most of them were Buddhist works of persuasion, and the forms were novel, incorporating talking and singing, and this started in the 8th century continuing into the 11th century.[13]

---

13 Wang Chuan, "On some Dunhuang Nestorian manuscripts bearing certain resemblances to the type of Buddhist rituals", Proceedings of Conference at Princeton University, Sep-

If Jingjiao was to compete for believers in areas of Dunhuang and Turfan, it had to borrow the Buddhist methods. Although it could not use folk songs of their homeland, it certainly could adapt the Chinese terminology so as to produce chants. As pointed out by the German scholar 克里木凯特 (Hans-Joachim Klimkeit) with respect to the martyrdom story of St. George preserved in Uyghur documents, according to Syriac tradition, if one called out St. George's name, he would receive help, the same as the Buddha in Central Asia rendered help to their believers.[14] For Jingjiao, in the propagation of faith, its documents such as Sanwei Mengdu Zan, Zunjing, and Xuanyuan Zhiben Jing incorporated a large amount of Buddhist vocabulary and content. Its absorption and re-interpretation of the Buddhist culture needs to be studied, but the mutual influences between them should also not be underestimated.

In evangelism, nothing would have been worse than "dry chanting". Written in seven or five-character quatrains, the chants had patterns of tones and rhymes that produce vocal variations, making them easy to sing. Therefore, chants of seven or five-character quatrains were used in Buddhism, Manichaeism and Jingjiao. The same for Taoism, where casual reciting turned into chanting, thus easy to memorize and recite. I believe that the literary expression used in Buddhism no doubt had some influence on Jingjiao when translation was rendered in the form of poetry.

The leaders in chanting used "throat voice" like that used in other regions such as Siberia, Mongolia, Tibet, etc. It was not because they had a unique vocal chord, but because they used overtones which could be learned by all. It was similar to those uninterrupted Sanskrit chants, which required continuous and stable vocal precision, something people vocal cent, which added to the body and harmony in a choir's chant.

In the cultural traditions of China and the West, the relationship between poetry and music is very important, because the beauty of sounds is always treasured. Therefore, there is this saying that "poetry and music are twins." Although there are major differences in the phonetics between the Eastern and Western languages, and the rhythms of speaking are different (there are four tones for each character of the Chinese), in chanting and singing, which are the "voice of languages", languages share the same essence. This is particularly true during worships. The sound is the life in liturgical singing, and thus the wording in the liturgy sometimes takes the back seat. The parishioners, when listening to such liturgical singing, would for sure avoid ravings, gossips, mumblings or sudden noise, because any incoherent and coarse sounds would upset the

---

14 tember 6-8, 2014: Prospects for the Study of Dunhuang Manuscripts: The Next 20 Years.
Hans-Joachim Klimkeit, Christianity in Central and Southern Asia before Vasco da Gama, trans. Lin Wushu, Taiwan Shuxin Chubanshe, 1995.

beauty of the words, and would be seen by the bishops and missionaries as signs of a corrupted soul. Therefore, when the missionaries translated documents, they paid a lot of attention to the elegance and beauty of the rhymes in words and expressions. Even when the dialects change, they would have tried to maintain the beauty of rhymes, and would not overly restrict themselves to the strict rules of language.[15]

Summing up the above contrast analysis and taking into consideration also the musical symbols of chants in the Christian documents in Turfan, it can be seen that after the entry of Jingjiao to China, celebration of liturgy was not some simple vocalization by the people. Especially after a re-interpretation and deepening by the Uighurs and other racial groups, it had an uplifting effect on the mainstream concepts amongst the believers, stimulating Jingjiao followers to, in the midst of a myriad of religions, even more firmly believe in their own religion. In helping to make the faith of believers complete, liturgical singing definitely plays an undeniably important role.

The author has been at the liturgy celebration of the Church of the East (the Nestorian Church) several times to listen to the demonstration of overtones in liturgical singing. As there were many parts in the catalogue, it is not possible to introduce them one by one.[16] However, the resonance of their voice and the unison of their breath could fill empty valleys and rise to exuberant heights. Although it is not extremely elated, its effect in the church can readily be felt, as it manifests a sacred realm, allowing the pleasure of the hearing of faith. As those who study history of art can testify: a religious ceremony and religious art not only lead believers to be closer to God, but also, through liturgical singing, to be more willing to listen, have self-respect, penitent, and willing to seek salvation.

---

15 Zhou Xiaojing, Studying Christian Music from the Perspective of Faiths and Liturgies, Journal of Tianjin Conservatory of Music, Issue 2, 2011.
16 Ge Chengyoung, "The Study of Music in the Tang and Yuan Jingjiao Chants", The Journal of Chinese Literature and History, Issue 3, 2007 (87th series).

PART 2

Practical Theology in Chinese Context

CHAPTER 3

The Multiple Identities of the Nestorian Monk Mar Alopen: A Discussion on Diplomacy and Politics

Daniel H.N. Yeung

According to the Nestorian Stele inscriptions, in the ninth year of the *Zhenguan* era of the Tang Dynasty (635 AD), the Nestorian monk Mar Alopen, carrying with him 530 sacred texts[1] and accompanied by 21 priests from Persia, arrived at Chang'an after years of traveling along the ancient Silk Road.[2] The Emperor's chancellor, Duke[3] Fang Xuanling, along with the court guard, welcomed the guests from Persia on the western outskirts of Chang'an and led them to Emperor Taizong of Tang, whose full name was Li Shimin. Alopen enjoyed the Emperor's hospitality and was granted access to the imperial palace library[4], where he began to undertake the translation of the sacred texts he had

---

1 According to the record of "Zun jing 尊經 Venerated Scriptures" amended to the Tang Dynasty Nestorian text "*In Praise of the Trinity*," there were a total of 530 Nestorian texts. Cf. Wu Changxing 吳昶興, *Daqin jingjiao liuxing zhongguo bei: daqin jingjiao wenxian shiyi* 大秦景教流行中國碑 – 大秦景教文獻釋義 [*Nestorian Stele: Interpretation of the Nestorian Text*] (Taiwan: Olive Publishing, 2015), 195.

2 The inscription on the Stele reads: "Observing the clear sky, he bore the true sacred books; beholding the direction of the winds, he braved difficulties and dangers." "Observing the clear sky" and "beholding the direction of the wind" can be understood to mean that Alopen and his followers relied on the stars at night and the winds during the day to navigate. Tradition has it that Alopen traveled along the Silk Road. "When the Nestorians headed east, they would travel through Tokhgra, which lay south of the Wuxu River… They would set out from Tokhgra to the mountains of Badakh and then head for Pamirs, eventually arriving at Khotan, from where they followed Monk Xuanzang's trail all the way to Chang'an." Feng Chengjun 馮承鈞, *Jingjiao bei kao* 景教碑考 [*Study of Nestorian Stele*] (Shanghai: Commercial Press, 1931), 58. It is also plausible, however, that Alopen traveled, at least part of the way, by sea along the ancient Maritime Silk Route, a possibility discussed in the latter part of this article.

3 "During the Tang Dynasty, the office of the *shangshulin* (head of the Department of State Affairs), or "grand chancellor," was sometimes left vacant, so that the position had to be filled by a head of one of the ministries under the Department of State Affairs (*shangshusheng*). There were six ministries under the Department: the Ministry of Personnel, the Ministry of Revenue, the Ministry of War, the Ministry of Justice, the Ministry of Works, and the Ministry of Rites, which dealt with foreign relations. Li Hu 黎虎, *Han tang waijiao zhidu shi* 漢唐外交制度史 [*History of the Diplomatic System of the Han and Tang Dynasties*] (Lanzhou: Lanzhou University Press, 1998), 347-354.

4 The Hongwen Library, which Emperor Taizong erected next to the imperial palace, housed a collection of 200,000 volumes and was comparable to the famous Library of Alexandria. Cf.

brought with him. Taizong not only read the translated scriptures, but also discussed their religious doctrines in face-to-face consultations with Alopen so as to ascertain the credibility and merit of the foreign religion. In the twelfth year of *Zhen'guan* (638 AD), after three years of study and observation, Taizong sent out an imperial decree[5] granting permission to the Persian priests to proclaim their religion. At the same time, Taizong's court financed the building of a Nestorian church (*Daqin si*) in Chang'an's Yi Ning Fang District, providing a long-term settlement where Alopen and his followers could establish their monastic order[6] and continue their work of translating and preaching. Over the next 150 years, the Nestorians translated a total of 35 volumes of sacred texts, a task that lasted well into the reign of Emperor Dezong of Tang.[7]

Alopen's elaborate welcome along with the personal attention he had received from Emperor Taizong far exceeded the hospitality ordinarily shown to

---

Samuel Hugh Moffett. *Yazhou jidujiao shi* 亞洲基督教史 [*A History of Christianity in Asia*] (Hong Kong: Chinese Christian Literature Council, 2000), 3.

5   The inscription on the Stele reads: "Right principles have no invariable name, holy men have no invariable station; instruction is established in accordance with the locality, with the object of benefiting the people at large."

6   The Nestorian Stele itself offers a description of the monastic life led by Nestorians such as Alopen: "By the rule for admission, it is the custom to apply the water of baptism, to wash away all superficial show and to cleanse and purify the neophytes. As a seal, they hold the cross, whose influence is reflected in every direction, uniting all without distinction. As they strike the wood, the fame of their benevolence is diffused abroad; worshiping toward the east, they hasten on the way to life and glory; they preserve the beard to symbolize their outward actions, they shave the crown to indicate the absence of inward affections; they do not keep slaves, but put noble and mean all on an equality; they do not amass wealth, but cast all their property into the common stock; they fast, in order to perfect themselves by self-inspection; they submit to restraints, in order to strengthen themselves by silent watchfulness; seven times a day they have worship and praise for the benefit of the living and the dead; once in seven days they sacrifice, to cleanse the heart and return to purity." For a modern Chinese translation, cf. He Guanghu and Daniel Yeung 何光滬, 楊熙楠, *Hanyu shenxue duben (shang)* 漢語神學讀本(上) [*Sino-Christian Theology Reader, Volume I*] (Hong Kong: Logos and Pneuma Press, 2009), 20.

7   They brought with them a total of 530 volumes of scriptures, most of them not translated into Chinese. Only six of these – 13,500 words in all – are extant. Cf. Ge Chengyong 葛承雍, "Tangdai jingjiao chuanjiaoshi ru hua de shengcun fangshi yu liuchan wenming 唐代景教傳教士入華的生存方式與流產文明 [The Lifestyle of Nestorian Preachers and Their Cultural Influence on China during the Tang Dynasty]," in *Jingjiao: The Church of the East in China and Central Asia*, ed. Roman Malek (Sankt Augustin: Institut Monumenta Serica), 171. On the translation of these 35 volumes and how the first Syriac-speaking Nestorians creatively adapted the Scriptural accounts to the Chinese context after their arrival in China, cf. Matteo Nicolini-Zani, "Tangdai jingjiao wenxian 唐代景教文獻 [Tang Dynasty Nestorian Texts]," in *Studium Biblicum Annual Report* (2006-2007): 113-123.

members of a foreign religious group[8]: in its extravagance it rather resembled the official diplomatic welcome extended to envoys of an allied kingdom. This observation raises three important questions: first, is it possible that the Nestorian delegation was in fact a diplomatic one in the service of the Persian Empire? Second, was the diplomatic relationship between Tang Dynasty China and Persia such that the Tang court would welcome visitors from Persia with highest state honors? Thirdly, if Alopen was in fact a secret Persian envoy, what might his purpose have been? Nestorianism was certainly not the state religion of Persia, so why was a Nestorian monk sent to China to represent the affairs of the Persian Empire?

Alopen came to Tang Dynasty China from Persia at the time of the Sasanian Empire – also known as the "Neo-Persian" Empire (AD 224-651) – when Persia, the Roman Empire, and the Byzantine Empire coexisted side by side as competing world empires, each seeking to secure its hold on power. When the Roman Empire persecuted its Christians during the first two centuries AD, a large number of Ayana-speaking Jews and Christians fled across the Persian border, starting settlements along the Euphrates River, where the Syriac Church was able establish itself without initial interference. Although Emperor Aldashir I (ca. 226-240 AD) established Zoroastrianism as the Persian state religion, Christianity was granted relative freedom under his reign.[9] Decades later, however, the reign of Sasanian Emperor Shapur II (309-379 AD) ushered in a wave of religious persecution that lasted nearly 40 years. Hostilities had begun when Shapur II received a letter from his rival, the Byzantine Emperor, demanding that the Persian Emperor show kindness to the Christians in his territory. As a result, Shapur II became deeply suspicious of the Persian Christians under his rule[10] and began levying heavy taxes on their churches, hoping to limit the fur-

---

8   The hospitality Emperor Taizong extended to Alopen and his followers went far beyond the customary imperial welcome given to foreign guests. Cf. Lucette Boulnois, *Si chou zhi lu* 絲綢之路 [*The Silk Road*], trans. Geng Sheng 耿昇 (Jinan: Shandong Pictorial Press, 2001), 177.

9   There are three reasons Moffett considers for the instatement of his tolerant religious policy: first, Ardashir I was too busy fighting Byzantium to concern himself with minority religions; second, both the Jews and Christians were refugees who fled from Rome and Byzantine to Persia, where their loyalty to the Persian Empire might have proven useful; third, the legacy of the Saharan Emperors had left Zoroastrianism much neglected. Cf. Moffett, *Yazhou jidujiao shi*, 112.

10 Two years after Emperor Constantine of Rome issued the Edict of Milan granting tolerance to Christians in 313 AD, he wrote to the Sasanian Emperor Shapur II, demanding that kindness be shown to the Christians in Persia, whom he referred to as his people, which Shapur II took to mean that Persia's Christians were loyal to Rome. Cf. Zhu Xinran 朱心然, *Anshen yu liming: dongfang jiaohui zai hua xuan jiao shi* 安身與立命- 東方教會在

ther expansion of Christianity.[11] His scheme proved unsuccessful: a number of Zoroastrians converted to Christianity, which so infuriated the Persian Emperor that he ordered the immediate execution of any convert from Zoroastrianism to Christianity, without trial or reprieve. Sixteen thousand Christians were killed in the violent years of persecution that followed (339-379 AD).[12] Every one of Shapur's successors continued persecuting Christians until ca. 401 AD.[13] Far from extinguishing the Christian Church in Persia, the half-century of violence against Persian Christians not only revealed their faithfulness, resilience and strength of character; the Persian nobility also discovered that Christians tended to be far better educated than the Zoroastrians due to the traditional ideals of theological education, which the Persian Christians deeply valued and which by this time had extensively absorbed both Greek and Roman learning.[14] Persian converts to Christianity, as well as the descendants of earlier Christians in Persia, combined theological education with Persian culture to the enrichment of Syriac traditional learning. Observing this phenomenon, the Neo-Persian rulers eventually decided to make use of the talents of Christian Persians, routinely appointing learned Christians to take up important govern-

---

華宣教史 [*Being Human: The Church of the East Mission in China*] (Hong Kong: Baptist Press, 2009), 76-77.

11 Shapur II levied heavy taxes on the Archbishop Shimun of Persia (329-341), which the latter refused to pay. As a result, the Archbishop, five bishops and one hundred priests were executed. Zhu Xinran, Ibid., 77.

12 Cf. Moffett, *Yazhou jidujiao shi*, 142-50. Cf. also B.A. Litvinski, *Zhongya wenming shi, di san juan* 中亞文明史，第三卷 [*History of Civilizations of Central Asia*, Vol. III] (Beijing: China Translation Corporation, 1996), 360.

13 As many as 190,000 Persian Christians are thought to have been martyred. Cf. Moffett, ibid., footnotes 24-26, p. 151. Iranian scholars acknowledge that there was substantial religious persecution in that period, but think that the estimate of 190,000 seems exaggerated. Cf. Abdul Hussein Zarinkoob, *Bosi diguo shi* 波斯帝國史 [*History of Persian Empire*], trans. Zhang Hongnian 張鴻年 (Shanghai: Fudan University Press, 2011), 371-372.

14 The main seminaries in Persia, such as Edessa, Nisibis and Seleucia-Ctesiphon, made important contributions to the formation of Syrian and Persian cultures. Seminary lectures covered subjects such as Bible study and teaching, theology, Greek philosophy, Roman and Greek Patristics, medicine, natural sciences, history, music and linguistics. The Seychelles-Taisi Maple Theological Seminary was well-known for its medical studies in particular, while the Oriental Christian theologians translated the Greek Bible, Greek and Latin philosophy and theology, history, geography, astronomy and other classics into Syriac. Cf. Zhu Xinran, *Anshen yu liming*, 81-87. The Oriental Christian intellectual priests not only won the favor of the Persian rulers, who elevated many of them to important government positions; when the Nestorian monks came to China in the seventh century, their skills and knowledge in the fields of medicine, astronomy, mathematics, mechanical manufacturing and other areas also won them the favor of the Tang Court. Cf. Ge, "Tangdai jingjiao," 168-169.

ment positions. Some of the Persian emperors[15] were so well-disposed toward Christianity that, as in the case of Sasanian Emperor Yazdegerd I (399-421 AD), they alienated the Zoroastrian priests while implementing policies affording greater tolerance to Christians. In order to secure the allegiance of the Persian churches and gain their support, the Sasanian Empire in 410 AD officially recognized the Syriac-speaking eastern churches,[16] which had already existed in the Persian Empire since 315 AD. Later, in 431 AD, the Council of Ephesus condemned the teachings of Nestorius as heresy and the churches following him as heretical; as the Roman Empire began expelling all Nestorians, many of them fled to Persia, seeking refuge with the Persian Emperor, who selected the most gifted and learned among their ranks to serve as officials at the Persian court. When Alopen set out for China, Ishoyahb II was Patriarch of the Church of the East (628 – 644 AD), and the last Sasanian Emperor, Yazdegerd III (632-651 AD), had just ascended the throne. Ishoyahb II was a uniquely eminent religious leader of his time. He was the first representative of the Church of the East to persuade the Islamic Army to sign a peace treaty. He possessed the foresight to invest in the development of a Hindu parish and went to the Central Asian Turkic tribes to preach Christianity; it was Ishoyahb II who sent Alopen to China.[17] Ishoyahb II had himself been sent as a diplomatic envoy to Constantinople by Yazdegerd III, a mission that ended successfully with the signing of a peace treaty with the Eastern Roman Empire and during which he

---

15 These included Yazdegerd I, Khosrow II and Ishoyahb III with Arroyo. Cf. Moffett, *Yazhou jidujiao shi*, note 9, 117.

16 In 315 AD, the Persian Church had instated its first Archbishop in Ctesiphon, the capital of the Sasanian Empire. However, the Sasanian Empire never granted legal status to the Persian Church, persecuting the Christians more than half a century. In 410 AD, with the approval of Yazdegerd I, the Bishops' Meeting of the Eastern Church was held, which discussed and established the parish system of the Eastern Church. The Third Episcopal Conference in 424 confirmed the Archbishop of Seleucia-Ctesiphon, granting him the same title and authority as the western bishops in Jerusalem, Antioch, Constantinople, or Rome. Cf. Zhu, *Anshen yu liming*, 76-78. See also Litvinski, *Zhongya wenming shi*, 360.

17 Ishoyahb II was one of the most prominent patriarchs in the history of the Eastern Orthodox Church. The geopolitical situation he faced was very complicated. While the Arab Islamic armies were gradually occupying the borders of Persia, the Church in Persia had to deal with in-fighting to the point that the Patriarch's position became vacant for more than two decades. Ishoyahb II was the first Christian to negotiate a peace treaty with the invading Islamic armies. He was also enthusiastic about the Church's mission and founded an independent diocese in India, which was to be directly responsible to the Persian Patriarch so as to avoid in-fighting within the church. It was also Ishoyahb II who sent missionaries to China on a large scale, which enabled the establishment of mission stations throughout in Central Asia and the major provinces of China over the next 700 years. Moffett, *Yazhou jidujiao shi*, 272-274.

also spoke with Emperor Heraclius (610–641 AD) in defense of the orthodoxy of his Church.[18]

From the historical backdrop briefly sketched above, Nestorianism can be seen to have emerged from the Syriac Orthodox Church, which originated in Persia during the Sasanian Empire. Although Nestorianism never became the state religion of Persia and at times suffered violent political persecution within the borders of the Empire, Nestorianism by means of the merit of some of its leading representatives nonetheless won the favor and official recognition of the Persian court in the late Middle Ages. Due to the brilliance of Ishoyahb II, who enjoyed the trust of the last Sasanian Emperor, the Archbishop – or one of his disciples – would have been a likely candidate for a diplomatic mission had the Persian Emperor sought an envoy to lead a delegation to Tang Dynasty China to discuss secret business between the two Empires. Another, more practical, consideration would have been the journey itself. At that time, one could travel from Persia to China either by the Silk Road or by the Maritime Silk Road. As Basrah[19], the most famous port in the Persian Gulf, was not far from Ctesiphon, the capital of the Sasanian Empire, the most likely route[20] to take for someone setting out from the Persian capital would have been to sail from the Persian Gulf to the South Indian coast and then on to Guangzhou in southern China.[21] More interestingly, the working language on the vessels

---

18 At that time, the Byzantine Emperor Heraklonas was deeply interested in theological debates. When he met with Ishoyahb II, theyy even discussed questions of heresy pertaining to the Eastern Church. Interestingly, Ishoyahb II persuaded Heraklonas to accept the orthodoxy of the Eastern Church, and they entered a peace treaty. See Zhu, *Anshen yu liming*, 97-98.

19 "From the seventh century to the ninth century, the Indian Ocean was a safe and rich ocean, thronged with ships of every nationality. The Arabian Sea was protected by the power of Islam, and after the Abbasid Empire was moved from Damascus to Basra at the head of the Persian Gulf, the eastern trade flourished greatly." E.H. Schafer, *Tangdai de wai lai de wenming* 唐代的外來文明 [*The Golden Peaches of Samarkand: A Study of Tang Exotics*] trans. Wu Yugui 吳玉貴 (Beijing: China Social Sciences Press, 1995), 21.

20 "After the Tang settlement the merchants of Arabia and the Indies pointed their argosies at Canton or even further north." Schafer, Ibid., 25-28.

21 "But most of China's overseas trade was through the South China Sea and the Indian Ocean. And it was governed by the periodic shifts of the monsoon … the wind of departure from the great ports of the Persian Gulf port … in September or October … would be out of the Persian Gulf in time for the fair monsoon to carry them across the Indian Ocean … to catch the stormy southwest monsoon in June … from Malaya across the South China Sea to their destinations in south China." Schafer, Ibid., 21. Further, according to Chen Zhiqiang's research on the Maritime Silk Road, there were several maritime Silk Roads, originating in the east and passing through China's Quanzhou, Fuzhou, Guangzhou, to the south of Luzon, Indonesia's islands, Java, the Strait of Malacca, the southern tip of the Indian peninsula, Ceylon and along the Indian coastline to the very south of India, and there connecting the road to the sea port. The Indian Ocean-Arabian Gulf route followed

headed for India was Persian,[22] and Syriac Christians had long been well acquainted with this particular route due to their dealings with the Saint Thomas Christians in India,[23] with whom they had established contact[24] as early as the fourth century AD for purposes of discussing church affairs. The sea route was thus frequently used,[25] and it is likely that Alopen would first have traveled to South India by sailing from the Persian Gulf, and then on to China by land or sea.

Diplomatic Relations between Persia and Tang Dynasty China

The reign of Emperor Taizong (598-649 AD) was the most open era in Chinese history. Geopolitically, India was China's closest western neighbor, while Japan

---

the monsoon and the currents, ending in the Persian Gulf. One could spend years waiting for the proper monsoon and ocean currents. Cf. Chen Zhiming 陳志明, *Sheng shi yu hui: ge yong baizhanting wenmin* 盛世餘暉: 歌詠拜占庭文明 [*The Afterglow of the Great Leap: In Praise of Byzantine Civilization*] (Taipei: Shi Chao Press, 2002), 353-367.

[22] "From these ports, then, the ships of many nations set sail, manned by Persian speaking crews – for Persian was the lingua franca of the Southern Seas." Schafer, Ibid., 22. See also Lin Meicun 林梅村, *Si chou zhi lu kao gu shi wu jiang* 絲綢之路考古十五講 [*Fifteen Lectures on Silk Road Archeology*] (Beijing: Peking University Press), 221-244. Lin said "The route between the Indian Ocean and the South China Sea was initiated by the Persians. At the beginning of the Arab Empire, the Persians still dominated the route from the Persian Gulf to Guangzhou."

[23] All the early church literature stated that Thomas, one of the Twelve Apostles, had traveled to India for missionary work and established a church, which past historians, however, have largely considered purely legendary and not credible. With regard to travel routes, however, Strabo (ca. 64 BC-24 AD), a Greek geographer who lived around the 1st century AD, mentioned in his book *Geography* that he had been to Egypt at the time of Christ and discovered that about 120 vessels every year were headed for India from the upper Red Sea region in Egypt. We can thus conclude that Thomas would have had a convenient travel route to India from Egypt. See Moffett, Ibid., 32, 43. In recent years, there have been many new discoveries in research on the Silk Road. Cf. Lin, Ibid., 139-163. For further discussion on contemporary archeological findings, see Moffett, Ibid., 26-45.

[24] See also Indian scholars' perspectives regarding the origins of the Saint Thomas Christians in the first century and how the Syriac Orthodox Church reorganized their church system and tradition so that the Saint Thomas churches were eventually able to merge with the Eastern Church. Cf. "Origins of Christianity in India: The First Centuries," in *The St. Thomas Christian Encyclopaedia of India, Vol. 1*, ed. Geoge Menachery, (Madras: B.N.K. Press, 1973), 4-12.

[25] According to the records of the Persian Church, the Church of the East began to contact the Saint Thomas Christians in India in the fourth century AD, gradually establishing close ties with them. In the seventh century AD, Ishoyahb II even allowed them to establish a relatively independent archdiocese. The Bishop of India was then directly responsible to the Persian Patriarch. See Moffett, *Yazhou jidujiao shi*, 284-289.

bordered the formidable Chinese Empire to the east. The former was in a state of internal fighting and divisions, while the latter tried to send Japanese officials to study under the Chinese, perceiving that its own cultural accomplishment lagged behind those of its western neighbor. In western China, Islam was just beginning to establish a foothold. By contrast, Byzantium and the Eastern Roman Empire were gradually declining. On the Chinese borders to the north and northeast, the Eastern Turkic Khaganate on the Mongolian grasslands and the Goguryeo and Baekje Kingdoms, located in today's northeast China and North Korea, each in turn paid tribute to China. Emperor Taizong conquered the Turks and western tribes with a policy of "using foreign force to control foreign forces," and set up military checkpoints along the borders to regulate the secure flow of people and goods into his Empire.[26] An advanced city of its time, the ancient dynastic capital of Chang'an, today's Xi'an, had a taxpaying population of over two million. The capital was exquisitely constructed and well-run; the sewage system alone far surpassed that of any metropolitan area in the world at the time. With its bustling commerce and advanced culture, the Chinese capital drew visitors, statesmen, religious clergy and students from around the world to observe and learn from China's advanced engineering and cultural achievements. Businessmen and state officials from Persia, Arabia and even Byzantium succeeded in establishing diplomatic ties with Chang'an. Taizong adopted a policy of welcome and tolerance toward visitors while asserting his solid hold on regional power. During the Tang Dynasty, the central outer plains area was divided into the Fan tribes and the remote regions.[27] According to the records of *Zizhi Tongjian* 資治通鑒 [*A Comprehensive Mirror in Aid of Governance*], Emperor Taizong had come to see himself as a benefactor of the foreign tribes: "Since ancient times, China has been honored above all nations, yet we alone have loved them, who came to look at us as their parents."[28] Such a policy of relative equality allowed for the integration of different nationalities in an unprecedented way during Tang Dynasty China, with many foreigners appointed military or civil officials. In 630 AD, the leaders of the northwestern tribes gathered in Chang'an requesting Emperor Taizong to serve

---

26 Cf. Schafer, *Tangdai de wai lai de wenming*, 14.
27 According to "Xi yu zhuan 西域傳 [Biography of the Western Regions]," in *New Book of Tang, Vol. 221*, it was recorded that "these regions east of Goryeo, south of Kmir, west of Persia, Tubo and Genhun General Prefecture, north of Khitan, and Turkic Mohe were classified as the Fan tribes, while the regions beyond were called 'remote places.'"
28 Emperor Taizong ruled the world by the five principles, according to "Tang ji shi si 唐紀十四 [Chronicles of Tang, Vol. 14]," in *Zizhi Tongjian* 資治通鑒 [*A Comprehensive Mirror in Aid of Governance*], Vol. 198.

as arbiter in the northwestern region, praising him as the "Celestial Khan."[29] Northern minorities even constructed a trade road, which they named after him and which was conceived to promote trade and political relations between the neighboring border areas and the imperial court. At this time, Tang Dynasty China had undoubtedly become a leading imperial power of late antiquity. The Persian Sasanian Empire had established contact with the Northern Wei Dynasty as early as the middle of the fifth century AD,[30] which meant the latter was most likely well acquainted with Persian customs, as well as the

---

[29] In the spring of 630 AD, the northwestern tribal chiefs went to the court in Chang'an, asking Emperor Taizong to accept this honorary title, which was to signify his supreme sovereignty and grant him authority to arbitrate disputes among them. Cf., *Jianqiao zhongguo sui tang shi* 劍橋中國隋唐史 *The Cambridge History of the Sui and Tang Dynasties*, ed. Denis Twitchett (Beijing: China Social Sciences Press, 1990), 221.

[30] There is a fairly detailed account of the Persian Sasanian Empire in *Bei shi* 北史 [*History of the Northern Dynasties*] from the fifth century, which includes some very interesting descriptions about its location, politics, economy, religion and culture. "Persia, whose capital was Suli City, was located to the west of New Mi, which is ancient Syria, about twenty-two thousand two hundred and twenty-two *li* form Qudai. The city covers an area of about ten square *li* and provides residence for more than one-hundred thousand households; a river flows through the southern part of the city. The ground is level and produces gold, silver, copper ore, coral, amber, tridacna, agate, and large pearls, sphatika, colored glaze, crystal, emerald, diamonds, rubies, pinthieh, copper, tin, cinnabar, mercury, damask silk, brocade, cotton, carpet, blanketry, felt and red hydropot fur, as well as spices like frankincense, tulip, styrax and radix, as well as aristolochiae, pepper, long pepper, sucrose, date palm, cyperus rotundus, terminalia fruit, gallnut, atacamite, orpiment. The climate is hot, people stock ice at home, and there is a lot of sand and stone in the earth, so that people have to irrigate the fields with water from the river. The whole grains and animals are similar as the Central Plains, except without rice, proso and millet. There are famous horses, big donkeys and camels that can run 700 miles. The rice can feed thousands of people in rich and poor households alike. There are also white elephants, lions and bird that lay large eggs. One kind of bird looks like the camel: it has two wings, cannot fly very high, eats grass and meat and is given to fits of rage. The king is called Bo Si and sits on a bed of golden sheep, wearing a golden flower crown and an extravagant, half-length gown decorated with pearls and jewels. The custom dictates that husbands always cut their hair and wear white hats that are open on both sides. They also wear kerchiefs and short woven cloaks. The women usually wear long gowns and paint their foreheads. Their hair is worn long and loose and is decorated with golden or silver flowers. Women also wear armlets made of five-colored jewels. The king owns ten additional, smaller imperial palaces, just like the summer or winter palace in China." From this record we can see that the Persians had frequent economic and cultural exchanges with China, dealing in gems, coral, agate, spices and medicines. These trade activities are also confirmed by archaeological evidence. For example, more than 1,000 Sasanian silver coins were unearthed in China. The Tang Dynasty Chinese referred to the Persians as "rich Persians." Cf. *Gudai yilang shi liao xuan ji* 古代伊朗史料選輯 [*Ancient Iranian Historical Anthologies*], ed. Li Zhijiang 李鐵匠 (Beijing: Commercial Press, 1992), 206-207.

Empire's geographical location. In the early seventh century AD, after Emperor Yang of Sui had ascended the throne, he had sent an imperial emissary to Persia, who had returned to the Sui Emperor accompanied by Persian envoys carrying tribute[31]. At the time of Taizong, border policies had further relaxed, international relations were improved and all nations were understood to belong to one race, or "one world under heaven" (tianxia yijia). Not only did the Tang and Sasanian Empires enjoy good trade relations and cultural exchanges with each other; they also banded together as a political alliance against the Turks. If Alopen was indeed a secret envoy of the Sasanian Empire, an extravagant state welcome by the Tang Court would be in line with protocol.

If Alopen was a Secret Persian Envoy, What was His Purpose?

We can speculate that Alopen's secret mission was somehow related to the disastrous situation in his home country. At the time when Alopen visited the Tang Court, the Sasanian Dynasty was nearing its end: the Persian Empire, on the brink of collapse, was being besieged by Arab forces on all sides[32]. From the subsequent decline of the Sasanian Empire, we can conjecture that when the last Sasanian Emperor, Yazdegerd III, was facing Arab forces, he may have sought help from the "Celestial Khan" asking him to either send troops to rescue his country or provide shelter to him and the imperial household. The chronology of Persia's defeat supports this speculation: in 637 AD, just two years after Alopen's arrival in Chang'an in 635 AD, the Arab armies seized the Persian capital of Ctesiphon, and thousands of people, including Yazdegerd III and his men, fled for their lives. The general of the Iranian forces sheltered the emperor until Yazdegerd III made for Merv (in today's Turkmenistan),[33] where he waited for military assistance. According to the records of the Persian Islamic historian Tabari (838-923 AD), Yazdegerd III in 651 AD wrote to the Chinese Emperor, as well as to the kings of Bangalore, Gabriel (today's Kabul) and Khazars beseeching them to come to his rescue. As fate would have it, he was robbed

---

31 "Emperor Yang sent Yun Knight Li Yu to Persia as envoy, and Persia also sent envoys to the Sui Dynasty with Li Yu with tribute." Cf. "Xi yu zhuan 西域傳 [Biography of the Western Regions]", in *Book of Sui, Vol. 83.*

32 Arab armies were attacking the border in January 634 AD, and the capital Ctesiphon was on the edge of collapse. Two years after Alopen arrived in Chang'an in 635 AD, the Arab armies had moved into the Sasanian Empire's capital of Ctesiphon. Cf. Zarinkoob, *Bosi diguo shi*, 439.

33 Merv was located on the contemporary Afghan border and was a caravan site by the ancient Silk Road, as well as the easternmost diocese of the Syriac Orthodox Church. Cf. Moffett, *Yazhou jidujiao shi*, 353.

and killed by a mill owner in a remote mill outside of Merv before they came to his aid. His son Peroz fled east with about 1,000 men. He was able to secure the support of local tribal chiefs along the way before arriving in Tochari (today's Afghanistan), from where, after a short time of rest, he sent envoys to the Tang Dynasty to ask for immediate assistance. At that time, Emperor Gaozong of Tang was competing with the Western Turks for the right of governance in the western regions and thus unwilling to entangle himself in another war. He stated that he was unable to provide military assistance, explaining that the theater of war was too far away to send troops. All Peroz could do was ally himself with the Tochari tribal armies against the Arab troops and retake control of Jiling (today's northeastern Iran) as a temporary residence[34]. In the first year of Longshuo (661 AD), Peroz once again sought the help of the Tang Emperor. By this time, Gaozong had conquered the Turks, seizing the areas around the eastern and western Pamir Mountains and subjugating their inhabitants. After 659 AD, Emperor Gaozong began dividing the lands he had conquered in Central Asia into provinces, counties and prefectures, totaling 127 administrative regions throughout western Xinjiang, Uzbekistan and Afghanistan. Once word of Gaozong's victories reached Peroz, the Prince may have been persuaded to contact the Tang Emperor yet again, requesting aid in protecting his new headquarters at Jiling. Finally, in response to his request, Gaozong sent Wang Mingyuan to establish Jiling as a Persian protectorate general, which then became the westernmost outpost of the Tang Empire. In 663 AD, Peroz was appointed governor of the Persian protectorate general as a Persian Prince. To express his gratitude, the Prince regularly sent emissaries to Chang'an to pay tribute. Unfortunately for Peroz, the Arab armies eventually conquered Jiling in 674 AD, forcing him to flee to Chang'an, where his work of guarding the western border for so many years earned him Emperor Gaozong's grateful welcome. Peroz was treated to wealth and comfort and appointed an important general in the Emperor's army.[35] In the second year of the Yifeng era of Emperor Gaozong's reign

---

34 *Ce fu yuan gui* 冊府元龜 [*The Annals of the Northern Song Dynasty*], Vol. 995, are clear on this point: "In May of the fifth year of *Yonghui*, the Caliph attacked and defeated Persia and the Māymurgh. The Persian Emperor Yazdagird III was killed by soldiers of the Caliphate, and the son of Yazdagird III, Peroz, was forced to flee to Tochar, sending envoys to tell the Tang Emperor about his troubles. Gaozong replied that he could not help, citing geographical distance as the reason. Waiting for reinforcements at Tochar, Peroz hoped to return to Persia and take back the throne."

35 The *Xin tang shu* 新唐書 [*New Book of Tang*], Vol. 221 (completed in 1060 AD) provides a fuller historical account than the *Old Book of Tang Book* (completed in 945 AD). "At the end of the Sui Dynasty, Tong Yabghu Khan of the western Turkic tribes sent a punitive expedition against and destroyed Persia. King Khosrau II was killed, and his son Serge succeeded him. Tong Yabghu sent his general to govern the conquered territory. After

(677 AD), Peroz requested Emperor Gaozong to build him a Nestorian chapel in Chang'an's Liquan District, considering perhaps that many of the aristocrats of the imperial household who had accompanied the Prince were Nestorians.[36] Furthermore, a Persian religious site would serve the purpose of integrating Persian religious and political culture; importantly, it also resulted in uniting and reviving the exiled Persians. Regrettably,[37] Peroz died later that same year. His statue was erected in Qianling, where both Gaozong and Wu Zetian were buried, standing among the 61 ministers on both sides of the Road of the Gods outside the Rosefinch Gate, memorialized for posterity.[38]

From this dramatic historical narrative, we may venture the following speculation: apart from being a Nestorian monk, Alopen may also have served as a secret envoy of the Sasanian Empire, whose mission was to seek help from Emperor Taizong of Tang. The understanding was that, as the "Celestial Khan," Emperor Taizong had been charged with maintaining the peace and arbitrating disputes among the surrounding nations, as well as defending the sovereignty of allies and protecting them from external aggression. Political, commercial and cultural exchanges between the Chinese and Sasanian Empires had been

---

Serge's death, the Persians were reluctant to bow their heads. Then the daughter of Khosrau II was made queen and reigned until the Turks killed her. The son of Serge fled back to his own people, who crowned him King Hormizd VI. After he died, his brother's son, Yazdgerd III, was instated as king. In the 12th year of *Zhenguan*, Yazdgerd III sent an envoy to China to pay tribute to the Tang Emperor. The envoy presented him with a living snake of pure blue color; it measured 9 inches in length, and was able to hunt mice. After Yazdgerd III lost his throne and was banished by the Caliphate, he fled to Tochar. He later sent envoys to the Tang Emperor to request military assistance, but Gaozong sent the envoys back refusing help on grounds of distance. After the Caliph retreated, the people of Tochar protected him. In the beginning of *Longsuo*, Yazdgerd III sent another message to the Tang Emperor informing him that he had again been attacked by the Caliphate. The Emperor then sent envoys to the western regions to establish provinces and prefectures, and proclaimed Jiling a Persian Protectorate General, to be governed by Peroz. As Persia had been defeated by the Caliphate, not even Peroz was able to rebuild his country. He came to the [Tang] court in the middle of *Xianhen* and served as right guard general until his death." Cf. "Xi yu zhuan 西域傳 [Biography of the Western Regions]," in *New Book of Tang, Vol. 221*. Cf. also Zarinkoob, *Bosi diguo shi*, 439-441.

36 "It is remarkable that when Peroz's father, the Persian Emperor Yazdgerd III, died in Merv (木鹿), his funeral was conducted by the Archbishop of the Syriac Orthodox Church of Merv. According to later Persian sources, the wife of the Persian Emperor was a Nestorian, which shows the close relationship between the Persian royal family and the Syriac Orthodox Church, or Nestorianism, in that period." Cf. Matteo Compareti, *Tang feng chui fu sa ma er han* 唐風吹拂撒馬爾罕 [*Dawn of Samarkand*], trans. Mao Min 毛銘 (Guilin: Lijiang Press, 2016), 20-22.

37 Cf. Compareti, ibid., 20-22.

38 Edited by Twitchett, *Jianqiao zhongguo sui tang shi*, p. 278. Cf. also Compareti, Ibid., 18-25.

so common over the centuries that when the Sasanian Empire was facing its most serious national crisis, Persia naturally sought the aid of the Tang Emperor. To the detriment of the Persians, however, political self-preservation took priority over China's concern for foreign allies, and Alopen's hospitable reception in Chang'an did not signify the Emperor's inclination to send hundreds of thousands of troops across the mountains to fight the Arab forces for the survival of the Sasanian Empire. The Tang Emperor's priorities at the time were clearly elsewhere, fighting the western Turks in a region located between China and Persia, so that, geopolitically, he could hardly afford to become involved in another war. Yet history offers us this paradox: although Emperor Taizong might have rejected Alopen's request for military aid, he did become interested in the teachings brought to China by the Nestorian monk and, after three months' careful consideration, not only permitted him to preach Nestorian Christianity in China, but even built a Nestorian church for Alopen and his followers. These actions prepared the way for the remarkable development of the Nestorian Church in Tang Dynasty China over the next 200 years. The high-profile yet covert diplomatic mission also sheds important light on the complex issues surrounding the Tang Emperor's decision years later to assist the Persian royal family in exile on several occasions and to admit a number of Persian aristocrats to the Tang Court in the wake of the Sasanian Empire's downfall.[39]

Translated by: Dr. Xiong Jingzhi (Chengdu University)
Proofreading by: Dr. Naomi Thurston (Sichuan University)

---

39   Diplomatic contact between China and Persia's Sasanian Empire had been frequent since the Northern Wei Dynasty. However, it was Alopen's visit (635 AD) to China that received special attention and was recorded in great detail. "The Persian monk Alopen carried scriptures from afar and brought them to the royal court. The Emperor closely examined their teaching and discovered it to be most excellent and sublime, the scope of its meaning reaching back to the creation of the world. Offering salvation and goodness to mankind, the Emperor found that it merited propagation among all people. So he built a temple in Yining Fang which housed 21 monks." Cf. Wang Pu, "Daqian si 大秦寺 [Daqin Si]", in Tang hui yao 唐會要 [*Institutional History of the Tang Dynasty*], *Vol. 49* (Shanghai: Commercial Press, 1935). Over the course of the next few years (639 AD, 647 AD, 648 AD), China and Persia were in frequent contact and established close diplomatic ties. Cf. RONG Xinjiang 榮新江, Sichou zhi lu yu dong xi wenhua jiaoliu 絲綢之路與東西文化交流 [*The Silk Road and Cultural Interaction between East and West*], (Beijing: Peking University Press), 2015, 65.

CHAPTER 4

The Ethic of Love in Ancient Judaism and Early *Jingjiao* and Its Impact on Ancient China's Religious Narrative

Melville Y. Stewart

1 The Metaphysical Grounding of the Ethic of Love in Old Testament Judaism

As one reads the Old Testament, a sense of a divine metanarrative is likely to emerge, punctuated by central beliefs relating to God's place in human history, and his engagement with his covenant people Israel. Our first task is to single out those central beliefs which might be viewed as providing a *metaphysical grounding* for the Old Testament ethic of love. These beliefs are listed in order and identified as *belief statements*, S_1, S_2, S_3, etc. The first statement affirms God's creation of the heavens and the earth, and so we have,

S_1: There is a Creator God who brought into being the entire universe as we know it.[1]

As we proceed in our sketch of the ontological grounding of the ethic of love, the concepts and content of each statement are so formed as to avoid contradiction.[2]

Secondly, S_1 implies that since God created the entire universe, his agency is seen as the sufficient condition for human origin--he created the human species. This is affirmed in Genesis 1:26-31 and Genesis 2:7. In the latter, God is spoken of as creating humans from the dust of the ground, and breathing into them the breath of life, and thereby they became living beings. In the prior reference, God is spoken of as creating humans in his image. We have thus,

S_2: God created humans in his image.[3]

---

1   Melville Y. Stewart, *The Greater-Good Defence, An Essay on the Rationality of Faith*, (hereafter GGD), The Macmillan Press, 1993, Chapter 2.
2   S_1 may be taken as a properly basic belief in the sense Alvin Plantinga would affirm it, that is, S_1 is *de jure* rational – the concepts employed and the statement itself are not contradictory. Moreover, the *de jure rationality* of the metaphysical base may be taken as salutary to the reliability of the ethic that it grounds.
3   The passage adds, "in his likeness." This is taken as a Hebrew parallel, see GGD, 84.

While the concept of *divine image* is not clearly specified in the Old Testament, several associated elements are either directly affirmed or implied. The creation of Adam and Eve was accompanied by an endowment of *rationality* which included both *moral innocence* and *goodness*, and a yet-unspoiled *moral consciousness*.[4] Evil choices had not entered the picture in creation chapters 1 and 2. Moreover, in view of the probation in the Garden of Eden, the whole probation narrative during which Adam and Eve were warned to not eat of the fruit of the tree of the knowledge of good and evil, implies that both were *moral agents,* (1) with a *free-willing capacity,* and (2) a *reliable moral sensibility* allowing them to comply with the stated pivotal prohibition that they choose *not* to eat of the forbidden fruit. This brings us to another statement,

S_3: Adam and Eve were created significantly free; that is they could choose x or y, where x is good and y is evil, and they had reliable belief-forming mechanisms that enabled them to form correct moral judgments regarding moral options.[5]

This significant freedom made Adam and Eve's response to the probation open to either an *affirmative*, or a *negative*. The former would keep open the door to the Garden and *to love* for the Creator by doing what he commanded. Disobedience, *au contraire*, would open the door to a rejection *of* and *by* the Creator, and with this, a rejection of life as they knew it.[6]

Yet another element appears in clear relief in this melodramatic divine-human encounter. From all that one can gather, *divine love* descends and is *displayed* in the *availability of companionship with the divine*, attended by boundless provisions and pleasures in the Garden.[7] In the face of all these goods, the human narrative takes an horrendously tragic turn. All is quiet in

---

4   By *goodness* here, I have in mind an *unspoiled goodness*, because that which is spoken of comes into being directly from the *hand* of God. The statement, "God saw that it was good," (*tov*, תוב) implies a *flawless goodness*, since it came from God's direct fiat. Adam and Eve had as yet no flaws in *function* or *perception* with regard to their *belief-forming mechanisms*, and their *moral sensibilities*. All of which applied to the period before their fall. They had a clear moral grasp of the warning: "in the day that you eat thereof, you will surely die." So their original moral state involved a contingent goodness, subject to loss given moral failure.

5   See *GGD*, Chapter 5.

6   How a non-fallen agent created in God's image could fail to obey God's command in the light of such clear revelation and innocent goodness is indeed apologetically problematic. One possible response is, yes, God could have created a world without a fall; perhaps he has. This is one possible inference were one to opt for a variant multiverse hypothesis (which I affirm in "The Greater-Good Defense, O Felix Culpa, and the Multiverse Hypothesis" (a revision of the seventh chapter of the *GGD*). For our universe, perhaps evil is allowed so as to make possible greater-goods for our universe, one of which arguably might be the meaningful good of Redemption. See Chapter 7 of the *GGD*.

7   God is spoken of as making every tree pleasant to sight and good for food, Gen. 2:9.

the Garden. In the midst of that quietness, a voice calls out to Adam and Eve. It was a penultimate divine-human encounter, as God "walked in the Garden in the cool of the day." Amazing! The eternally transcendent God descends in a way that suggested in an anticipatory pre-Incarnate mode that he *walked in the Garden* with the first couple of the human family.[8] And what had they done? Because of their moral failure, and existential sense of it, *and* one immediate noetic consequence, they thought that they could hide themselves from their *omniscient* and *loving* Creator. The reader sees how sin darkens and blinds the mind. Perhaps for years, *we don't know*, God came down in *condescending walks*, like a parent might readily and frequently *fall to the floor to play* with a child to express love closely and concretely. One disclosure is immediate and transparent, *infinite love, compassion* and *care* in the midst of moral failure. It was a Garden filled to overflowing with good things. Even the nights exhibited a transcendent glory. David said, "The Heavens declare the *glory* of God!"[9] Still they turned their *minds* and *wills* away from a marvellously provisional, infinitely-loving God.[10] It's hard, if not nearly impossible to imagine. But that's what the Scriptures say happened. This is affirmed in,

S_4: Adam and Eve by a disobedient act of their respective willing capacities, disobeyed God's prohibition that they not eat of the fruit of the tree of the knowledge of good and evil.

There's yet another central affirmation that perhaps some Jews and most if not all Christians hold to be true. It issues from the earliest Messianic prophecy, what some call the first mention of the Gospel, the *protoevangelium*,

---

8   My read here is that since God shows himself to be omnipotent, he can incarnate if and whenever he chooses, even in the divine narrative of the OT.

9   Psalm 19:1. Psalm 97:6 adds God's *righteousness, tzideqov* (צדקו) *and glory* is thus revealed.

10 While I argue that God revealed himself passim as showing love, as we see in Hosea, some contend that God's *essence is love* isn't clear until specific disclosures in the NT, see *The Oxford Dictionary of the Christian Church*, editor, F.L. Cross, 2nd ed. By F.L. Cross and E.A. Livingstone, Oxford University Press, 1974, "Love," 839. But this contention can be challenged. At the very heart of the Ten Commandments is the core value of love, first to God, and then to one's neighbor. A summary of the Second Table of the Law in Lev. 19:18, declares, "Love your neighbor as yourself." If the law is taken as revelatory of God's nature, then it follows that *God is love*. Christ in the NT declares in summary fashion the Levitical principle in Mark 12:31, "Love thy neighbor as thyself." So loving God and one's neighbor is quintessentially the creature's *reflection of the divine nature*. It is important to also see that God's love needs to be understood in connection with his *justice*, both of which (in the New Testament) are eternal in his nature and so essential (necessary). Since God *is* both *love*, and *just*, the two are held to co-exist without contradiction in God *eternally*. As we shall see shortly, while his love is expressed eternally perichoretically among the Trinitarian threesome, love is expressed eternally toward creatures he determined from eternity to create, thus it is a love that is not merely potential.

appearing in Genesis 3:15, "it (her seed to follow) shall bruise thy head (Satan), and thou (Satan), shall bruise his (the Messiah's) heel."[11] The NT Christian interprets this as saying that God will bring about a descendent via the seed of the line of David, who will be called Messiah (משיח), the Anointed One, who will effect a redemption designed to rescue the human family. Thus we have,

S_5: God so loves the world that in due course he came in an Incarnation to bring about a Redemption remedy for a lost humanity.

I contend finally, that statements S_1-S_5 evidence above all else that God's metanarrative relative to the human drama of innocence and fallenness contains OT anticipatory moments evidencing God's overall patient and triumphal love, and that these statements provide a ground for an ethic of love, and that this divine love was to be the main ethical value analogously[12] reflected in all human relationships.

11 The Old Testament Teaching: Love as a Core Human Ethic

Thus far we have tried to show that the God of Creation behaved in such a way as to warrant the claim that he is manifestly *a God of love*. As the Old Testament metanarrative unfolds, God *continues* to show his love toward the covenant people of God, as for example on the occasion of his deliverance of Israel from the hand of Pharaoh recorded in Deuteronomy 7:8. What gradually becomes clear in the process of divine disclosures of love in the history of Israel, is that this regularity with which love issues from God clearly implies that love is his nature. O.T. disclosures may thus be taken as anticipatory moments of the essentialist love-statement of the New Testament, God *is* love (I John 4:8, 16).[13] And since, according to the Creation component of this metanarrative, God created the heavens and the earth *and* humans, *divine supremacy over all*

---

11   Words in parentheses are added.
12   Here, I prefer the analogy of *proportionality* rather than *attribution*, because the former allows a *univocity of meaning in some measure* with regard to the analogues. See GGD, 52-53.
13   Here, I need to acknowledge that there are those who *would* contend that the prevailing ethical descriptives of God in the Old Testament emphasize God's *holiness, righteousness*, and *justice*, rather than his *love, mercy*, and *compassion*. This tends to be the view of Dispensational exegetes. But I think that this take fails to see the motive behind Creation itself, *and* the motive behind the giving of the Law (as in Exodus and Deuteronomy). Creation's beauty was given for the enjoyment and good of all creation, including rational creatures. And the Law was given with the divine intent that people should try to promote peace, tranquility, harmony, and civility in any and all social groups and in all arenas, public and private. This divine emphasis clearly issues from *love and justice*, not just justice.

Creation conveys *with* this supremacy the creational extensional complement of this love which is to be instantiated via the *mode of obedience to divine command* on the part of *every creature bearing the divine image*. Thus how *God* behaves toward his creatures,[14] *analogously* models how creatures should respond to God and behave toward one another. So attention to the divine dimension regarding a first-order love has implications for a second-order love, i.e., the way the covenant people of God are to behave in society. That God is *essentially* a loving being explains the regularity with which God is motivated to act in behalf of his covenant people.[15] Divine love is also *logically prior* to the ethic of love that humans are to show to one another. Humans are to show love because they are image bearers, and as such they are to reflect the love of their Maker. Up to this point, we have not paid attention to the meaning of *ethics*. The term is a derivative of the Classical Greek term, εθος, meaning, *custom, usage, manner, habit*.[16] While there may not be a Hebrew counterpart term, much of what falls under Jewish ethics has to do with what is now called *normative ethics*, the ethic of normative or *law-like* principles, such as for example, the Ten Commandments. Other foci include law and ethics and rabbinic religious law (*halakhah,* הלכה), which focuses on *duties*. But the terminological gap doesn't warrant by itself the conclusion that Judaism doesn't work with an ethic or doesn't have ethical principles. The language of the Old Testament is

---

14   It needs to be pointed out here that how God deals with Creation, and Creatures in that Creation, is *always* according to divine *love, justice* and *goodness*. But this statement needs to be followed quickly by another. God is always working with an *eternal perspective* and plan for all of creation. For example, death happens according to God's plan, in terms of which, whatever may appear on the surface in human history, and in terms of human perspective and understanding, may not coincide with the way God sees and wills things (Isaiah 55:8, 9). The point to be drawn here is, the principles of *justice, goodness* and *love* ultimately and eternally instantiated in God are perfect in every respect. Here, *note bene*, history doesn't always report back an accurate picture of God's perspective, or actions. Only God can finally answer for God in history, no matter what defensive strategy an apologist might dream up.

15   So while the *essentialist read* isn't explicitly stated in the OT, the regularity of divine expressions of love implies it. And the NT believer could rightly argue, that since God never changes, if he is described as essentially a God of love in the New, then he was that same God in the Old. If one takes revelation as an in-process account of God's metanarrative, one can expect an increase of information regarding the fullness of God's being over time.

16   Henry George Liddell and Robert Scott, *A Greek-English Lexicon* (based on the German work of Francis Passow, New York: Harper & Brothers, Publishers, 1870), 397. The Koine Greek lexicon, *Greek-English Lexicon of the New Testament and Other Early Christian Literature*, includes the term εθος, but there are no references in the Old Testament Septuagint that includes the term, and there are few in the New Testament that do such as Heb. 10:25, which translates the term as "habit," and ten passages that translate it as "custom."

known for its simplicity of style and terms.[17] Nevertheless, the moral laws leave little if any doubt as to the intended teaching. In terms of content and context, the reader is confronted with what is called in contemporary ethical theory, a variant *divine-command ethic*.[18] The Ten Commandments (*shi jie* 十诫) in the Old Testament list 10 moral principles which define by a list of eight prohibitions and two affirmatives God's principles for just, good, and holy living. The first part of the law focuses on moral principles pertaining to God himself, namely laws 1, 2, 3, and. Laws 1, 2, and 3 are prohibitions, and 4 is the affirmative, "remember the Sabbath to keep it holy." In the second part of the law, namely 5, 6, 7, 8, 9, and 10, 5 is the affirmative, "honor your father and mother", while the remaining laws are prohibitions. An agent's being morally wrong or morally blameworthy is understood as an agent's violation of one or more of the commands. A parallel to the Exodus account of the Ten Commandments is found in Deuteronomy 5:7-21. Both sources make it clear that God requires that humans walk a certain walk, in response to God, in response to Creation, and in response to the self and other human agents in Creation. We have thus far seen that the Ten Commandments are a disclosure mostly in the negative, of God's code for human moral uprightness. Both accounts divide the Ten Commandments into two sections, the first dealing with four moral principles dealing with human moral obligations to God as God. The second table of the law pertains to human moral obligation toward other humans. The first set says that every human should rightfully hold God to be the only true God, worthy of all worship, while allowing *no other* to share this unique recognition, service, and devotion. The second table, by contrast, focuses on human obligations to other humans in the ethical sphere.

The positive behaviour that humans are to show *others* is to include *respect* for others, because every human is created in the *image of God*, regardless of

---

17 The early Hebrew language developed in the context of a culture and at a period of human history that took place a century and a half before the Golden Age of the Greek city-states of Athens and Sparta, and the appearance of the philosopher heroes of the Greeks, Socrates, Plato and Aristotle. The discourse of these ancient Greek philosophers (especially Plato and Aristotle) generated an expansive taxonomy of terms that allowed greater degrees of precision in the expression of ideas pertaining to reality, knowledge and values.

18 See Robert M. Adams, *The Virtue of Faith, and Other Essays in Philosophical Theology* (Oxford: Oxford University Press, 1987), cp. 7, "A Modified Divine Command Theory of Ethics," and cp. "Divine Command Metaethics Modified Again." Adams draws attention to the problem of circularity that may face certain renditions of this view of ethics. If one defines the term "wrong" as "what is contrary to what God commands, this will not work as a theory for those who do not believe in God. So the simple version of the theory assumes God's existence.

gender, wealth, race, intelligence, age, or any other potentially differentiating criterion pertaining to humans. God himself views every person as an image-bearer.

The first command in the second table of the law requires that one honor one's father *and* mother. Note, both parents are to be honored: there is no differentiation such that one is *above* or *before* another. Both are equally image-bearers. But note further, this command, unlike the others pertaining to human behavior toward other humans, involves a *two-fold promise*: (1) "that thy days may be prolonged" – that you may enjoy a long life, and (2), "that it may go well with each one who obeys in the land of promise."[19] We have thus the motive of a *consequential good*. The remaining five commands are negative prohibitions that rule out murder, adultery, stealing, bearing false witness, and coveting. These prohibitions are to be guiding principles in all social contexts. The law thereby takes on a very practical mode.

Note that each command in the negative mode may be transformed into a positive if one were to grasp the deep meaning of each of these negative commands as a *thou shalt* thus: thou shalt preserve life, thou shalt be faithful and pure toward one's spouse, thou shalt respect the ownership of the property of others, thou shalt always tell the truth, and thou shalt be happy with your lot in life. Taken together, one might say that they represent a *variation of the Golden Rule*, "do unto others, what you would have done unto you." As I state in my earlier paper,[20] Confucius expressed a negative variant of the same rule in the *Analects*, "Do not do to others what you would not like yourself."[21] Christ's positive version has existential import. One is to treat others in a friendly-loving way. Within the family unit, a husband loves his wife just in case in every situation and condition of life he does to her what he would like done to himself. This is a real, authentic, and powerful principle. Were it to be followed most if not all the violence and abuse that happens in homes in the contemporary world would disappear. Similarly, most if not all of the nefarious in societal relationships would be eliminated. We currently witness a world marked by extreme abuses of civility – instances where persons use language in mean, savage ways in both the private and public sector. Were each to follow the Golden Rule, undoubtedly this would lead to a pleasant, harmonious and peaceful world. The public square, the private home, every dimension of human existence could be transformed by a positive personal obedience to the

---

19 Deuteronomy 5:16.
20 "Ancient Chinese, Hebrew and Christian Monotheism."
21 *Ji suo bu yü wu shi yü ren* 己所不欲勿施于人. Confucius, *The Analects*, Books 5 and 12. The New Testament account is yet to be discussed in the second part of this paper.

Golden Rule. Notice, that the Golden Rule, albeit brief, is really a summation of all of the *second table* of the Law dealing with humans. The commands issue from a God of love, a God who wants creatures to live happily, reflecting his righteousness, justice, and mercy. So, the Golden Rule is really a summary of the six commands applicable to human behavior, in private and in societal contexts. You might say, it assumes friendly responses to others expressing thereby friendship love *and* self-love. So, we might summarize the laws in terms of the singular value of *love*, which is the *underlying principle* of the Law. That *love is the summation* of the second table of the law is clear in Leviticus 19:18, "thou shalt love thy neighbor as thyself." This very same moral principle appears in Mark 12:31, "Thou shalt love thy neighbor as thyself." After having stated that love to God is prior, Jesus then summarily comments on the two thus, "There are no other commandments greater than these."

We've briefly explored the *metaphysical* basis for the ethic of love. That metaphysical basis is the *ground* for the ethic in question. And while we've explored some of the consequences of obedience to the law we haven't directly considered the question as to *why one should show love*. One might immediately respond with the answer, because God's existence is the ground of ethics. But this doesn't spell out *the* motive--the *why* one is to respond to ethical principles grounded in a metaphysic of divine love, though the ground might hint at it. So there remains the question, what is the *appropriate and primary motive* (assuming that there is one) in terms of which one pursues kind, friendly, loving behaviour? Are we to treat others with love and respect because it is the *virtuous* thing to do? Or is it because it is one's *duty*? Or is it because of some *good pleasurable result* or *consequence* such actions/behavior bring about, or perhaps because of some combinatorial order or arrangement of all of the above? Let's begin our response to the question with a brief philosophical approach to ethics, and then shift into a practical mode. There are two main approaches as to *why* or *what motive* is to be uppermost regarding a justification of moral behavior in contemporary Western ethical theory, the *deontological*, and the *teleological*. The former focuses upon *duty*:[22] so in the case of command theory, one simply follows the commands because it is one's duty. For the Hebrew mind, the Ten Commandments comprise covenant stipulations

---

22   *Duty* or *deontological ethics* works with the root idea expressed in the Greek term, *denotes* (δηοντες), or *duty*. That is, behaving in a certain way is one's duty, and this is the primary reason for doing it. So a divine command theorist's approach to the Ten Commandments might take it that the primary motive for keeping the commands is, it is one's duty because God is the Ultimate Sovereign, hence the duty as such, is rooted in this metaphysical foundation or base.

that one is to follow as a duty as *covenant heir*.[23] The second is the teleological approach: one obeys the commands because doing so brings about a positive, perhaps pleasurable *end*. There have been other accounts, such as the virtue ethic approach.[24] This view has been given at least two readings, the deontological, which says, one follows after virtue as a *duty*, and the other, the teleological which says, one follows after virtue because of the *good results or pleasure*(s) that obedience brings about. So, when it comes to motive, *prima facie*, the answer as to primary motive appears to end up being a choice among a number of options or a combinatorial approach with an ordering or ranking of the motives.

The question we need to raise now is, Is the Jewish believer in the Old Testament to show love to others because it is one's *duty*, or because *obedience benefits/profits* those who pursue this end? The answer may appear easy at first glance. Since God is the ultimate Moral Covenant Sovereign, then what humans are to pursue in terms of a *primary motive* is spelled out in terms of *duty* – humans *must obey God, regardless of outcomes*. But note here another important and central truth, one that is affirmed way back in the Deuteronomic-codal context, as in Deuteronomy 6:24, which says, "And the Lord commanded us to do all these statutes, to fear the Lord our God, *for our good always, that he might preserve us alive*, as it is at this day." Another translation reads as follows: "so that you may always prosper and be kept alive…" The Hebrew text uses the word, לטוב (*letov*), which literally translates, "good." This means that *following the commands of God brings about one's good*. This line is affirmed in the call to honor and obedience to one's parents. So two motives are affirmed, one clearly *deontological*, another clearly *teleological*. Now the question is, which if any is prior? Or is there an equivalence of some sort? Isn't duty prior, because whether things appear for our good at some point as a result of a good choice issuing from an obedient mode of the will, one is to show love *no matter the consequence*. But note, the promise that such choices will always bring about good ends *always follows*, whether in an immediate consequence, or at some future time in this life, or the next.[25] Note, good consequences may not always

---

23   Hebrew covenant theology works with the concept of *covenant* (the Hebrew term is, *beriyth*, ברית). God is viewed as having established various covenants, marked by sacrifices, which in ceremonial practice involved a cutting of the animal, and then the human passed between the parts divided, committing in effect to the idea, "so be it done unto me if I do not obey the conditions of the covenant". Various covenants in the history of Israel, include the Abrahamic, in Genesis 17, and following. On the positive side, God promises to confer blessing and provision, and closeness.

24   Linda Zagzebski offers such a position, along with a virtue approach to epistemology.

25   The good always follows because God who is *loving, good* and *just*, ultimately controls outcomes in history.

show themselves immediately upon the completion of the duty to love. Ecclesiastes 8:11 explains why; "Because sentence against an evil work is not executed speedily, therefore the hearts of the sons of men are fully set in them to do evil." God *does not intervene* to counter/correct every act of evil in the world at least for the reason that this would make God so evident as to eliminate the reality of human free choice. But we need to observe another central point. God has issued commands for the *human good*, for ethical practices and behavior in societal contexts. Divine commands are *not arbitrarily contrived*. Divine commands reveal something of the nature of God himself, in respect to his *internal holiness* goodness and order. But further, Creation *is, and should be*, reflective of *God's order* in the world, both moral and physical. Humans were created with minds, and a moral capacity (a *conscience* bearing witness to the *works of the law* in the New Testament).[26] So in the light of the forgoing, a *pure* deontological motive doesn't cover all of the bases. The more one gets to know God, the more one comes to know that laws aren't just out there to *obey*. They are issued from Above for one's *good*, always, by divine promise, whether that good is realized immediately, or at some time far off into the future. And perhaps it is also relevant to say that the young Hebrew mind might because of inexperience, think that duty isn't the best path, because of pressing immediate pleasures associated with an unwise teleological mind-set. In the OT, with age often, but not always, comes *wisdom*. Over time, one comes to know that God[27] does come through for the obedient, richly, clearly and overflowingly.[28] Perhaps pure duty is to be set down a notch outranked by the motive of *love*. Perhaps *Divine love* should be the paroxysm whereby humans are to be moved to love one's neighbor. Perhaps growth in the Christian life leads to a wisdom that values love to God and one's neighbor as the highest and most excellent motive.

So we may conclude that the Judaic ethic of love, shown by a loving-obedience to divine commands for those bearing the divine image, is a model for human behavior that can result in peace and harmony in society because the God who created humans gave them the capacity to respond to commands he designed to promote that peace and harmony. Note further, that the laws given by God to promote peace and harmony in society, also work personally

---

26   Such as in Romans 2:14, 15, principally 15, which contains the word for *conscience*, συνειδήσεως. Paul adds the point that the conscience bears witness to *the works of the law* (το εργον του εισιν νομος).

27   God is to be seen here as *omnisapient*, that is, he is *all wise* in his setting forth covenant stipulations.

28   John 14:21 declares that those who keep the commands, truly show love, and they will not only experience his love, but he will show himself to them.

internally. Persons who obey the law generate an internal calmness and peace, because the Creator has structured humans to live this way in external relations, as well as for internal heart and mind practices and states. Hence *practitioners of the law* thereby show love, a love which can *permeate* and flavor all of society, and further, extend it to each member of that society, offering thereby *consequent pointers* to the Maker. Since the world is *one* by the creation mode, God wanted to make a oneness/togetherness of the human family possible via good ethical choices, thereby giving the dictum, *one world, one dream*, both a transcendent and immanent meaning.

III Early Christianity's Ethic of Love, Grounded in an Ultimate Christian Monotheism

A *Ultimate Christian Monotheism*

The mainstream of Christian theism embraces three main traditions, the Roman Catholic, Protestant, and Orthodox. All three hold that God has revealed himself as a Trinity, Father, Son, and Holy Spirit. Trinitarianism can be found in the main creeds and confessions,[29] and writings of the Church.[30] Two main views of the Trinity have been defended historically, the Latin view, and the Social Trinity view. Regarding the latter, Peter van Inwagen in "The Trinity"[31] summarily describes possible worrisome identity transivity claims that might occur if one makes improper transfers of identity with regard to the individual persons of the Trinity and the all-embrasive Trinity.[32] With regard to both views of the Trinity, the main concern is to keep *distinct* the *three Persons* of the Trinity, and at the same time affirm the *oneness of God*, thereby avoiding both a modalism and a tritheism. The Latin view of the Trinity works with an abstract *formal relation* of the Father to the Son, and the Father and Son to the Holy Spirit.[33] The Social Trinitarian view sees all three as eternally in a loving/

---

29 See for example, the Nicene Creed of 324 AD, J.N.D. Kelly, *Early Christian Creeds*, 3rd ed., 2006, London: Continuum.

30 See for example, *A Discourse In Vindication of the Trinity: With an Answer to the Late Socinian Objections Against It from Scripture, Antiquity and Reason*, Edward Lord Bishop of Worcester, London, printed by J.H. for Henry Mortlock at the Phoenix in St. Paul's Churchyard, 1697.

31 In the *Routledge Encyclopedia of Philosophy* (ed. Edward Craig, Vol. IX: Routledge Publishers, 1998), 457-461.

32 *The Trinity:East/West Dialogue* (Melville Y. Stewart ed.), 55.

33 The Latin view has two readings: the Son proceeds from the Father, and the Holy Spirit proceeds from the Father *and* the Son (the *filioque* clause translates "and the Son"), or from the Father *only*.

perichoretic relationship.³⁴ That is, the Social view of the Trinity stresses a *perichoretic love* within the Trinity, to draw attention to the *centrality of love* ascribed to God as a *metaphysical descriptive* of an *eternal, internal* divine love. Thus the unity of the Trinity is affirmed in a way that allows *distinctions within*, but avoids dividing God into separable parts, thereby permitting an accounting of love *internal* to God in a *unified eternal* (circuminsession) intermingling (circumincession) mode.

But there's yet another dimension to divine love if one takes into account the *eternality of the divine decree*.³⁵ That is, it can be argued that since God decreed to create from eternity, he also expressed his love to that Creation *from eternity past*. Love was *eternally* (in eternity past) *instantiated in the decree*. Infinitely later, it is *actualized* say at time t after the act of Creation.³⁶ The former is both logically and chronologically prior to the latter. Divine love was also *eternally instantiated* in his decree to offer Redemption via Christ, and then *temporally instantiated* in the actualization of Redemption. *Decretive love* can thus viewed as flowing from an *internal-perichoretic* love from *eternity*, whereby decretive self-giving love is expressed in *due time*--the time of Creation and Redemption.³⁷ But if the Latin view is assumed, then it is difficult to see how love can be seen as *internal* to God from eternity, if the Trinity is viewed primarily as an *abstract relation* of a *processional* sort where the Son *proceeds* from the Father, and the Holy Spirit *from the Father and Son*. There's a sense that God's love, said to be infinite (without boundaries), on the Latin view, is bound by time in the sense that, before Creation, there was nothing, no being besides God, to which he could show his love. Hence, divine love as outward going, would only be prevenient, a potentiality for God, waiting for the

---

34   *Perichoresis*, meaning an *intermingling of love within the Trinity from all eternity*, expressed by the terms, *circumincession* (meaning *rotation, to go around*, signifying the *dymanic circulation of Trinitarian life from each to the others*, appealing to the Greek mind), and eternally, *circuminsession* (meaning *an insitting* or *indwelling from eternity*, appealing to the Latin tradition because it emphasized the divine essence). See "Trinitarian Willing and Salvific Initiatives", *The Trinity: East/West Dialogue* (Melville Y. Stewart, ed.), 52-53.
35   Some take the decree of God as plural, decrees.
36   It is assumed here that there is a before and after with regard to God's decree and his actualizing of that decree. The *before* refers to something that had existence eternally in the past.
37   There's a sense in which the perichoretic love within the Trinity, may be said to overflow toward humanity, since the redeemed, the *Church*, is viewed in the NT as the "body of Christ" (εκκλησια...σωμα αυτου) Eph. 1:22, 23). Hence the self-giving love of Christ retains its proper focus in respect to *perichoretic love*, and his *self-giving love*. The logical prius of perichoretic love is never compromised or mitigated by another love.

moment of Creation for love to become a reality.[38] This brief excursus examined briefly two views of the Trinity, the Latin formal account, and the Social view. It was argued that the Social view provides a more transparent accounting of God as expressing love, inwardly from eternity, and outwardly via his divine decree with regard to Creation and Redemption. The account of divine love above gives attention to two central manifestations of God's self-giving love both in decree, and in the carrying out of his decree with respect to Creation and Redemption. One of the most formidable challenges to the Christian faith calls into question the *rational consistency* of some its central beliefs spelled out in the following Set_1:

1. God exists.
2. God is omniscient, omnipotent, and perfectly loving.
3. God created the world.
4. Evil exists.[39]

The *inconsistency strategy* involves the charge that the entire set S_1 cannot be true because (4) is inconsistent with (1)-(3). An expansion on statement (4) that includes, horrendous evils,[40] suffering[41] and the fallenness of the human race make (4) very difficult to deny. Furthermore, statements (1)-(3) are historic core beliefs for the Christian theist. Further discussion on this main issue takes us too far afield for this study. Instead our attention is given to a topic falling under (4), *Evil exists*, namely *the Fall*. It is argued that the Fall may be viewed as God opening a door to a dimension of his love not existentially meaningful in a *prefallen* world. In the GGD, the argument is made that a fall might have been allowed so as to make meaningful, a *redemptive particularization* of divine self-giving love to a *fallen* humanity thereby bringing about a greater-good, hence the *O felix culpa* (*oh happy fault*) locution.[42] No doubt, an infinitely loving and all-powerful God could have brought about a world where *no fall* occurs. But just maybe, if one assumes a variant *multiverse hypothesis* a fall of some sort just might be a divine option. That is, assuming a *multiverse*

---

38 A defender of the Latin view of the Trinity who holds that God is outside of time in some sense, might affirm the *eternal actuality* of divine self-giving love since *all of creation* is in his *eternal present*, hence his self-giving love to humans is *eternal*.
39 See the GGD, Chapter 3, "The Greater-Good Defence." *Defence* is the British spelling.
40 See Marilyn Adams, *Horrendous Evils and the Goodness of God*, Ithaca: Cornell University Press, 1999.
41 See Eleonore Stump's *Wandering in Darkness*, Clarendon Press, 2010.
42 *O Felix Culpa* (*Oh happy fault*), "*O certe necessarium Adae peccatum, quod Christi morte deletum est! O felix culpa, quae talem ac tantum meruit habere redemptorem!* (*O fortunate crime* or *happy fault, which merited* [*to have*] *such and so great a redeemer!*)." GGD, 145.

hypothesis (many universes), perhaps there are also *many planets* out there in the many universes that would be friendly to the flourishing of human life (such are called *exoplanets*).[43] Then one might further argue that there might very well be a universe (or many universes) that contain(s) an exoplanet (or exoplanets) like our exoplanet$_1$ (which seems to evidence a fall of some sort), and another kind, say exoplanet$_2$ (or many such exoplanets) which include(s) humans (or some sort of intelligent agents) who never fall morally, in which case there would be an exoplanet (or exoplanets) where no evil occurs.[44] Arguably then, God could thus create a universe (or universes) which include(s) at least one exoplanet$_1$ (Earth), where a Fall *does* occur, so that he could show his infinite love towards a lost humanity and at least one other exoplanet$_2$ (or many such exoplanets) where his love can be shown to a non-fallen creation. So, with both *kinds* of exoplanets, those of the exoplanet$_1$ kind and of the exoplanet$_2$ kind, God makes possible the showing of love to an *unfallen humanity*, *and* love to a *fallen humanity*, thereby *expanding* the *ways* whereby he shows an infinite love overflowing from the divine perichoretic Source. In both cases, divine love is affirmed in and through that which he brings about. I hasten to add, that a universe and single exoplanet where no fall occurs likely embraces a *greater-good* than the universe and single exoplanet where a fall occurs.[45] The point is, perhaps God wanted both, so as to maximize his outgoing self-giving love.

B   *The Early Christian Ethic of Love*

As we begin, it's important to note that New Testament revelation isn't *all* new. There is in fact an amazing connectedness between the Testaments, and such a continuity as to warrant affirming the existence of a *divine metanarrative*. The divine Word delivers a Sermon on the Mount,[46] and a Sermon on the Plains, both containing an expository account of the truths of the Law. Notice what Christ says in the seventh chapter of Matthew, "Therefore all things whatsoever ye would that men should do to you, do ye even so to them: for this is the Law and the Prophets." Christ here summarizes the second "table" of the Ten Commandments in his offering of the Golden Rule. Whereas Christ offers a

---

43   See Owen Gingerich's article, "Designing a Universe Congenial to Life, in: *Science and Religion in Dialogue*, Volume II, 618-627.

44   I argue thus in a new paper, "The Greater-Good Defense, O Felix Culpa, and the Multiverse Hypothesis" (a revision of the 7th chapter of my book, *The Greater-Good Defence, An Essay on the Rationality of Faith*, London: Macmillan//New York: St. Martin's Press, 2003).

45   Augustine, Anselm, and Aquinas held that an Earth without a fall is a greater-good than an Earth with a fall, GGD, 189, n. 34.

46   Matthew 5-7.

positive framing in the Sermon on the Mount 登山宝训 Confucius offers a contrasting negative variant of the Golden Rule in Books V and XII of his *Analects*. But there's a substantial difference between Christ's positive read and Confucius' negative turn. Christ's positive version is more demanding. The negative prohibitions that characterize Confucius' moral directive don't cover the positives that Christ's version does. *Not doing* what one would not want done unto oneself, doesn't go as far as, *doing* what one would want done unto oneself. Not lying, which would count as an instance of "not doing something I would not want done unto me," doesn't go to the other higher level of positively being honest in every dimension of human engagement.

John knew well what he had in mind when he said in I John, 4:8, and 16, *God is love*. The term he chose for *love* in the Greek, is αγαπε. One, if not its most basic meaning is, love that is *self-giving*, because God in his essence, is viewed as a God of *self-giving love*. This truth is expressed clearly in John 3:16 which says, that "God so loved (ηγαπησεν) the world (via a self-giving love expressed in the giving of his Son) that whosoever believes on him will not perish but have everlasting life." Taking God as one's model of love, provides an understanding that allows and helps enable the recipient of divine love to then offer a self-giving love in return by *keeping the commandments*. John expresses it in John 14:21 thus, "He/she that has my commandments, and keeps them, he/she is one that loves me, and he/she that loves me, shall be loved of my Father, and I will love him/her, and manifest myself to him/her." The term used in this passage is *agape* (αγαπη). It is a love that involves a *giving of the self in obedience to the commandments of God*. Notice that God again gives of himself, to such a degree, that he promises to *manifest himself* to the person who affirms God's commands in his/her life. *One way* to see the truth of this promise is, if a person loves others, they will find out that the commands have a pragmatic value, they *work*. They evidence a *divine moral order in the cosmos*, such that, when that order is followed, humans experience a flourishing because there's a Providential God who affirms and upholds that order. But more yet follows. The truth of the Word becomes ever more evident to the practitioner. Over time, one finds a happiness and contentment in the presence of the One who made the promise. *Wisdom* may thus be said to issue from experience.

There's a problem that faces the whole issue of the pursuit of virtue, and of love in particular. It arises both in connection with God's expression of love in a self-giving way, and with humans responding to God with the motive of imitating the divine Giver of love. It can be expressed by the question: Does God as the divine agent have significant or real freedom in the showing of agape love? Mainstream Christian theism affirms that God is *perfectly good*. That is, he is *free to choose* x or y, but both x and y are good. So, his freedom is *confined* to perfectly good choices. Do his choices, because they issue from a perfect nature, come about *necessarily*? Moreover, has he not *decreed* what is to take place in human history from an eternity past? The answer depends upon a number of considerations, one having to do with whether a Sovereign God can allow humans to have *significant freedom*, say with regard to x or y, where x is good and y evil? If so, then doesn't his creation of such creatures bring about the *possibility* of evil? And if he did do this, doesn't this make him *ultimately responsible* for evil in bringing about sets of states of affairs that make evil possible? There's yet another question, is human significant freedom compatible with God's decreeing the course of history? One possible answer to the last question is conceivably yes. But *just in case* in creating such creatures, he doesn't deny his *ultimate sovereignty, and deny himself* in *what he creates, sovereignly rules over,* and *ultimately bring about in terms of final overbalancing goods*. As to the question whether God is free in his self-giving love, one possible answer is, he is free to show his love to whomever and whatever he wills from eternity to create.

Now it can be argued that God could not have avoided some sort of redemptive plan, say something like the Atonement for exoplanet$_1$, since he allowed the Fall by giving Adam and Eve enough *freedom* so as to make it possible. Earlier it was argued that as an earthly father wouldn't give an offspring enough freedom when they are young, so as to make possible a choice that could end with their demise, so by *analogy*, a Heavenly Father wouldn't have given so much freedom to Adam and Eve so as to risk the end of a *final* death. That is, unless he had a plan that would bring about a final *greater-good* in response to such a devastating human failure. In my book, *The Greater-Good Defense*, I argue that the greater-good is Redemption. Redemption would have had no meaning without a *fall* of some sort. Hence it was arguably an *O felix culpa*, a *happy fault*. One possible way to frame the greater-good defense argument runs as follows:

S_6, GGD: Every evil that God allows is logically necessary to some at least *counterbalancing* good *set* of states of affairs, and some evil is *overbalanced* by all of the good set of states of affairs to which the evil in question is logically necessary.

The GGD affirms that God, being perfectly good, might with regard to exoplanet$_1$ Earth, allow a Fall, so as to make possible a *greater-good* than the evil of the Fall, namely the good of Redemption. This final good end God would have to bring about, because, greater is he who is in the believer, than he (Satan) who is in the world,[47] and secondly, because God cannot deny himself.[48] These two Biblical statements imply a greater-good must come about if God allows

---

47   I John 4:4, "Greater is he who is in you, than he that is in the world."
48   2 Timothy 2:13, "If we believe not, yet he abides faithful: he *cannot deny himself*."

evil into a world he created and declared to be good. So, while space doesn't permit an expansion on the brief accounting of God's allowance of evil, it does suggest a plausible and consistent response to the inconsistency strategy.

IV   Nestorianism-the Nestorian Relic, and the Ethic of Love in Early *Jingjiao* (Christianity) in China

Thus far, careful attention has been given to the ethic of love in Judaism and Christianity. We shift now to how the earliest Christian outreach initiative to China emulated the ethic of love. Jean-Pierre Charbonnier, drawing attention to this discovery in his first chapter, "Relics from China's Past," of his tome, *Christians in China, A.C. 600 to 2000*, observes that the Christian religion has been "rooted in Chinese soil since the Tang Dynasty, more than thirteen centuries ago. The monks of the Syrian Church who came from Persia in the seventh century…brought with them the message of *Jingjiao* (Christianity)--of God's kingdom.[49]

The Christian Xi'an stele was erected in 781. The priest in residence was Jingjing. The inscription containing 1,756 characters in vertical lines, lists his name as Adam, and he is referred to as Chorbishop and Papash of Chinastan.[50] He was a member of one of the four great Christian monasteries in China at that time. The text includes the core beliefs of the Christian faith, including the Trinity, and other teachings which were viewed as so transcendent and difficult to understand and describe that the text refers to the religion as the "Luminous Religion."[51] Various descriptions of the Messiah contain Mahayana Buddhist images, such as, the "shining Lord of the universe," and the "ship of mercy carrying its passengers toward the dwelling place of light."[52]

There is some sort of relationship closer than coincidence that can sufficiently explain the hermeneutic situation of Jingjing's transplantation strategy. Zhu Donghua's survey of parallels between Buddhist explanations of Ying/ Nirmana and Jingjing's understanding of Ying/ 應 shows how much Jingjing's efforts in Christian inculturation were rooted in both traditions of Chinese Buddhism and East Syriac Christianity. Ingeniously, Jingjing borrowed the Buddhist conception of "compassionate response" as the basis for under-

---

49   This is Jean-Pierre Charbonnier's point made in the opening to his book, *Christians in China*, AD 600 to 2000 (Trans. by M.N.L. Couve de Murville, San Francisco: Ignatius Press, 2002), 19.
50   Ibid., 24.
51   Ibid., 26.
52   Ibid., 27.

standing and translating such theological claims as God is love, and Holy Son embodied and fulfilled the economic love of God. Jingjing grasped deeply the functional and soteriological significance of both Agape and maitri-karuna as the fundamental religious motifs.[53] All of which shows, that even if there is a cultural and religious pluralism, if there is enough *loving care* and *concern* to reach out to one's neighbor, a society marked by diversity has the potential thereby to learn to live in peace and harmony.

The Christological controversies that alienated the Church of the West and the East, involved extensive allegory with regard to Old Testament exegesis. The full human nature of Christ was center stage. Jesus was viewed as having a *human soul* and free moral activity, exercised in his redemptive work. The famous Jingjiao Stone Pillar features the Cross symbolizing the theme of love instantiated in God's metanarrative as it unfolded in central episodes of love expressed in an anticipatory mode in Messianic prophetic utterances in the Old Testament, and as it is brought to fulfillment in the Messiah Incarnate in Jesus of Nazareth, who was the Word God spoke in Creation, who lived a life in obedience to the Law and the Prophets, and who sacrificed his life to be the Second Adam. He thereby reinstated a lost humanity by offering the grace of salvation by faith. As the NT writers reported, he was also raised again for the believer's justification. And he is to appear in a final denouement--a Second Coming and Final Resurrection. This metanarrative, acted out in human history by divine decree,[54] Providence, and divine acts, is to culminate in a Kingdom marked by peace, harmony and love, in a life of everlasting felicity with the Maker and Redeemer.

Conclusion

Love, as we have seen, has various meanings in both the divine metanarrative, and its human counterpart in history. The giving of the Ten Commandments in the Old Testament, and their reaffirmation in the Sermon on the Mount, embraces the love, justice and righteousness of the God of the Hebrew and Christian faiths. The Christian theist, as we've seen in the unfolding of history, takes both Testaments as exhibiting a continuity, with the Old embracing anticipatory moments of revelation, and the New, embracing both retrocipatory and

---

53 Zhu Donghua, "Ying/應/Nirmana," in: *Winds of Jingjiao* (edited by Li Tang and Dietmar Winkler, LIT Verlag, 2016), 427, 432.

54 Some speak of *decrees* (plural). Note, the decree of God issues from eternity, but when it is carried out in human history it happens an eternity from the original decree.

anticipatory divine disclosures. Both of which offer a progressive and continuous disclosure of divine truth as significant for the human condition. The core statements at the beginning (S_1-S_5), present a summary of the divine-human narrative. Love is at the center of the divine nature along with an eternally existing complementary justice. The divine Law expresses a moral order intended for humans created in God's image that might properly be called a *divine moral cosmic code*. The divine Law was given as an expression of compassion and self-giving love, so as to aid humans in their effort to live together in peace, harmony, love and justice. These virtues distinguishable and internally woven together in God, are to be reflected in the created human counterpart, again woven together in every strata of society, and in the private sector. Complicity is to be rendered, not merely as a *dutiful response simpliciter*, but as a response of obedience to the divine will expressed in law, designed and intended for the practitioner's good, and in terms of which the human agent is to bring the dutiful response of obedience to show love full circle, by reflecting the love God extends back to him and to others he has created.

PART 3

Church History in China

CHAPTER 5

The Church of the East in China (Jingjiao)

Mar Aprem Metropolitan

The **Christianity in China** is generally believed to be going back to the 7th century during the Tang dynasty. The famous Nestorian Pillar erected in 781 AD is written in Chinese language. But the names of the heads of the Church in China from 635 AD to 781 AD are inscribed in Syriac language.

Ian Gillman and Hans-Joachim Klimkeit in their book **Christians in Asia before 1500** refers to the possibility of St. Thomas, the disciple of Jesus to India had evangelised China. Referring to the Breviary used in Kerala these authors think of the possibility of St. Thomas evangelising China. The Syriac Breviary known as Hudra we read:

> By the means of St. Thomas the Chineeses and the Ethiopians were converted to the truth...... By the means of St. Thomas the Kingdom of Heaven flew and entered into China... The Chineeses commemoration of St. Thomas do offer their adoration unto the most holy name, O God.

Some recent writers think that the Church in China was founded by St. Thomas, the doubting disciple of Jesus Christ during 65 to 68 AD. It is generally believed St. Thomas was in India from 52 to 72 AD. There is a well-researched and documented book in French language captioned THOMAS FONDE L'EGLISE EN CHINA, Pierre Perrier & Xavier Walter published in 2008 ISBN (978-2-86679-482-8). The authors give a lot of illustrations to support their arguments for the existence of Christianity in China already for five and a half centuries before the general belief of the founding of Christianity in 635 AD by Alopen, a Nestorian missionary. This book written in French has not found a deserving place in the discussion of Christianity in China in the early centuries.

Generally speaking, the Church of the East known as the Assyrian Church or Persian Church does not like the name Nestorian Church because of the stigma of heresy attached to it. Nevertheless, the present writer has used the name Nestorian Church in many of his books during the past five decades. The main reason is that the name Nestorian Church is not without honour in the missionary history of the Church, East of Jerusalem. Moreover, the present writer has claimed that Nestorius was not a Nestorian. Especially in China, the name of the Nestorian Church is an honourable name.

The chronicles of Han Emperor Mingdi and other attestations fix the trip of Apostle Thomas to China in 65- 68 AD.

Pierre Perrier writes: p. 299 of his book **'Thomas Fonde L'Eglise En Chine'**.

> As we have now better knowledge of Judeo-Christianity in France, Chinese scholars should turn towards recognition of the first Christian mission in China during the third part of the first century. A major contributor to such recognition is the new analysis of the Parthian reliefs, among many not so older Buddhist figures, on Kang Wong Cliff. The site is located near the imperial road leaving the ancient harbour of Lianyungang for the capital Luoyang of later Han dynasty; there, the travellers coming from south India and western countries allowed to travel to the capital Luyoyan continued their trip on foot. In fact, for the second part of the first century, the Silk Road was almost closed by continuous wars over land and the large trade between Roman, Parthian and Chinese empires used sea transportation; so the connection between the Buddhist area in north-west India and China was broken off.

Translation from the book written in French by Pierre Perrier & Xavier Walter, pages 276 and 277.

Cities Evangelized by Thomas in South India (duration and years)

Southwest Coast

Maliankara: 8 months (52-53 AD); 1 month (54); 5 months (55); 2 weeks (59)
Quilon: 1 year (55-56 AD)
Chayal: 1 year (56-57 AD)
Triepalesuram: 2 months (55 AD), 2 months (57 AD)
Niranam: 2 months (57 AD); 1 year (60-61 AD)
Kokkamangalam: 1 year (57-58 AD)
Kottakavu-Parur: 1 year (58-59 AD)
Palayur: 1 month (59 AD)
Maleatur: 2 months (60 AD)

Southeastern Coast

Meilapouram and surroundings: 4 months and ½ (53 AD); 1 month (54 AD); 2 months (59 AD); 3 years (70-72 AD)

South Coast and Ceylon (Tamilnadu) Trivandrum and Tabropane (61-64 AD)

Cities evangelized in China: the dates are approximate, except beginning and end, following expectations on the ground of favorable winds; previously Thomas made preparations and attempts (from summer 53 to Kalah and Malacca, then to 59); finally, he had a trained interpreter, probably from Tabropane, the busiest port for his sales facilitating the circumvention of India on the sea route.

The sabbatical years 61-62 and 68-69 did not give chance to go on a pilgrimage to Jerusalem being in latent insurrection which was to be aggravated, but there were exchanges of letters carried by the merchants.

Cities evangelized by Thomas in China
Lianyungang (65)
Xushou (65-67)
Kaifeng (67)
Luoyang (67-68)
The one-year long evangelization was from Pentecost to Pentecost:
– 8 months of Tents at Pentecost
– 4 months or 4 months or more from Pentecost to Yom Kippur
– 2 months or less on a summer mission or in a trip

The cycles of three passages made it possible to install a bishop who was trained during winter session and by his collaboration with the missions of the apostle according to the model of the teaching of Jesus himself. Thus, Thomas formed in India two bishops whose names have been preserved by tradition, more than seven priests and thirty deacons. At least two of the priests are Rabbans, that is, successors capable of forming deacons and priests. The same structure must have taken place in China. Baptisms took place at Easter or Tents after raising a mission cross and ordinations at Pentecost after edification of a church at the feast of Dedication. The liturgical cycle is that of Matthew and the liturgical language Aramaic, with simultaneous translation into vernacular language by the deacon-translator, in this case the collaborator of Thomas called Shofarlan.

There were Jewish merchants not only in the south west coast of India but also in China and Ceylon in the early centuries of the Christian Era. In Ceylon the present writer went to visit the famous Persian Cross at Anuradhapura, which was the capital city of Ceylon at that time. The researchers have to work hard by digging up the historic places in Ceylon.

FIGURE 5.1
The Nestorian Stele is a Tang Chinese stele erected in 781 AD that documents 150 years of history of early Christianity in China.

South coast and Ceylon (Tamil country)
Trivandrum and Tabropane (61-64 AD)

Cities evangelized in China: dates are approximate, except beginning and end, following expectations on land of favorable winds; previously Thomas made preparations and attempts (from summer of 53 AD to Kalah and Malacca, then to 59 AD); finally, he has a trained interpreter, probably from Tabropane, the busiest port for his sales facilitating the circumvention of India on the road to the sea.

We do not have enough evidences of the existing and functioning of this Christianity until the arrival of Alopen in China in 635 AD.

The first definite documentation of Christianity entering China was written on an 8th-century stone tablet known as the Nestorian Stele. It records that Christians reached the Tang dynasty capital Xi'an in 635 and were allowed to establish places of worship and to propagate their faith. The leader of the Christian travellers was Alopen.

In 635 AD when the news of the expected arrival of Alopen reached China the Emperor Tai Tsung sent his own brother to receive him. What was the interest of the emperor to receive a stranger with such warm welcome.? Raymond Oppenheim who published a book The First Nestorian Mission to China and its Failure, Berkeley 1971 observes that the emperor did not have any worldly motive, as he had completed successfully his conquest of the people in the North West.

Emperor's motive was spiritual because Islam was formed a new religion at that time. It could spread from Arabia to China. Alopen was allowed to stay in the Royal Palace and use the Library to translate the religious books he had brought with him. Three years after the arrival of Alopen, the emperor issued an edict of toleration in 638 AD.

> The way had not at all times and in all places, the self same name, the sage had not at all times, and in all places, the self same body. Heaven caused a suitable religion to be instituted for every region and clime so that each one of the races of mankind might be saved. Bishop Alopen of the Kingdom of Ta-chin, bringing with him the sutras and images has come after and presented them at our capital........ So let it have free course throughout this Empire. (**The Luminous Religion**, page 32)

In 649 AD Emperor Tai Tsung died. His ninth son Kao Tsung succeeded. He ruled China for 34 years with prosperity.

The Christians survived the difficult time of about half a century. After Wu Ho had abdicated in AD 705, one of her deposed sons, HsuanTsung, came to the throne in AD 712. His reign was important for the Christians as a period for rebuilding. A bishop named Chi-lieh3 was honoured by the Emperor in AD 732, and his relationship with the court probably continued.4 The church regained the ground it had lost under Wu Ho during the reign of Hsuan Tsung which lasted until his abdication in AD 756.

Towards the end of the eighth century, Christianity in China was at its zenith. But in the ninth century it began to decline. After the edict of 845 AD, two or three thousand monks were sent back to civil life. But what happened to the Christian population is not known. Mrs. C.E. Couling in her book *The Luminous Religion* p. 34 suggests the following possibilities.

> 1. The Nestorians may have merged themselves in the Mohammedan community, which was larger and less molested. Their common worship of the One True God would tend to draw the two sets of religionists together, especially in time of trouble; and it is said that the increase in the number of Chinese Moslems, who do not proselytize, has been such greater than natural increase could account for. Another consideration is that in those times the Saracens in Persia were very friendly with the Christians, who were indeed high in favour at Baghdad.

> 2. A better-known suggestion is that the Nestorians after they fell from favour hid themselves in certain secret sects, such as the "White Lily", and the "one Stick of incense" sects, and very specially in the "Chin Tan Chiao"

the Pill-Immortality sect- which claims to have even to-day ten or eleven million followers.

If none of the Nestorians actually turned Buddhists, there is proof that they greatly influenced Chinese Buddhism. There is abundant evidence that Buddhists and Nestorians were on very friendly terms in Xian Foo: the very man who composed the inscription on the Nestorian Tablet-Adam, otherwise Kingtsing- is found shortly afterwards helping an Indian monk to translate a Buddhist sutra into Chinese. The Emperors, it is well-known, were friendly with both cults for a long time.

The Nestorian influence on Chinese Buddhism, it is claimed, is shown in the great impetus given in China at this very time to the Buddhist All Souls' Day, and to the Pure Land School of Buddhism.

But suppose all these suppositions true; that many Chinese Nestorian Christians entered Islam instead of reverting to paganism-that others hid their teaching in secret sects-that an immense influence from them was felt by Chinese Buddhism and new elements introduced into Chinese thought-do we not all agree that it is a poor, paltry, pitiful result, of two attempts to Christianize the Middle Kingdom? Can we say other than that they failed? 1

Unfortunately, there is no monument to give us the details of the period after AD 781. However, we know something of the latter period from the imperial edicts. After the Tang Dynasty the Nestorian Missionary Enterprise died out in China. Nevertheless, Christianity did not disappear completely.

John of Monte Corvino, who arrived in Canbalac (Peking) in AD 1294 speaks of the Nestorians as a powerful community. He managed to convert King George, e descendant of Prestor John 'When King George, died, his brothers and all his people reverted to Nestorianism again, or as Corvino puts it, "to their original schismatic creed."2 A Nestorian called Mar Sergius was governor of the province of Kiang Su in China, during AD 1278-1280 and is said to have built two churches.3

---

1. Mrs CE Couling, *The Luminous Religion*, p. 34, 35, 3, 38, 41
2. *John Stewart, The Nestorian Missionary Enterprise*, p. 193
3. Ibid., *p. 195*

By the end of the 13th century the Nestorian Church was widely spread. Assemani gives a list of no less than twenty-seven Metropolitan seats extending over the whole of Asia at this time. Two hundred bishops were connected with these mission areas. 3 In the year A D 1369 Ming dynasty replaced the Tartar dynasty of the Mongols. This resulted in the final eclipse of Nestorianism in China.

In 845 AD, at the height of the great anti-Buddhist persecution, Emperor Wuzong decreed that Buddhism, Christianity, and Zoroastrianism be banned, and their very considerable assets forfeited to the state.

In 986 AD a monk reported to the Patriarch of the Church of the East:

> Christianity is extinct in China; the native Christians have perished in one way or another; the Church has been destroyed and there is only one Christian left in the land.

Karel Pieters noted that there were some Christian gravestones dated from the Song and Liao dynasties, implying that some Christians remained in China.

Medieval period

Christianity among the Mongols

The 13th century saw the Mongol-established Yuan dynasty in China. Christianity was a major influence in the Mongol Empire, as several Mongol tribes were primarily Nestorian Christian, and many of the wives of Genghis Khan's descendants were Christian. Contacts with Western Christianity also came in this time, via envoys from the Papacy to the Mongol capital in Khanbalik (Beijing).

The Assyrian Church of the East was well established in China, as is attested by the monks Rabban Bar Sauma and Rabban Marcos, both of whom made a famous pilgrimage to the West, visiting many Nestorian communities along the way. Marcos, the younger of the two monks, was elected as the Catholicos Patriarch of the Church of the East, and Rabban Bar Sauma went as far as visiting the courts of Europe in 1287-1288 AD, where he told Western monarchs about Christianity among the Mongols.

Rabban Marcos became famous as Patriarch Mar Yahballaha III (1281-1317 AD), the only ethnically non-Assyrian Patriarch of the Church of the East nicknamed Nestorian. It is believed that the site of the Cross Temple near Beijing in China is the place where Patriarch Mar Yahballaha III prayed when he started his journey to the Holy Land.

Actually, during the period of Patriarch Mar Yahballaha III (1281-1317 AD), the Nestorian Church had spread widely in Asia. J.S. Assemani in *Bibliotheca Orientalis* published in Rome in 1719 AD gives a list of twenty-seven Metropoli-

FIGURE 5.1 Nestorian priests in a procession on Palm Sunday, in a 7th- or 8th-century wall painting from a Nestorian Church in China, Tang dynasty.

tan seats in Asia at that time. There were 200 bishops. The collapse of the Nestorian Church in China was in 1369 AD when the Ming dynasty replaced the Tartar dynasty of the Mongols.

In 1289 AD, Franciscan friars from Europe, who are Roman Catholics, initiated mission work in China. This is the first entry of the Roman Catholic church in China It was the time when the only Chinese Patriarch of the Assyrian Church of the East was very much active as the head of this great missionary Church. For about a century they worked in parallel with the Nestorian Christians. The Franciscan mission disappeared from 1368 AD, as the Ming dynasty set out to eject all foreign influences.

The Chinese called Muslims, Jews, and Christians in ancient times by the same name, "*Hui Hui*" (*Hwuy-hwuy*). Christians were called "*Hwuy* who abstain from animals without the cloven foot", Muslims were called "*Hwuy* who abstain from pork", Jews were called "*Hwuy* who extract the sinews". "*Hwuy-tsze*" (*Hui zi*) or "*Hwuy-hwuy*" (*Hui Hui*) is presently used almost exclusively for Muslims, but Jews were still called "*Lan Maou Hwuy tsze*" (*Lan Mao Hui zi*) which means "Blue-cap Hui zi".

At Kaifeng, Jews were called "*Teaou-kin-keaou*", "extract-sinew religion". Jews and Muslims in China shared the same name for synagogue and mosque, which were both called "*Tsing-chin sze*" (*Qingzhen si*), "temple of purity and truth", the name dated to the thirteenth century. The synagogue and mosques were also known as "*Le-pae sze*" (*Libai si*). A tablet indicated that Judaism was once known as *"Yih-tsze-lo-nee-keaou"* (Israelitish religion) and synagogues known as *"Yih-tsze lo née leen"* (Israelitish temple), but it faded out of use. In my mother-tongue Malayalam, not only the Jewish synagogue and Muslim mosque but also the Christian Church too is translated as *Palli*. Nevertheless, the Hindu Temple is never translated as *Palli*.

It was also reported that competition with the Roman Catholic Church and Islam were also factors in causing Nestorian Christianity to disappear in China; the Roman Catholics also considered the Nestorians as heretical, speaking of "controversies with the emissaries of Rome, and the progress of Mohammedanism, sapped the foundations of their ancient churches."

The Ming dynasty decreed that Manichaeism and Christianity were illegal and heterodox; to be wiped out from China, while Islam and Judaism were legal and fit Confucian ideology Buddhist sects like the White Lotus were also banned by the Ming.

The number of Chinese Christians has increased significantly since the easing of restrictions on religious activity during economic reforms in the late 1970s; Christians were four million before 1949 (three million Catholics and one million Protestants).

It is not easy to find accurate data on Chinese Christians today. According to the most recent internal surveys there are approximately 31 million Christians in China today (2.3% of the total population). On the other hand, some international Christian organizations estimate there are tens of millions more, which choose not to publicly identify as such. The practice of religion continues to be tightly controlled by government authorities. Chinese over the age of 18 are only permitted to join officially sanctioned Christian groups registered with the government-approved Protestant Three-Self Church and China Christian Council, and Chinese Patriotic Catholic Church. On the other hand, many Christians practice in informal networks and unregistered congregations, often described as house churches or underground churches, the proliferation of which began in the 1950s when many Chinese Protestants and Catholics began to reject state-controlled structures purported to represent them. Members of such groups are said to represent the "silent majority of Chinese Christians and represent many diverse theological traditions.

After the arrival of the Jesuit Missions in China in the 16th century Eastern Christianity in China either disappeared or went underground. It may be one of the secret sects not recognised.

In conclusion, it is necessary to trace the history of the Christians founded by St. Thomas from 65 to 68 AD with the second Mission of Alopen in 635 AD. It is also necessary to study what happened to the Eastern Christianity after the Jesuit Missions began to work in China in the 16th century.

Raymond L. Oppenheim, *The first Nestorian Mission in China and its Failure*, Berkeley, Shires Bookstore, 1971, p. 32.

The 13th century saw the Mongol-established Yuan dynasty in China. Christianity was a major influence in the Mongol Empire, as several Mongol tribes were primarily Nestorian Christian, and many of the wives of Genghis Khan's descendants were Christian. Contacts with Western Christianity also came in this time period, via envoys from the Papacy to the Mongol capital in Khanbaliq (Beijing).

Nestorianism was well established in China, as is attested by the monks Rabban Bar Sauma and Rabban Marcos, both of whom made a famous pilgrimage to the West, visiting many Nestorian communities along the way. Marcos was elected as Patriarch of the Church of the East, and Bar Sauma went as far as visiting the courts of Europe in 1287-1288, where he told Western monarchs about Christianity among the Mongols.

In 1289 AD, Franciscan friars from Europe initiated mission work in China. For about a century they worked in parallel with the Nestorian Christians. The Franciscan mission disappeared from 1368 AD, as the Ming dynasty set out to eject all foreign influences.

In conclusion, I would like to see that more scientific research is conducted in China to dig deeper for more archaeological evidence to support the missionary labours of St. Thomas in China from 64 AD to 68 AD. We need to find out more of the activities of these early Christians after Apostle Thomas had departed from China back to South India in 68 AD.

We do not know whether the Christian Church in the first century ever attempted to write prayer books in the Chinese language. Had the first century Christian Church in China ever attempted to translate Bible or holy Books to the Chinese language as Alopen attempted in 635 AD.

I do not find a single Syriac book connecting it to the Church in China in the archives of the Metropolitan's Palace, in Trichur, India which has several Syriac books copied in Iraq and Iran.

Was there an exchange of bishops and priests between India and China?

How was the end of the Nestorian Christianity in China?

After the arrival of the Portuguese in China in the 16th century, were the Nestorian Christians persecuted by the Non-Christians as happened in India?

During the 2nd international conference on "the history of Early Christianity in India with parallel developments in the other parts in Asia" sponsored by the Institute of Asian Studies in Chennai held in Chennai in 2008 some participants requested us to research and find out the activities of St. Thomas outside the Kerala State. They wanted to know more details about his activities in Tamilnadu where he was martyred in 72 AD. Have St. Thomas established churches in and around Madras before he was martyred? Now, I feel that the students of the Church history of St. Thomas have to search for the churches which St. Thomas established not only in Kerala and Tamilnadu but in China, too.

In the Hudra (Syriac Prayer Book of the Church of the East printed in Trichur in 1960) volume III, page number 336 we read in the prayers for the Rogation of the Ninavites on the prayer on Wednesday: "Receive our Lord requests of the Chinese and the Indians (*the Sienaye Vad Hinduvaye*) in the language of their land, honouring thy name and to thee they worship". As these prayers were composed in the sixth century we can believe that there were Christians in China at that time. This makes us to go deeper searching for Christianity in China prior to the arrival of Alopen in 635 AD.

CHAPTER 6

Fangshan Cross Temple (房山十字寺) in China: Overview, Analysis and Hypotheses

Xiaofeng Tang and Yingying Zhang

There are at least three Christian relics or remains in the Beijing area: One is a copy of the Syrian hymn of the Yuan Dynasty discovered in the Beijing Meridian Gate tower in 1925, which was partly taken over by Peking University. The other two are located in the Fangshan District, Beijing. One is the inscription of the Ming Dynasty left by Nestorian monks who traveled to Shijingshan (石经山, also known as Xiaoxitian 小西天); the other is the cross temple at the foot of Maoer Mountain (猫耳山) at Chechang village (车厂村). In the course of its history, the Cross Temple has been related to Buddhism, and it has also been connected with the existence of Christianity during the Tang and Yuan Dynasties. This paper will discuss the Christian identity of the Cross Temple.

1   Overview of the Fangshan Cross Temple

According to the historical data, the name "Cross Temple" first appeared on the Monument of the Yuan Dynasty (*we will abbreviate it to Yuan Monument,* Yuanbei 元碑) in the Cross temple. The name was bestowed by the Yuan Shun Emperor (Yuan Shundi 元顺帝) during the renovation of the temple at the end of the Yuan Dynasty. However, we haven't any further information about whether the temple was known as the Cross Temple before the Yuan Dynasty. This name was used throughout the Ming and Qing Dynasties, and the Republic of China (1911-1949), because there is the entry of "the Cross Temple" in the "*Chronicle of Fangshan County*" (*Fangshan xian zhi* 房山县志), which was edited during the Ming Wanli period and reedited in the Qing Emperor Kangxi period. It was simply recorded that the Cross temple was located in the northwest of Chechang Village and was listed with other Buddhist temples without any detailed descriptions. In the 6th year of the Republic of China, there was still a plaque for the "Ancient Cross Buddhist Temple" over the gate, which is currently housed in the Beijing Stone Carving Art Museum.

The relics of the Cross temple seen by visitors today include only the faintly visible ground of the main hall, the building elements scattered in the courtyard and two monuments (from the Liao and Yuan Dynasties) under a large ancient ginkgo tree. The wall of the Cross Temple was set up again in the 1990s by Christians in Beijing. The new courtyard covers about 2,200 square meters.

Japanese scholar Yoshiro Saeki surveyed this site in 1931. At that time, there was still a main building in the temple. In his book *The Study of Chinese Christianity*, he described the architectural layout of the temple.

> The central part of the whole building is supposed to be a closed gate of the temple. If you went through the original gate, you would first come across the Heavenly King Hall (天王殿), where there is a plaque of "Ancient Cross Buddhist Temple" over the side door, which has fallen to the ground. Entering the door, there are two rows of rooms for Monks ... facing the gate, the main hall was erected with a stone-paved road leading to it.[1]

The main indications that the Cross Temple used to be a Christian one come from two directions.

On the one hand, archaeologists have two stone carvings in the temple, which were transported to Nanjing and preserved in the Nanjing Museum in November 1931; currently one stone replica is displayed in Beijing's Capital Museum. The size of the two stone is the same (68.5 cm in height, 58.5 cm in width, 22 cm in thickness on the end, and 14 cm in thickness on the side), but the contents of the inscriptions are slightly different. Although both sides are engraved with crosses, the ornamentation of the crosses is different. One cross has two peach-shaped ornaments on both ends, with its intersection decorated with dots on the tip of petals. The bases are also different, except for the same double-layered lotus. One of the bases is equipped with auspicious clouds, while the other base is decorated with single-layered lotus roots with waists. The base with the clouds was engraved with a line in ancient Syriac "ܚܘܪ ܠܘܬܗ / ܡܗ ܣܒܪ" (translated as "Those who look to him are radiant."[2]), which can be regarded as formulaic language of Nestorians.[3] The style of the crosses carved on these two stone inscriptions has many similarities with those unearthed in Quanzhou and Inner Mongolia, and therefore, they can basically

---

1 Yoshiro Saeki 佐伯好郎, *Zhina Jidujiao de Yanjiu* 支那基督教的研究 [*The Study of Chinese Christianity*], volume 1, (Toyko: Chunqiushe Songbaiguan Press 春秋社松柏馆, 1943), 500-502.
2 Scholars usually hold that this line came from Psalms 34:5, but also noticed the discrepancy between them.
3 See Psalms 34:5

be regarded as Christian. The bouquet ornaments on the side of the stone carvings are also slightly different, one with a round-belly short-necked vase and the other with an open flower pot; the plants engraved on the inside are also different. According to Mr. Harding (H. I.) whose words are recorded in the *New China Review*, the monk in the temple told him that the two stone inscriptions were discovered in 1357 when people restored the Temple of Heavenly King Hall.[4]

On the other hand, the contents of the inscription of Yuan Monument and the style of the monument can also indirectly prove that the building was once associated with Christianity. Although the inscription says that the temple was rebuilt as a Buddhist one, the name of the "cross temple" and the striking "cross" sign on the top of monument can naturally be associated with its Christian identity. The inscription also mentions that after the "Godly man" (*shenren* 神人) became obscure, the cross on *ancient Chuang* (*guchuang* 古幢) glowed brightly. It can be imagined that there were some cross symbols in the temple at that time, and it was most likely the cross which the Christians believed in.

2 Overview of Related Research on Fangshan Cross Temple

The studies of the Fangshan Cross Temple mainly focused on the description and introduction of the stone carvings and inscriptions. Meanwhile, some articles have focused on issues related to the relics, including the authenticity of the inscriptions, the change between Buddhist and Christian identities, and the origin of the temple as a Christian church etc. These issues will be discussed below.

2.1 *The Authenticity of the Inscription*

In 1930, the British scholar A.C. Moule pointed out that there was an error in the year-dating on the Monument from the Liao Dynasty (*we will abbreviate it to Liao Monument,* 辽碑), and the date "Yingli the 10th year, BingZi[5] （应历十年，丙子）" was wrong, due to the 16-year time difference between Yingli the 10th year and Bingzi. The other two years mentioned in this Monument

---

4 See A.C. Moule, *Christians in China Before the Year 1550* (Beijing: Zhonghua Book Company, 1984), 99.

5 Yingli the 10th year (应历十年) and Bingzi (丙子) are supposed to be the same year named with the two different Chinese year numbering methods. Bingzi is the year designated by Ganzhi (*Ganzhi jinian* 干支纪年), Heavenly Stems and Earthly Branches, a way of numbering the years in the Chinese Lunar calendar. Yingli is the reign title of Emperor Muzong in the Liao Dynasty. Yingli the 10th year (应历十年) is the 10th year in the period of Yingli.

also added 16 years.[6] Prof. Chen Shu also stated that in the commentary on "The Inscription of the Dadu Chongshengyuan" （大都崇圣院碑记）in *Complete Works of the Liao Dynasty* （全辽文）(volume 4) that the Liao monument had some mistakes having to do with the year; that is, according to the Ganzhi (Heavenly Stems and Earthly Branches) system of calculating years: "Yingli the10th year should be Gengshen (庚申), not Bingzi (丙子)."[7] Professor Xu Pingfang of the Chinese Academy of Social Sciences held that these errors were made by people from the Ming Dynasty (AD1368-1644) when they rebuilt the monument and engraved the inscriptions again. He also pointed out that the inscription on the Yuan Monument included the names of some donors from the Ming Dynasty, such as Madam Zuo, the director of Jin Yiwei, Gao Rongtai's wife (*Jinyiwei zhihui Gao Rongtai furen Zuoshi* 锦衣卫指挥高荣太夫人左氏) and Madam Zhang, Nan Gaoru's wife.[8] In this regard, Prof. Wu Menglin and other scholars also provided epitaph rubbings of Gao Rongtai and his wife Madam Zuo in the book "*Research on Christianity in the Beijing Area*."[9]

In response to the above statements, Tang Gengsheng from the Chinese National Library claimed that these incomprehensible mistakes in the Yuan monument were not made by accident: First, the author of this inscription was not Huang Jin (黄溍). According to the works of Song Lian (宋濂) who lived in Ming Dynasty, Huang Jin had passed away in the year 1357, which was several years before the erection of Yuan Monument. Second, there was also a problem with the abbreviation of the title of Huang Jin. Huang Jin was a "Hanlinyuan Shijiang scholar" (翰林院侍讲学士), which could be simplified as "Shijiang" (侍讲) or scholar (学士), not as "Hanlinyuan Jiangxue" (翰林院讲学) as inscribed on Yuan Monument. Third, The King Huai Tie Muer Buhua (淮王铁木儿不花) and Prime Minister Qingtong (丞相庆童) who were mentioned twice in the inscription hadn't been appointed to their positions at the time when the monument was erected. According to Tang Gengsheng, both the writing style and narrative sequence of the Liao and Yuan Monument are very

---

6 A.C. Moule, *Christians in China Before the Year 1550* (Beijing: Zhonghua Book Company, 1984), 101.

7 Chen Shu 陈述, *Quan Liao Wen* 全辽文 [The Whole Liao Texts] (Beijing: Zhonghua Book Company, 1982), 79.

8 Xu Pingfang 徐苹芳, "Beijing Fangshan Shizisi Yelikewen Shike 北京房山十字寺也里可温石刻 [Nestorian Stone Carvings at Fangshan in Beijing]", *Chinese Culture* 2(1992): 187.

9 Wu Menglin, Xiong Ying 吴梦麟、熊鹰, "Beijing Diqu Jidujiao Shiji Yanjiu 北京地区基督教史迹研究 [*The Study of Christian history and relics in Beijing*], (Beiing: Cultural Relics Publishing House, 2010), 39.

similar. Therefore, she concluded that most of the contents of these two stone monuments were forged in the Ming dynasty.[10]

2.2 The Temple's Relationship with Buddhism and Christianity

If we look only at the contents of the two tablets, it would seem that the temple can only prove to be a Buddhist temple. In the *Chronicle of Fangshan County*, the temple was also juxtaposed with other Buddhist temples. According to Dr. Yoshiro Saeki, there was a plaque with the words of "Ancient Cross Buddhist Temple" near the gate of Monastery during the period of the Republic of China. However, as mentioned earlier, the "segmented words" on the Yuan Monument, the cross on the top of it, and especially the two stone inscriptions unearthed in this place, point to their previous Christian identity. Then, we might ask, in the history of the temple, what kind of interaction existed between Buddhism and Christianity?

Moule thought that the two inscriptions preserved by the temple indicated that "this temple was built in the Jin and Tang (晋唐) dynasties, and we have reasons to speculate that these crosses (or one of them) may have been there before 960 AD.... Moreover, the fact that there was Christianity in Beijing in the 13th century has already been fully proved, but as far as I know, there has been no clear proof of its existence before it. Neither these inscriptions explicitly mention Christianity. The name "the Cross Temple" was bestowed by the emperor upon a purely Buddhist temple, which may have caused confusion, because "the Cross Temple" is a proper name for a Christian church. However, there is no doubt that it used to be a Buddhist temple, and was still a Buddhist temple after its rebuilding in 1365".[11] As for the question when the monastery became a Christian Temple, Moule did not give a clear answer. Japanese scholar Saeki also offered some hypotheses about this question. If the ancient Chuang (古幢) mentioned on the Liao Monument was the stone Chuang (幢) with the sparkling "cross" mentioned on the Yuan monument, it showed that there was already a cross on the ancient building in the Liao dynasty. In addition, he also mentioned the possibility that during Huichang the 5th year in the Dang Dynasty (唐会昌五年), when Emperor Wu Zong suppressed Buddhism, Nestorians also attacked, resulting in the wipeout of Nestorianism. Some Nestorians fled to You Zhou (幽州, near Beijing). Certainly, Saeki be-

---

10   Tang Gengsheng 汤更生, Beijing Fangshan Shizisi Liao Yuan Bei Zhiyi 北京房山十字寺辽元碑质疑 [Questions on Liao and Yuan Monuments in Fangshan Cross Temple in Beijing], *Beijing Library Journal* 1(1998): 61-64.

11   A.C. Moule, *Christians in China Before the Year 1550* (Beijing: Zhonghua Book Company, 1984), 100-101.

lieved that there was not enough evidence to account for being a Christian building.¹²

Professor Xu Pingfang held that from the Liao Dynasty, when the Chongsheng Buddhist temple (崇圣院) was in ruins, to the Zhizheng 8th year (至正八年) in the Yuan Dynasty when the Yuan Monument was built, it was highly likely that Christians conducted some activities in the Cross temple. Jingshan (净善) mentioned that in the Yuan Tablet was a Buddhist monk. According to the inscription, after witnessing the appearance of the godly man and the glowing sign of the cross, Jingsan visited influential officials, such as Tie Muer Buhua, Qing Tong, and Zhao Boyan Buhua and raised enough funds to renovate the Buddhist temples, making it slightly larger than in the Liao Dynasty. Because the fundraising was based on the myth of the illumination of the cross, and these influential officials were mostly Mongolians and Semu people (色目人) who were familiar with Nestorian beliefs, the newly built Buddhist temple was named "The Cross Temple" by the emperor, and the cross on the monument and some Christian features were also preserved. Professor Xu believed that it was likely to be Jingshan's intention to designate the temple as a Christian one, and the great philanthropists and monk had come to a compromise about this. And in professor Xu's view, it was most likely to be another proof of the fact that Nestorian temples could be replaced by paganism, just like what happened to the Zhenjiang (镇江) Cross Temple mentioned in the *"Examination of Nestorians in Yuan Dynasty"* (元也里可温考) by Prof. Chen Yuan (陈垣). Although Tang Gengsheng questioned the authenticity of the two inscriptions, she did not deny the fact that the Cross Temple was a Christian monastery in the Yuan Dynasty. Likewise, it cannot be denied that it became a Buddhist temple during the Jiajing period (嘉靖年间) of the Ming Dynasty. The reason why the Ming people "tampered with the inscription" is that Buddhists worshiped in the ancient temples and tended to trace the source when rebuilding the temple. "Two hundred years have passed from the time when Zhu Yuanzhang banned Christianity to the Jiajing period, when the ruins of the ancient temple were preserved. The name of 'the Cross Temple' has also been passed down. The Syriac stone inscription and the cross mark of the Yuan monument had not been destroyed, probably because the later generations believed in the spirit of the ancients and dared not change the rules. Consequently, the Buddhist temple and the "Cross Temple" were combined into one. In this case, in order to gain trust from people, inscriptions writers in the Ming

---

12 Yoshiro Saeki 佐伯好郎, *Zhina Jidujiao de Yanjiu* 支那基督教的研究 [*The Study of Chinese Christianity*], volume 1 (Toyko: Chunqiushe Songbaiguan Press 春秋社松柏馆, 1943), 101, 175.

Dynasty made use of the name of the ancients and wrote on the basis of some rumors."[13]

3 Analysis and Hypotheses about the Cross Temple

Based on the introduction to the Cross temple, the overview of related studies on its identity and the authenticity of the stone inscriptions, we propose hypotheses.

3.1 Hypothesis 1: During the Jin and Tang Dynasties (晋唐), the Cross temple was a Buddhist temple and was renovated in the Liao Dynasty. At the beginning of Yuan Dynasty, it was changed into a Nestorian monastery, and then restored as a Buddhist temple at the end of Yuan Dynasty

This hypothesis is in line with the contents of the unearthed relics and inscriptions found in the ruins, and accepted by most academics. According to the inscription on the back of the Liao Monument, the temple was built by the monk Hui Jing (惠静) in the first year of the Jianwu period (建武元年) in the Eastern Jin Dynasty (晋, AD 317-420). During the period of the Jin and Tang Dynasties, the name of the monastery cannot be verified. It was a Buddhist temple named Chongshengyuan (崇圣院) in the Liao Dynasty. The rebuilding process can refer to the contents of the Liao monument. The expansion of the Buddhist temple in the Liao Dynasty is plausible because most of the Khitan emperors followed Buddhism, which could be proved by the words recorded in the 40th volume of the *History of Liao Dynasty* (*Liaoshi* 《辽史》): "Nanjing Xijinfu (南京析津府) was the ancient state of Yizhou ... there is the Yanjiao building in the Northeast. Markets, governmental buildings and temples are countless."[14]

The temple that was expanded during the Liao Dynasty had undergone the vicissitudes of changes for four hundred years, and was a ruin at the beginning of the Yuan Dynasty. During the rapid development of Nestorianism during early Yuan Dynasty, the Nestorian Cross Temple was rebuilt on the Buddhist ruins. The construction process can be tracked from the two stone carvings currently stored in the Nanjing Museum, because the two carved stones have

---

13   Tang Gengsheng 汤更生, "Beijing Fangshan Shizisi Liao Yuan Bei Zhiyi 北京房山十字寺辽元碑质疑" [Questions on Liao and Yuan Monuments in Fangshan Cross Temple in Beijing], *Beijing Library Journal* 1(1998): 64.
14   Tuo Tuo 脱脱, *Liao Shi* 辽史 [*History of Liao Dynasty*], volume 2 (Beijing: Zhonghua Book Company, 1984), 493-494. Nanjing Xijinfu once refered to Beijing in Liao Dynasty.

the obvious Nestorian sign of cross, and the style of the carved pattern was popular during the Liao and Jin Dynasties, according to Prof. Xu Pingfang's analysis. After nearly one century, the temple ceased to flourish. With the decline of the Nestorianism in the area, this temple was reused by Buddhist monks. However, the symbols of Christianity were still quite obvious. At that time, the monk Jingshan happened to come to the place and heard about the history of temple, and then made up a story of the presence of the Godly man and the illumination of the miraculous cross to the court officials. Those important officials, as Professor Xu Pingfang said, were familiar with the Nestorian beliefs, and therefore said "it confirmed the miracles of the ancient temple" and "donated their money to" rebuild the temple. However, it was used by Buddhists and rebuilt as a Buddhist temple. The only thing related to Christianity was that it retained the cross and the name "the Cross Temple" was bestowed by the emperor upon their request.

3.2 Hypothesis 2: It was a Nestorian Temple in the Tang Dynasty and then changed into a Buddhist one

This viewpoint has been mentioned in the works of the Moule and Saeki. Although Moule was skeptical about this opinion, he pointed out that the temple in Liao Dynasty had the same name "Chongshengyuan" as the name of the temple where the Nestorian stele "Daqin Jingjiao Liuxing Zhongguo Bei" (大秦景教流行中国碑) was located in the Tang Dynasty. This coincidence was "very interesting, but it may not be important."[15] Corresponding to this, Saeki considered that it was possible for the monastery to have been a Nestorian Temple at late Tang or after the Tang dynasty. In the process of the suppression of Buddhism by Emperor Wuzong, Nestorianism was also attacked. Some Nestorians fled from the Chang'an area (the capital city at that time) to Youzhou (幽州) and Liaodong (辽东), and built a monastery there. But Saeki admitted that there was no solid evidence for this claim, and it was only the speculative. I believe that the temple was Nestorian in and just after the Tang Dynasty, is based on the following reasons.

First, in the inscriptions on the two monuments, the same Chuang (幢) was mentioned. According to the Liao Monument, Monk Huicheng observed an ancient stone Chuang which surrounded with the ruins of the temple. However, according to the Yuan Monument, Monk Jingshan saw the ancient Chuang and the monument in the yard, and he related that he saw the illumination of the cross on the ancient Chuang (幢) after a Godly figure disappeared. If the

---

15   A.C. Moule, *Christians in China Before the Year 1550* (Beijing: Zhonghua Book Company, 1984), 100-101.

Chuang (幢) in the Yuan Monument refers to the same one mentioned in the Liao monument, it could be speculated that the cross on the ancient Chuang (幢) had existed in the temple in the Jin and Tang Dynasties. If this Buddhist monastery had been a Nestorian one before the Liao Dynasty, it would be most likely to have existed in the Tang Dynasty, when Nestorianism was popular.

Second, in 845 AD, Tang Wuzong promulgated the Decree of the Eradication of Buddhism, "Since Buddhism has been eliminated, then, other evil religions cannot exist". Consequently, Nestorianism and other foreign religion were implicated.[16] According to the records of *Tang Hui Yao* (唐会要, Volume47), "More than 3,000 Nestorians, Muslims, and Zoroastrians have been ordered to be secularized, so that the atmosphere in China would not be affected". The Nestorian monks, who did not want to change their faith, took refuge in remote areas. In Suining County, Shaoyang City, Hunan Province (湖南省邵阳市绥宁县), there is a mysterious ancient temple called Shenpo Nunnery (神坡庵). A manuscript of tablet inscription "The Lingbao Temple Ji" (灵宝寺记) published several years ago resolved the mystery of Shenpo Nunnery (神坡庵). The inscription records that the temple was built by the descendants of Xianjue, a Persian monk from Chang'an in the 6th year in the Huichang (会昌六年) period during the reign of Tang Wuzong, just one year after the religious persecution. The possibility that the temple belongs to Nestorianism cannot be ruled out.[17] Youzhou (幽州) in the Tang Dynasty was inhabited by ethnic minorities, such as Turks (突厥), Khitan (契丹), Mohe (靺鞨), and Huihe (回纥), etc. Moreover, this region used to be a traffic artery that connected the Central Plains with the Outskirts (塞外) and Liaodong area (辽东). It is possible that the Nestorians in the late Tang Dynasty fled to this area, and that the monks would build a monastery there.

Third, on the Yuan monument, there were descriptions of "the appearance of the Godly-man, the glowing cross, and the confirmation of the legend of the ancient temple". These descriptions seem to indicate that there must have been many legends about the appearance of the Godly man, or the legend of the cross. It does not rule out the connection with the spread of ancient Christian beliefs. It also seems to confirm the close relationship between the Nestorianism and Buddhism in the history of the temple and the replacement by Buddhism with the destruction of Nestorianism.

Fourth, during the Tang Dynasty, Youzhou belonged to Nanjing Road (南京道). In Nanjing Road, Li Zhongxuan's "Monument for the Founding of Youtang

---

16 Wang Pu 王溥, *Tang Hui Yao* 唐会要 [*Important Documents of Tang Dynasty*], Volume Zhong 中卷 (Beijing: Zhonghua Book Company, 1955) 841.

17 Please see *China Cultural Relics News*, December 17 (2000).

Temple" (《佑唐寺创建讲堂碑》) was found and it recorded that "the person in charge of the monastery belonged to the Jing sect. When tracing their origins, their gods were unfathomable. "This monument was set up in 987, in which the 'Jing'(景), 'God' (神) and other arguments all gave rise to the speculation associated with the Nestorianism.[18]

Finally, according to the analysis made by Gai Shanlin, a scholar from Inner Mongolia, crosses in China are divided into two forms. Generally speaking, there were ornaments on the crosses in early Chinese history (that is, from the Tang to the Five Dynasties), while there were no ornaments on the crosses in the Song and Yuan Dynasties. In the Song and Yuan Dynasties, the crosses were Islamic-style with firelight-windowed trims. He believes that the cross's style on the carved stone in the Fangshan Cross temple resembles the cross found in earlier periods, such as the Five Dynasties. These crosses with ornaments were common in Central and East Asia.

From the above perspectives, we can propose a hypothesis that the cross temple in Fangshan was a Nestorian church in the later Tang Dynasties or Five Dynasties. With the decline of Nestorianism, it gradually became dilapidated and was eventually replaced by Buddhist monasteries. The temple was repaired in the Liao Dynasty, and with the rise of Nestorianism in the early Yuan Dynasty, it was rebuilt according to the ancient legends.[19] However, it was changed back to the Buddhist temple after about a hundred years, and then renovated at the end of the Yuan Dynasty.

3.3 Hypothesis 3: It Was Rebuilt as a Nestorian Temple during the Period of Great Mongolia

Among various hypotheses, one is often neglected: the cross temple was built during the time of the Great Mongolia period. The rulers of the Jin Dynasty (A. D.1115-1234) believed in Shamanism, Buddhism, and Taoism. There is less evidence to prove that there were traces of Christianity in Zhongdu (中都, now Beijing).[20] However, it is possible that there were Christians in this area at that time, because during the Liao and Jin eras, some Christians from central Asia moved their families to China for business reasons. The famous Semu

---

18   Li Zhongxuan 李仲宣, "Youtangsi Chuangjian Jiangtang Bei 佑唐寺创" [Monument for the Founding of Youtang Temple], in *Liao Wencun* 辽文存 [*Cultural Heritage of Liao Dynasty*], volume 5 (Taipei: Chengwen Publishing Company, 1967), 166-170.

19   Gai Shanlin 盖山林, *Yinshan Wanggu* 阴山汪古 [*Ongut in Yin Mountain*] (Hohhot: Inner Mongolian People's Publishing House, 1991), 282-286.

20   See Wu Yuhuan 武玉环, Lun Jindai Nüzhen De Zongjiao Xinyang Yu Zongjiao Zhengce 论金代女真的宗教信仰与宗教政策 [Nüzhen's Religious Beliefs and Policies in Jin Dynasty], *Collected Papers of History Studies*(2)1992.

(色目) literatus Mazuchang (马祖常) came from a Nestorian family. His ancestors came to China in during the reign of Liao Dongzong (辽道宗). But it can be assumed that their beliefs were mostly individual, and there was no political support or a large number of believers. Therefore, it is not possible to think that they could have built the Cross Temple.

After the Mongolian army captured Jinzhongdu (金中都, near Beijing) in 1215, Christians were much more likely to build monasteries there. As mentioned above, Professor Xu Pingfang believed that the style of potted plants on the stone carvings unearthed in the Cross Temple had a distinctive Song and Jin style. He inferred that the stone carving might be the work of the early Yuan Dynasty. Chances are that Nestorian temple was rebuilt in the Great Mongolia period, that is between the year of 1215 when Jinzhongdu (金中都, near Beijing) was captured and the year of 1271 when Kublai Khan founded the Yuan dynasty. During this period, many Christians came to Yanjing (燕京). As early as the 11th to 12th century, some ethnic minorities in the border areas of northern China, such as Ongut, Kereyid, Naimans, etc., became Nestorian Christians and later spread their faith to China's hinterland. According to Dr. Paul Pelliot's research, these ethnic minorities lived in the area from Gansu to Nanman (南满) during the Liao and Jin Dynasties, and some even became Sinicized (汉化). Born in the Yanjing area around 1225, Ba Shuma (巴扫马) came from a Christian family. His father was a church patrolman. In 1248, Beijing became the bishopric of the Nestorians[21] and had a permanent archbishop of the Nestorian church by 1275. Therefore, regardless of whether the former temple was a Nestorian one, it is plausible that there was a Nestorian temple in the Fangshan area during the Great Mongolia period.

Remarks

Why were there so many mistakes made in rewriting the inscriptions in the Ming Dynasty? For one thing, the contents of the original inscriptions are not recognizable; for another, it is mainly due to the Buddhists' tendency to worship at the ancient temple.

The bigger reason is likely to be that the re-builders intentionally avoided the history associated with Christianity of the temple. The glowing cross, the presence of the Godly man, and the cross on the Yuan monument all lead us to speculate that there might have been something related with the cross temple

---

21   Wilhelm Baum and Dietmar W. Winkler, *The Church of the East*, (London and New York: Routledge Curzon, 2003)86.

before the original monument was rubbed, and therefore the writer of the tablet inscription had no choice but to avoid it in the Ming Dynasty. It is not difficult to understand. With the demise of the Yuan dynasty, the Cross Temple was inevitably impacted. In the Ming dynasty, the closed-door policy and national assimilation were implemented. Foreigners were prohibited from intermarriage, and foreign languages were forbidden. Christians, Zoroastrians, and Manichaeans were all Sinicized (汉化). In such an atmosphere, it is understandable that inscription writers intended to avoid the part of history related to Nestorianism.

The suppression of Christianity by the Ming government obliged the Buddhist temple with a Christian history to rewrite the tablets to enhance its Buddhist characteristics in order to escape persecution. A bold hypothesis can be made that the temple was always a Christian church before the Ming dynasty. It was only because of the suppression of Christianity at the beginning of the Ming dynasty that monks had to hide their beliefs and hastened to rewrite the inscriptions. Eventually, it really evolved into a Buddhist temple, left with only a few legends and the crosses on the carved stones. Similarly, Christianity in Quanzhou was once glorious in the Yuan Dynasty, but disappeared in the early Ming Dynasty. In 1943, Mr. Wu Wenliang discovered green bricks and slate outside the East Gate of Quanzhou. According to folk legend, this area was known as the "Dacu" (大厝, mansion), but later it was demolished by the soldiers of the Ming Dynasty because of some "crime."[22] The building was once inferred by the scholars as a Nestorian temple, and its charge was related to its religious background. In conclusion, the identity of Fangshan cross temple in the Tang, Liao, Yuan and Ming Dynasties is still an unsolved mystery. These issues have yet to be analyzed and studied with more historical data collected and further archaeological work done in the future.

---

22 Niu Ruji 牛汝极, "Fujiansheng Quanzhou Jingjiao Beiming De Faxian Jiqi Yanjiu 福建泉州景教碑铭的发现及其研究" [The Discovery and Research of Nestorian Inscriptions], *Maritime History Studies* 2(2007): 4.

PART 4

Biblical and Scriptural Studies

∴

CHAPTER 7

Yishu (Jesu) Worship in Xiapu Manichaean Manuscripts[1]

Fuxue Yang and Wengjing Xue

1 The Name and Its Origin of Yishu 夷数 in Xiapu Manichaean Manuscripts

Since October 2008, a large amount of Manichaean manuscripts and cultural relics have been discovered near the Shangwan Village 上万村, in Baiyang Borough 柏洋乡, Xiapu County 霞浦县, Fujian Province 福建省. This was the second largest discovery of texts on Manichaeism in China, following the Manichaean literature discovered in Turfan and Dunhuang since the end of the 19th century and the beginning of the 20th century. Among these texts are manuscripts, such as *Moni guangfo* 摩尼光佛, *Xingfuzu qingdanke* 兴福祖庆诞科, *Diandeng qiceng kece* 点灯七层科册, *Mingfu qingfowen* 冥福请佛文, and so on. The *Moni guangfo* is one of the longest manuscripts written with rich contents and a witness of the Manichean belief from the late Tang to modern Fujian locals and the worthy survivor in the history of Manichaeism.

The *Moni guangfo* is a worthy masterpiece in the Xiapu Manichean manuscripts. It belongs to Priest Chen Peisheng 陈培生, who used it as a rules and liturgies book during his religious ceremonies. Priest Chen was the progeny of Chen Pingshan 陈平山, who was the orthodox disciple of the Manichaean Master Lin Deng 林瞪, the eighth-generation ancestor of the Lin family in Shangwan village, of Xiapu in Fujian. The manuscript includes 83 pages, 659 lines, and over 8,400 Chinese characters in total. Its length is close to *Monijiao xiabuzan* 摩尼教下部赞 (S. 2659), a Manichaean Manuscript from Dunhuang. Every page of the *Moni guangfo* generally is written in eight lines, except for page 83 (the last page) that is blank, page 82 (the ending of the text) has 5 lines and a few pages (such as page 5, 6, etc.) are written in 9 lines. The cover is in heavily worn, and reads "*Moni guangfo* Chen Peisheng *cunxiu* 摩尼光佛 陈培生存修". The term *cunxiu* (lit. to keep and to mend) signifies that the Priest Chen to some extent, made his supplements on this transcription, however, he was not the one that made the transcription. From the degree of wear, the

---

1 Thanks to Dr. Liu Yuxuan 刘毓萱 of Universität Göttingen to help with the English version of the paper.

transcript was likely copied in the late Qing Dynasty (1840-1912) or the Republic of China (1912-1949). Therefore, the manuscript draft was probably written much earlier. This manuscript was found in November 2009 and then published recently by Yang Fuxue 杨富学 and Bao Lang 包朗.[2] All references cited in this paper are based on the published version (2015), and we only give the number of the line(s).

In comparison with the older Manichaeism and other sinicised Manichaeism, the Xiapu Manichaean texts show an extreme worship towards the Yishu (namely Jesus). Take *Leshantang shenji* 乐山堂神记[3] (found in Xiapu) as example, Jesus, being called as *yYishu rulai* 夷数如来 (Jesus Tathāgata), is placed among those gods people should respectfully revere at the commencement of the text:

> tai shang ben shi jiao zhu mo ni guang fo 太上本师教主摩尼光佛
> dian guang wang fo 电光王佛
> yi shu ru lai 夷数如来
> jing feng 净风
> xian yi ru lai 先意如来
> tian di hua shen lu she na fo 天地化身卢舍那佛
> bei fang zhen tian zhen wu pu sa 北方镇天真武菩萨
> fa xiang hui ming ru lai 法相惠明如来
> jiu tian zhen ming da sheng 九天贞明大圣
> pu an zu shi 普庵祖师
> guan yin 观音 shi zhi 势至 er da pu sa 二大菩萨 (ll. 2-6)

> Supreme Lord, Original Master, Religious Leader, the Mani Buddha of Luminous,
> Buddha of the Lightning King,
> Jesus Tathāgata,
> Living Spirit,
> Tathāgata of the First Man,

---

2 Yang Fuxue 杨富学 & Bao Lang 包朗, 2015, Collation and Annotation of Xiapu New Manichaean Literature *'Moni guangfo'* 霞浦摩尼教新文献 «摩尼光佛» 校注, in *Hanshan Temple Buddhist Studies* 寒山寺佛学 (vol. x), pp. 74-115. See also, Lin, Wwushu 林悟殊, 2014, *The Explanation and Postscript on 'Moni guangfo'* 摩尼教华化补说《摩尼光佛》释文并跋, Lanzhou: Lanzhou University Press, pp. 457-492.

3 Yang Fuxue, 2011, *'Leshantang shenji'* and Fujian Manichaean – a Comparative Study of the Manichaean Manuscripts in Xiapu and Dunhuang Turpan «乐山堂神记»与福建摩尼教——霞浦与敦煌吐鲁番等摩尼教文献的比较研究, in *Literature and History* 文史 (No. 4), p. 138.

Locana Buddha, the Incarnation of Heaven and Earth,
Perfected Warrior Bodhisattva, the Celestial Guardian of the North,
Tathāgata of the Vijñaptimātra Wisdom,
Great Upright and Brilliant Saint of the Nine Heavens,
Master Pu'an,
two Great Bodhisattvas: Avalokiteśvara and Mahasthamaprapta.

Among the numerous deities, 'Jesus Tathāgata' ranks in third place after Religious Leader, the Mani Buddha of Luminous and Buddha of the Lightning King. This name is very common in Xiapu Manichaean texts, such as 'Dasheng yansheng yisuan yishu hefo 大圣延生益算夷数和佛' (Great Saint, Jesus the Buddha of Harmony, who lengthens life and prolongs lifespan) (l. 10) in *Xingfuzu qingdanke* 兴福祖庆诞科 (old version); 'Huoming shizun yishu hefo 活命世尊夷数和佛' (Lokanātha, Jesus the Buddha of Harmony, who saves life) (l. 12) and 'Yishu wang 夷数王' (Jesus King) (ll. 209, 364) in *Moni guangfo* 摩尼光佛; and 'Daci dabei zhengzhi yishu hefo 大慈大悲正智夷数和佛' (the greatly merciful and greatly compassionate Jesus the Buddha of Harmony) (ll. 9-10) in *Mingfu qingfo wen* 冥福请佛文.[4] Meanwhile, another name 'Disi shizun yishu hefo 第四世尊夷数和佛' (the fourth Lokanātha, Jesus the Buddha of Harmony) is written in the line 164 of *Zhenming kaizheng wenke* 贞明开正文科, a recently discovered Manichaean manuscript in Pingnan County 屏南, Fujian.

The appellation 'Yishu wang' (Jesus King) should receive particular attention. It is only seen in the *Moni guangfo* but not in Dunhuang and other Xiapu Manichaean manuscripts. We think that 'Yishu wang' may be derived from Nestorian Christianity, in which they addressed Jesus as 'Jingtong fawang 景通法王' (Dharma-King, of the Religious Mastery), 'Dashi fawang 大师法王' (Master Dharma-King), and so on. However, there is a large possibility that this expression derives from 'King of Jews' in the original *Bible* texts. Jesus Messiah has been frequently mentioned as the King of Jews in the *Gospel of Matthew*.

> After Jesus was born in Bethlehem in Judea, during the time of King Herod, Magi from the east came to Jerusalem and asked, "Where is the one who has been born king of the Jews? We saw his star in the east and have come to worship him. "…" In Bethlehem in Judea," they replied, "for this is what the prophet has written: "'But you, Bethlehem, in the land of Judah, are by no means least among the rulers of Judah; for out of you will

---

4 Yang Fuxue 杨富学, Shi Yajun 史亚军 & Bao Lang 包郎, 2014, A Study on Xiapu Manichaean Literature '*Mingfu qingfo wen*' 霞浦摩尼教新文献 《冥福请佛文》校录研究, in *Literature Research* 文献研究 (vol. 4), p. 85.

come a ruler who will be the shepherd of my people Israel.'" (*Matthew* 2: 1-7)

Meanwhile Jesus stood before the governor, and the governor asked him, "Are you the king of the Jews?" "Yes, it is as you say," Jesus replied. (*Matthew* 27: 11)

Although Nestorian Christianity was condemned as heretical in its time, there is credulity about Jesus as King of Israel or about Jews listed in the Scriptures. Based on the information in *Zunjing* 尊经 (a Nestorian Church canon), there are 30 Nestorian classics translated by Nestorian priests, Jingjing 景净, etc. Of these, *Asiqulirong jing* 阿思瞿利荣经 is the same as the *Four Gospels,* and *Ningyeting jing* 宁耶頲经 was rendered from the Persian's *Four Gospels*. Although we have not found these two classics in Dunhuang, we suspect that the Nestorians and the Manichaeans in the Tang Dynasty (618-907) should have been able to access them, which means the expression of the 'Yishu wang' should originate from that time. Similar to 'Yishu rulai' and 'Yishu hefo', this appellation is a particular terminology of calling Jesus in Xiapu Manichaean manuscript.

Besides the Xiapu Manichaean manuscript, the expression 'Yishu' is seen more commonly in Dunhuang Manichaean literature. For instance, 205th line of *Fragments of Manichaean Texts* (BD00256) collected in the China National Library, and ll. 6, 13, 29, 35, 45, 76, 126, 131, 138, 151, 152, 171, 176, 254, 367, 368, 381 of *Monijiao xiabuzan* 摩尼教下部赞 (S. 2659) kept in the British Library. In addition, in the *Moni guangfo*, a rather unfamiliar expression 'Moshihe 末尸诃' has appeared three times:

> ll. 219-221: wo jin qi shou li 我今稽首礼, gui ming mo shi he 皈命末尸诃. shi ci bei 施慈悲, shu wo deng 恕我等, zui xiao mo 罪消魔. yuan jin ye 愿今夜, xiao zai zhang 消灾障, jiang ji xiang 降吉祥.
>
> I sincerely worship and convert to Moshihe. I pray to You to be merciful and to forgive our sins. Tonight, (I) beseech (You) to eradicate disaster and spirit auspicious.
>
> ll. 526-527: na luo yan 那罗延, su lu zhi 苏路支, shi jia wen 释迦文, mo shi he 末尸诃, mo luo mo ni 末啰摩尼.
>
> Nārāyana, Zoroaster, Śākyamuni, Moshihe, Mār Mani.
>
> ll. 547-552: (see after).

The "Moshihe 末尸诃" here is one Chinese transliteration of the Messiah, and refers to the attribute of Jesus as the Saviour. This expression is not seen in the Chinese Manichaean manuscript of the Tang Dynasty, but often appeared in

Nestorian and Buddhist texts. Three wordings use in the Buddhist manuscript *Lidai fabao ji* 历代法宝记 (Record of the Dharma Jewel through Successive Generations) of Dunhuang: Mishihe 弥师诃 (S. 516), Mishihe 弥师何 (P. 3727v), and Mishahe 弥沙诃 (P. 2776).[5] In Nestorian manuscripts, moreover, similar transliterations are commonly seen. 23 times in the Dunhuang *Xuting mishisuo jing* 序听迷诗所经 (the correct title should be *Xuting mishihe jing* 序听弥施诃经), written as Mishihe 弥师诃 or Mishihe 迷师诃[6]; 38 times in the Dunhuang *Yishenlun* 一神论, all written as Mishihe 弥师诃[7]; and transliterated term Mishihe 弥师诃 appeared in the Xi'an's 'Daqin jingjiao liuxing zhongguo bei 大秦景教流行中国碑' (Nestorian Stele) in Xi'an, the Nestorian Stone Pillar at Luoyang, and the *Laozi huahu jing* 老子化胡经, the *Daqin jingjiao sanwei mengdu zan* 大秦景教三威蒙度赞 and the *Zunjing* 尊经 from Dunhuang.[8] Moshihe 末尸诃 written in the *Moni guangfo*, however, is relatively similar to 'Mishihe 弥师诃' in *Zhenyuan xinding shijiao mulu* 贞元新定释教目录 (*juan* 17), text written as 'Jing ying chuan mi shi he jiao 景净应传弥尸诃教' (Priest Jingjing should disperse the teachings of Messiah).[9] Jingjing 景净 was a Persian Nestorian missionary who came to China. In Chang'an (today Xi'an), he not only translated the Nestorian canon into Chinese at the command of Aluoben 阿罗本 (Alopen), but also composed the famous *Daqin jingjiao liuxing zhongguo bei*. Thereafter, we can only find Mishihe 弥师诃 in the *Dayuan zhiyuan bianwei lu* 大元至元辨伪录 (*juan* 3) compiled in the Yuan Dynasty[10], which is a mistaken copy from old classics. After the discussion above, we can reach the conclusion that similar terms to Mishihe 弥施诃 were mostly prevalent in the Tang Dynasty, as the appellation of the Saviour whom Nestorian Christianity sincerely worshipped. It spread widely along with Nestorianism, and even Buddhists were aware of it. However, after the Great Anti-Buddhist Persecution in Huichang era (841-845?/847?), the three major foreign religions involved from Persia ('*sanyi jiao* 三夷教': Zoroastrianism, Manichaeism, and Nestorian Christianity) were also destroyed and even disappeared. Henceforth none knew the Name of the Nestorian Saviour, let alone the Song and Yuan

---

5   Rong Xinjiang 荣新江, 1999, The Momanni and Mishihe in *Lidai fabao ji* – It also discusses the origins of Manichaeism and Nestorian elements in Tibetan literature «历代法宝记»中的末曼尼和弥师诃 —— 兼谈吐蕃文献中的摩尼教和景教因素的来历, in *Tibetology Periodicals* (I) 贤者新宴·藏学论丛 (I), pp. 130-150.
6   Kyōu shooku (杏雨書屋) (ed.), 2012, 敦煌秘笈·影片冊 (Secret Documents of Dunhuang: The Film Copies), Vol. 6, Oosaka: Takeda Science Foundation, pp. 84-87.
7   ibid. pp. 89-96.
8   Wang Lanping 王兰平, 2016, *A Study of Chinese Nestorian Manuscript in Dunhuang during the Tang Dynasty* 唐代敦煌汉文景教写经研究, Beijing: National Press, pp. 71-72.
9   *Taisho Tripitaka* 大正藏, No. 2157, 891c.
10   Xiangmai 祥迈, Dayuan zhiyuan bianwei lu 大元至元辩伪录, *juan* 3,

Dynasties, and afterwards. Until the Nestorian Stele at Xi'an was unearthed in the late Ming Dynasty, people were beginning to learn about it. However, information about the Nestorian Stele is only limited to missionaries during the Ming and Qing Dynasty and a handful of literati. In other words, under no circumstances could those local village Masters (*fashi* 法师) in Xiapu (afar from the Capital) learn about such information. Therefore, we can trace the 'Moshihe 末尸诃' in the *Moni guangfo* without question to the Tang Dynasty. Lin Wushu 林悟殊 believes that after the Great Anti-Buddhist Persecution, the Uighur Manichaeans, such as Hulu 呼禄 (Uighur: Qutluɣ) etc., took refuge in the region of Fujian, and it is very probable that Nestorian missionaries might have sought refuge there as well.[11] Even if the Nestorians did not take refuge in Fujian, the Nestorian Stele describes the popularity of Nestorianism as 'this doctrine was established in the ten provinces' and 'every city was full of monasteries', Nestorianism rose to prominence. It is not surprising that some Manichaean monks would become dependent on Nestorian church(s). Therefore, under such influence they certainly did entitle Yishu (Jesus) with Moshihe 末尸诃 (Messiah).

2 The Image of Jesus Yishu in Xiapu Manichaean Manuscripts

The Yishu is relatively complicated in Xiapu Manichaean manuscripts. As mentioned above, Yishi is Jesus and therefore about his image. So, we need to look at Jesus' image in Christianity from the start.

According to F. Burkitt, Jesus' epithet can be divided into three roles, namely redeemer, sufferer, and nourisher.[12] Werner Sundermann, however, distinguishes at least six different aspects, which are Jesus the Splendour, the suffering Jesus (Jesus Patibilis), the historical Jesus (Apostle of Light), the risen, or eschatological Jesus (final judgment), Jesus the Child, and Jesus the Moon.[13] Rui Chuanming interprets that the Jesus the Splendour is the Apostle of Light, which is close to the historical Jesus. Jesus the Splendour, who appears in human form, is sent into the world by the Supreme God — the Father of Greatness — for saving sentient beings by disseminating the truth and performing

---

11 Lin Wushu 林悟殊, 2016, *Exploration the Information of Zoroastrianism in Xiapu Manuscripts* 霞浦抄本祆教信息探源, in *Literature and History* 文史, No. 2, p. 284.

12 F. Crawford Burkitt, 1925, *The Religion of the Manichees*, London: Cambridge University Press, pp. 38-42.

13 Werner Sundermann, 1991, "Christianity v. Christ in Manichaeism," in *Encyclopædia Iranica*, Vol. V, fasc. 5, Costa Mesa, pp. 335-39; available online at <http://www.iranicaonline.org/articles/christianity-v>.

miracles.[14] The record related to Moshihe 末尸诃 can be seen in the *Moni guangfo* ll. 547-539:

> zhi xin li huo ming yi shu he 志心信礼活命夷数和,
> cong fan tian jie tian yao mo 从梵天界殄妖魔;
> teng kong ru ge xia 腾空如鸽下,
> huo yan qi liu bo 火焰起流波;
> shen tong yan fu lin guo sheng wu guo 神通验, 拂林国, 圣无过,
>
> ying hua he sha shu 应化河沙数,
> tian di ji sen luo 天地及森罗,
> jiang ren ru jie du da po 将忍辱戒度怛婆.
> wo jin qi shou li 我今稽首礼,
> gui ming mo shi he 皈命末尸诃.
> shu wo deng, zhu qian jiu, jin xiao mo 恕我等, 诸愆咎, 尽消魔.
> yuan jin ye, jian wang ling, sheng jing tu 愿今夜, 荐亡灵, 生净土.

(We) worship Jesus the Buddha, who exterminates demons from the Brahma-world. He is soaring like a dove in surrounding with running flames. His has such efficacious might that many sacred sites left in the Rome Empire. He can transform himself to numerous Ganges River sand, and also to the world and the Hell. He will endure humiliation in order to save *dapo*. I perform *kotow* rite and pledge allegiance to Moshihe: please forgive our sins entirely, and lead souls of departed to born in the Pure Land tonight.

This passage describes a story that Jesus missionarised in the Roman Empire while the Holy Spirit inhabited him. The term *renru* 忍辱 is used to describe Jesus' crucifixion, namely "the Fourteen Via Crucis". The same term also appears in the line 459 of the *Moni guangfo*: "zhen chang ren ru 真常忍辱, wo deng tong cheng shen gong yang yi shu he fo 我等同诚伸供养夷数和佛" (We faithfully make offerings to Jesus the Buddha of Harmony because he sacrificed himself for us.) These tell us that the Manichaeans in the imperial China have already understood and acknowledged the story about the Passion of the historical Jesus. On how people eulogised the suffering spirit of the Jesus, we can compare the book *Isaiah* 53: 4-6 of the *Old Testament*.

---

14 Rui Chuanming 芮传明, 2014, *Interpretation and Research on Dunhuang – Turfan literature in Manichaeism* 摩尼教敦煌吐鲁番文书译释与研究, Lanzhou: Lanzhou University Press, pp. 226-227.

> Surely he hath borne our griefs, and carries our sorrows; yet we did esteem him stricken, smitten of God, and afflicted. But he was wounded for our transgressions, he was bruised for our iniquities; the chastisement of our peace was upon him; and with his stripes we are healed. All we like sheep have gone astray; we have turned every one to his own way; and the LORD hath laid on him the iniquity of us all.

But until now, we do not find similar usage of positioning *renru* before Yishu in other Xiapu Manichaean manuscripts. The author/compiler of the *Moni guangfo* might have had access to the Nestorian Christianity and/or Manichaeism books. Either the original version, or Chinese translations, or both. The *mo* 末 in the Moshihe 末尸诃, as the *mo* in Momoni 末摩尼, means 'mighty'. Line 515 of The *Moni guangfo* is listed the Prophets with names, and the fifth is "Mo shi he mo luo mo ni 末尸诃末啰摩尼", in which *mo luo* should be Persian *Mār* transliterate into Chinese.

For Jesus, there are more examples in the *Moni guangfo*, such as "*Tiannü zhou* 天女咒" (Heavenly Maidens Spell):

> a tuo li ye he fa mi ye li xian na luo xi zhi ji wen ji luo jian xin mo luo shi zhi qi na li suo he yi zai Yishu ji he jin ni lu shen hu min hu se. 发弥耶哩诜那啰悉致咭吻咭啰健心默罗师致讫那哩娑和夷在夷数精和谨你嚧诜护泯护瑟 (ll. 231-234)
>
> True creation, bright and vigorous, heart silent soul, fair and just, the Third Messenger, Savior Jesus, Immortal Virgin, Great Nons!

The text tells us a story about the Third Messenger who once transformed into a virgin boy, and in cooperation with the Buddha of the Lightning into a maiden, in order to seduce male and female demons.

Although in the original Manichaean doctrine, it was only the Third Messenger who did transformation and seduced all demons. "…when the Ships went up and reached the middle of the heaven, the Messenger then revealed his forms, male and female, and was seen by all the Archons, the Sons of Darkness, males and females. And at the sight of the Messenger, who was beautiful in his forms, all the Archons became filled with lust for him, the males for the form of the female, and the females for the form of the male, and in their lust they began to emit that light which they had swallowed from the Five Luminous Gods."[15] Another viewpoint is that the Third Messenger and the sum-

---

15   A.V. Jackson, 1932, *Researches in Manichaeism – with Special Reference to the Turfan Fragment,* New York: Columbia University Press, p. 244.

moned Light Maiden (*viz.* Buddha of the Lightning) appeared separately in the forms of naked male and female.[16] However, those deeds of the Third Messenger were placed upon the Jesus in the Dunhuang manuscripts. Take the *Monijiao Xiabu zan* 摩尼教《下部赞》 (Hymnscroll for the Lower Section of the Manichaeism) as instance, in the section of the "*lanzan Yishu Wen* 览赞夷数文" (*In Praise of Jesus*):

> da sheng zi shi ji xiang shi 大圣自是吉祥时,
> pu yao wo deng zhu ming xing 普耀我等诸明性.
> miao se shi jian wu you bi 妙色世间无有比,
> shen tong bian xian fu ru shi 神通变现复如是.
> huo xian tong nan wei miao xiang 或现童男微妙相,
> dian fa wu zhong ci mo lei 癫发五种雌魔类,
> huo xian tong nü zhuang yan shen 或现童女端严身,
> kuang luan wu zhong [xiong mo dang] 狂乱五种[雄魔党]. (ll. 42-43)
> The Great Saint is no other than the auspicious hour (or Hours),
> Shining universally upon our many Natures of Light:
> Thy wonderful colour finds no compare in the World,
> Thy divine power of transfiguration is just the same:
> Sometimes appearing in the delicate and wonderful form of the virgin boy (or Boys),
> To strike with madness the five kinds of female devils;
> At other times in the dignified and solemn body of the virgin girl (or girls),
> To throw into wild confusion the five male devils.[17]

This piece of the text is similar to the contents of the "*Zan Yishu Ji* 赞夷数偈" (This *Gāthā is used to conclude the Wishing, after praising Jesus*):

> cheng zan jing miao zhi 称赞净妙智,
> yishu guang ming zhe 夷数光明者,
> shi xian tong nü 示现仙童女,
> guang da xin xain yi 广大心先意. (l. 369)

> We laud and praise the pure and wonderful Wisdom,
> Jesus the bright one,

---

16 Rui Chuanming 芮传明 2014: pp. 226-227.
17 Tsui Chi, 1943, *Mo Ni Chiao Hsia Pu Tsan* "The Lower (Second?) Section of the Manichaean Hymns", in *Bulletin of the School of Oriental and African Studies*, 11: p. 179.

> The self-revealing Angelic Virgin girl,
> And the broad and great Mind, the Anticipator of Thought.[18]

Jesus here becomes the embodiment of the Third Messenger and/or the Light Maiden, and hence his image was entangled with both. The above-mentioned "Yi shu xian tong nü 夷数仙童女" (Jesus served as Angelic Virgin girl) obviously identifies that it is Jesus himself who transforms into a beautiful maiden in the nude to seduce the male demon(s). This piece of eulogy represents characteristics of a combination of the Middle Persian and Parthian languages, which proves that the Jesus-transformed-himself-for-seducing-demon belief existed as early as the period during which Manichaeans did missionary work in Persia and Central Asia, and the Chinese believers afterwards accepted this belief as well.

In an Old Uighur Version of the *Great Hymn to Mani*, which was probably written in the Mongol period, in the thirteenth or fourteenth century:

> We…
> Who had been in the fetters of Suffering,
> Were rescued from this Samsaāra
> In order to see the Buddhalike Sun God.
> … similar to you.[19]

Hans-Joachim Klimkeit thinks that the Sun God here is Jesus the Splendor, one of the Lord God of Manichaeism.[20] It appears that Uighur Manichaeans in the Middle Ages already combined the image of Jesus with the Third Messenger (*viz.* the Sun God). Consequently, the "*Zan Yishu Ji*" and the "*Lanzan Yishu Wen*" from the *Monijiao Xiabu zan* and the "*Tiannü zhou*" from the *Moni guangfo* should have same source.

The spell texts of the *Tiannü zhou* in *Moni guangfo* appear exactly in the *Xingfuzu qingdanke* 兴福祖庆诞科 (Ritual Manual for the Celebration of the Birthday of the Ancestor of Promoting Well-being[21]) (*old version: ll. 41-45*), but under the title of "*Tiandi zhou* 天地咒" (Heaven and Earth Spell). The latter book is composed for celebrating the birthday of "Xingfuzu 兴福祖", which has an old and new version. Since the new version is compiled of relatively new

---

18   Ibid., p. 210.
19   Hans-Joachim Klimkeit, 1993, *Gnosis on the Silk Road: Gnosis Texts from Central Asia*, San Francisco: Harper, p. 281.
20   Ibid. p. 287, note 14.
21   Xiaohe Ma, 2015, On the Date of the *Ritual Manual for the Celebration of the Birthday of the Ancestor Promoting Well-being* from Xiapu, in *Open Theology*, 1: 455-477.

texts, we take the old version as a reference. "Xingfuzu" is the designation of Lin Deng 林瞪, who was the hierarch of Xiapu Manichaeism (also known as *mingjiao*). It is said that he was conferred by an emperor as the "Xingfu leishi zhenjun 兴福雷使真君" (Immortal Thunder Apostle of Promoting the Wellbeing) of Northern Song Dynasty. This old version of the *Xingfuzu qingdanke* is probably a product of the Northern Song Dynasty (960-1127), or later.[22] It can be seen from the Persian translation of *Tiandizhou* 天地咒 above, there is no single word mention of "heaven and earth". The eulogy which praises of Mani, Bright World and Bright Messenger at line 34 of *Xingfuzu qingdanke* 兴福祖庆诞科 (the older version) with "A fu lin mo he fu li ye 阿孚林摩和弗哩耶" may have some relations with "the heaven and earth". Bue it is labelled as *Tiannüzhou* 天女咒, this may be the wrong place to copy each other's name at the time of transcribing the *Moni guangfo*. At the end of *Xingfuzu qingdanke* (the older version) (ll. 229-235) praised the *Tiannüzhou* 天女咒 again, although incomplete, but it is the same with *Tiandizhou* 天地咒 and *Tiannüzhou* 天女咒 from *Moni guangfo*. However, the Master did not find the aforementioned wrong and the post amble is right, this may state that the copywriter may not understand the true meaning of the incantation. At least, he did not take a correct approach toward the Ming God, and did not take solemn attitude toward the text in order to please the Ming God. But we did not find the similar mistakes in the *Moni guangfo*, therefore, it might be possible that the *Moni guangfo* was composed earlier than the *Xingfuzu qingdanke*. Judging from the usage of Manichaeism terminology, the completed time of the *Xingfuzu qingdanke* should be earlier than the *Leshantang shenji* and *Zousanqing* 奏三清 (Memorial to Three Pure Ones). To conclude, the *Moni guangfo* might be the archetype of all Xiapu manuscripts.

As mentioned before, there is also description about the "shingling 圣灵" (Holy Spirit") in the *Moni guangfo* (ll. 535-536):

zhi xin li huo ming yi shu he 志心信礼活命夷数和,
cong fan tian jie tian yao mo 从梵天界殄妖魔.
teng kong ru ge xia 腾空如鸽下,
huo yan qi liu bo 火焰起流波.

---

22 Yang Fuxue 杨富学, 2014, Lin Deng and His Position in the History of the Chinese Manichaeism 林瞪及其在中国摩尼教史上的地位, in *Journal of Chinese Historical Studies* 中国史研究, No. 1, pp. 109-124.

> (We) worship Jesus the Buddha, who exterminates demons from the Brahma-world. He is soaring like a dove in surrounding with running flames.

This piece of text might have taken several terms from the *Bible* and Nestorian classics and then combined them. Dove in general is represented as the Holy Spirit in Christianity, and similarly in Nestorian Christianity. In the ll. 133-135 of *Xuting mishisuo jing* 序听迷诗所经 (*Sutra of Hearing the Messiah*):

> Mi shi he ru tang le 弥施诃入汤了,
> hou chu shui 后出水,
> ji you liang feng cong tian lai 即有凉风从天来,
> rong yan si bo he 颜容似薄阁,
> zuo xiang mi shi he 坐向弥师诃上.[23]

We can compare this piece of text with the *New Testament*:

> And Jesus, when he was baptized, went up straightway out of the water: and, lo, the heavens were opened unto him, and he saw the Spirit of God descending like a dove, and lighting upon him. (*Matthew* 3:16)

The sentence 'teng kong ru ge xia' 腾空如鸽下 seen in *Moni guangfo* certainly originates from *Matthew* 3:16, as same as the text: "Bai ge fei lai teng rui xiang, na neng su chu xian feng guang 白鸽飞来腾瑞相,那能俗处现风光". The phrase "huo yan qi liu bo 火焰起流波" appears to be related to Pentecostal, in of *The New Testament*:

> And when the day of Pentecost was fully come, they were all with one accord in one place. And suddenly there came a sound from heaven as of a rushing mighty wind, and it filled all the house where they were sitting. And there appeared unto them cloven tongues like as of fire, and it sat upon each of them. And they were all filled with the Holy Ghost, and began to speak with other tongues, as the Spirit gave them utterance. (*Acts* 2:1-3)

Similar words do not appear in the rest of the Xiapu manuscripts, although it appears to be Worship to Jesus, even have a tendency to go over Mani, the Buddha of Light.

---

23 Wang Lanping 王兰平 2016: 150.

3   Yishu Worship from "Five Buddhas" to "Three Buddhas"

The *Moni guangfo*, similar to its later manuscripts such as the *Zoujiaozhu* 奏教主 (*Memorial to the Hierarch*), also expresses extreme worship to the Yishu. Only one hymn for eulogising the Twelve Buddhas of Manichaeism occurred in the *Moni guangfo* – which might be identical to the one in the Dunhuang *Xiabu zan* – placed the Yishu almost to the ending, "*shi zhe zhi en yi shu fo, shi yi zhe qi xin dian guang fo* 十者知恩夷数佛，十一者齐心电光佛" (the Tenth, gratitude, Jesus Buddha; the Eleventh, unamnity, Lightning Buddha) (ll. 384-5). Except in this occasion, the Yishu is paralleled with the other four Prophets as the five Buddhas:

> da sheng yuan shi tian zun na luo yan fo 大圣元始天尊那罗延佛,
> da sheng shen bian shi zun su lu zhi fo 大圣神变世尊苏路支佛,
> da sheng ci ji shi zun mo ni guang fo 大圣慈济世尊摩尼光佛,
> da sheng da jue shi zun shi jia wen fo 大圣大觉世尊释迦文佛,
> da sheng huo ming shi zun yi shu he fo 大圣活命世尊夷数和佛. (*Moni guangfo*, ll. 8-12)
> Great Saint, the Celestial Venerable of the Primordial Heaven, Buddha Nārāyana;
> Great Saint, the World Venerable of the Variety, Buddha Zoroaster;
> Great Saint, the World Venerable of the Kindness, the Mani Buddha of Luminous;
> Great Saint, the World Venerable of the Awakening, Buddha Śākyamuni;
> Great Saint, the World Venerable of the Saviour, Buddha Jesus.

The same order appears in ll.482-488 of the *Moni guangfo*:

> (...) xian jie shi xian da ci da bei yuan shi shi zun na luo yan 贤劫示现大慈大悲元始世尊那罗延,
> xian jie shi xian da ci da bei shen bian su lu zhi fo 贤劫示现大慈大悲神变苏路支佛,
> xian jie shi xian da ci da bei shen bian mo ni guang fo 贤劫示现大慈大悲神变摩尼光佛,
> xian jie shi xian da ci da bei shen bian shi jia wen fo 贤劫示现大慈大悲神变释迦文佛,
> xian jie shi xian da ci da bei shen bian yi shu he fo 贤劫示现大慈大悲神变夷数和佛.
> Theophany in the Bhadrakalpa, the infinitely merciful, the World Venerable of the Primordial Heaven, Nārāyana;

Theophany in the Bhadrakalpa, the infinitely merciful, Buddha Zoroaster;

Theophany in the Bhadrakalpa, the infinitely merciful, the Divinity of Variety, the Mani Buddha of Luminous;

Theophany in the Bhadrakalpa, the infinitely merciful, the Divinity of Variety, Buddha Śākyamuni;

Theophany in the Bhadrakalpa, the infinitely merciful, the Divinity of Variety, Buddha Jesus.

In both texts, 'Mani, the Buddha of Light' is put at the centre, and the other four Buddhas are arranged in chronological order, which are Nārāyana (Hinduism) → Zoroaster (Zoroastrianism) → Śākyamuni (Buddhism) → Jesus (Christianity) → the Mani Buddha of Luminous. This arrangement intends to show an inherited relationship of the Five Buddhas, therefore the Mani Buddha of Luminous is the last prophet.[24] All of them follow the basic doctrine of Manichaeism.

In lines 207-207 of the *Moni guangfo* (ll. 207-209), only Three Buddhas are narrated, namely Yishu (Jesus), Dianguang fo (Buddha of the Lightning) and Dacizun 大慈尊 (*viz*. Damingzun 大明尊 Father of the Greatness):

> ying mu zhan yang da ci zun 盈目瞻仰大慈尊
> gui yi neng su yi shu wang 皈依能苏夷数王
> zhi xin xin li shen tong dian guang wang 志心信礼神通电光王
>
> look reverently at Father of the Greatness,
> convert to the Resurrection Buddha Jesus,
> respect to the Magic King of the Lightning.

These are the prototypes of the Three Gods – Guang ming shang tian 广明上天, Lingming datian 灵明大天, Taishang zhentian 太上真天 – seen in the Xiapu manuscripts *Zou sanqing* and *Zou jiaozhu*, but the latter has already replaced Mani, the Buddha of Light with Father of Greatness. Although Xiapu Manichaeism was introduced to Fujian by the Uighur Manichean master Hulu 呼禄 (Uighur: Qutluɣ) after AD 843, the Xiapu Manichaeism is neither the Manichaeism in the Tang Dynasty nor the Uighur's.[25] In the process of translation

---

24 Ma Xiaohe 马小鹤, 2013, Five Buddhas of Manichaeism based on the Xiapu Manichaean Manuscripts 明教 "五佛" 考 —— 霞浦文书研究, Bulletin of Fudan University 复旦学报, 3: 100-114.

25 Yang Fuxue 杨富学, 2013, The Supplement of Uigur Manichean mage preached to Fujian 回鹘摩尼僧开教福建补说, in *The Western Regions Studies* 西域研究, No. 4, pp. 109-117.

and inheritance, Fujian Manichaean classics should accept and refer to the popular Manichean literature of the Tang Dynasty, especially *Monijiao xiabuzan*.[26] It can be asserted that these changes in the Manichean texts in Xiapu form a special product that adapted to the local conditions of Fujian.

In the original Manichean doctrine, there was no special symbolism on number "three". After it entered China, cases appeared in which Laozi 老子, Śākyamuni and the Mani Buddha of Luminious have been mentioned as the 'Three Saints', but it was only for convenience. We cannot think that these three gods were dominant in Manichaeism at that time. On the contrary, the Buddhism and Taoism in the East and the Christianity in the West have their own tradition on worshipping the "Three". Buddhism has the Three Buddhas of the Three Times (*sanshen sanshi fo* 三身三世佛), Taoism has the Three Pure Ones (*sanqing* 三清 or *santian* 三天), while Christianity has the Trinity of the Father, the Son and the Holy Spirit. However, when Manichaeism came to China during the Tang Dynasty, it did not adopt this concept. Lin Wushu considers that, even until to the Song Dynasty (960-1279), Manichaeism still did not develop a tradition of the Trinity gods, because the popular belief in the Song Dynasty was the "Five Buddhas" instead of the "Three Buddhas" or "Three Deities".[27] The Three-Buddha Worship might be the outcome of the further Sinicisation and Taoistisation during the Ming and Qing Dynasties, based on the "*Zousanqing* 奏三清" which composed/compiled in the late Ming Dynasty.[28] Since Mr. Lin Wushu never saw/read the manuscript *Xingfuzu qingdanke*, which was composed around in the Song Dynasty and copied in the Qing Dynasty, the formation year of the "Three Buddhas" was correspondingly much delayed.

Seeing that the Three Buddhas, which are Buddha of the Lightning King, the Mani Buddha of Luminous and Jesus Buddha of the Harmony, are invited in the opening chapter of the *Xingfuzu qingdanke*, it indicates that at least the Three-Buddha Worship was starting to flourish at that time. Moreover, compare the absolute Three-Buddha Worship in the *Xingfuzu qingdanke* and the *Zou sanqing* to the one in the *Moni guangfo*, it is certainly that the latter, no matter the format or the contents, is different, because the main worshipped objects of the latter still belong to the systems of the "Five Buddhas" and the

---

26 Yang Fuxue 杨富学 & Bao Lang 包朗, 2015, The Relationship between *Moni Guangfo* and Dunhuang Manichean Literature «摩尼光佛»与敦煌摩尼教文献之关系, in *Dunhuang and Turfan Studies* 敦煌吐鲁番研究, XV, Shanghai: Shanghai Chinese Classics Publishing House, pp. 416-418.

27 Lin Wushu 林悟殊, 2013, Dating on the Formation Period of Xiapu Scripture *Zoujiaozhu* 霞浦科仪本«奏教主»形成年代考, in *Jiuzhou xuelin* 九州学林, XXXI, pp. 117-121.

28 Ibid. pp. 131-132.

"Twelve Buddhas". In summary, during the time when the *Moni guangfo* was composed, its theogony was mainly the Five Buddhas, but did not abandon the old theogony of the "Twelve Buddhas" completely. Instead, it simultaneously began to evolve from the "Five Buddhas" to the more concise and powerful "Three Buddhas" system. Thereafter, once the Three-Buddha Worship of was established, Xiapu Manichaeism has finished its Sinicisation and Taoistisation. In this process of transformation, Nārāyana, Zoroaster and Śākyamuni disappeared, but Jesus Buddha of the Harmony survived together with the Mani Buddha of Luminous. After adding Buddha of the Lightning King, the Three Buddhas concept was completed. Through this process, we also can see clearly that the lofty status of the Jesus Buddha of the Harmony in Manichaeism was exalting.

The completion of the *Xingfuzu qingdanke* took place between the Southern Song and Northern Song dynasties, or a bit later. The *Moni guangfo* however was in the transitional stage of from the "Five Buddhas" system to the "Three Buddhas" systems, in the interchangeable system of Buddhistisation and Taoistisation. Its composed/compiled time should be ranged from the late Tang Dynasty to the Five Dynasties and Ten Kingdoms Periods, or latest to the early Song Dynasty. Considering various factors, such as taboo words, god names, the application of terminology, etc., it is better to place its composition at the beginning of the Song Dynasty.

CHAPTER 8

Spirit in *Atrahasis*

Donald Wang

1 Introduction

Atrahasis is the protagonist of an 18th-century BC Akkadian epic comprised in various versions on clay tablets. It is one literary form of Sumero-Babylonian traditions about the creation and the early history of man.[1] The *Atrahasis* epic was comprised of three main tablets, included both were a creation myth and a flood account. The story is one of three surviving Babylonian deluge stories. Until 1965 about one fifth of the epic was known, now four fifths of the whole story has been restored.[2] The first tablet contains the most important single witness to Babylonian speculation on the origins and nature of the creation of man.[3] It is remarkable to note that "spirit" occurs four times in it,[4] there is only one article that solely discussed the role of spirit in *Atrahasis*.[5] In light of this, it is of great importance to study the role of spirit in the creation of human beings in *Atrahasis*. This paper focuses on studying the meaning and usage of spirit in *Atrahasis*. The point is that spirit in *Atrahasis* plays a vital role in the creation account of human beings and the spirit performs a bridging role in the overarching narrative of rebellion, creation and flood.

2 The Double Creation of Human Beings

It is highly significant that *Atrahasis* has two successive parallel accounts of the creation of man.[6] Kikawada suggests that it is a literary convention in the

---

1 W.G. Lambert and Alan Millard, *Atra-Ḫasīs: The Babylonian Story of the Flood* (Winona Lake: Esienbrauns, 1999), 1.
2 A.R. Millard, "A New Babylonian 'Genesis' Story", in Hess, Richard S., and David Toshio Tsumura ed., *"I Studied Inscriptions from before the Flood." Ancient Near Eastern, Literary and Linguistic Approaches to Genesis 1 11* (Winona Lake: Eisenbrauns, 1994), 115.
3 William L. Moran, Ronald S. Hendel (ed.), *The Most Magic Word: Essays on Babylonian and Biblical Literature* (Washington, DC: Catholic Biblical Association of America, 2002), 75.
4 line 215, 217, 228, 230.
5 Tzvi Abusch, "Ghost and God: Some Observations on a Babylonian Understanding of Human Nature." *Studies in the History of Religion* (1998): 363-383.
6 Isaac M. Kikawada, "The Double Creation of Mankind in *Enki and Ninmah*, *Atrahasis I 1–351*, and *Genesis* 1–2." in in Hess, Richard S., and David Toshio Tsumura ed.. *"I Studied Inscriptions*

Ancient Near East to telling the story of the origin of humankind in a doublet: the first part of the story of the creation of humankind in more general and abstract terms, while the second part of the story depicts it in more specific and concrete terms.[7] The two creation accounts of human beings are found in the tablet I of *Atrahasis*. Kikawada divides the two creation accounts in this as follows:

> Atmhasis 1 1–351
> 1–4 Introduction: A long time ago, "When the gods were man..."
> 5–245 Part I: The First Creation of Mankind (General)
> 5–6 The Anunnaki make the Igigi work; division of labour
> 7–38 Work of gods; administrative and labour classes
> 39–69 Complaint of the Igigi against Enlil; the Igigi call for a war
> 70–83 Enlil is frightened; Nusku tries to calm him
> 84–100 Ann and Enki are summoned together with the Anunnaki
> 101–185? Anu advises Enlil to find out the cause for the uproar, but the Igigi make themselves responsible collectively for the rebellion because of the excessive workload
> 186?–191 Anu gives a solution to the problem, that is, to ask Belet-ili/Mami/The Motherwomb to create oflspring (*li–gim?ma?-a*)
> 192–234 Marni with the help of Enki creates mankind (*lullu*) from the flesh and blood of a slain god, mixed with clay
> 235–243 Marni completes her task and imposes labour on man
> 244–245 Gods rejoice
> 246–248 Transition: Marni is praised; her name is called *Bélet–kala-ili*
> 249–351 Part II: The Second Creation of Mankind in Seven Pairs; Marriage, Procreation and Work (Specific)
> 249–271? Enki and Marni come to the house of destiny to create seven pairs of people by snipping off clay
> 272?–276 Marriage is instituted (text broken badly)
> 277–282 The ten-month gestation period is established by Marni
> 283–295 Marni performs midwifery and childbirth is perfected
> 296–304 Marni is praised for instituting marriage and childbirth. Nine days of rejoicing is decreed and Mami's other name, Istar, is now changed to Ishara

---

from before the Flood." Ancient Near Eastern, Literary and Linguistic Approaches to Genesis 1 11 (Winona Lake: Eisenbrauns, 1994): 170

7   Ibid., 169.

305–351 The people begin to labour for gods; "With picks and spades they built the shrines. They built the big canal banks. For food for the people, for the sustenance of the gods"[8]

Kikawada's division of the first creation account of human beings is in line 5-245 and the second creation account is line in 249-351. According to Kikawada's list, in both accounts, the two processes of the creation clay is recorded as the same element in the creation of human beings.[9] Both accounts make the same point that humankind was created of clay and destined to perform work.[10] Moreover, Millard claims that "the underlying idea of the Atrahsis' Epic and other Babylonian Creation stories is that man was made to free the gods from the toil of ordering the earth to produce their food."[11] There is no doubt that both accounts have some similarities, however, there are also some differences. One difference is that the creation account two focuses on fertility and sexuality in marriage. The human race does not start with a human being in abstract as in the first creation account. The account begins with seven pairs, giving the humans the possibility to multiply seven times faster.[12] Another difference that Kikawada misses in his list in the first creation account is the element of "spirit" (*etemmu*),[13] which is uniquely recorded as an important element in the creation of the human beings.[14] Therefore, it is necessary to

---

8   Isaac M. Kikawada, "The Double Creation of Mankind in *Enki and Ninmah, Atrahasis I 1–351,* and *Genesis* 1–2." in Hess, Richard S., and David Toshio Tsumura ed.. *"I Studied Inscriptions from before the Flood." Ancient Near Eastern, Literary and Linguistic Approaches to Genesis 1 11* (Winona Lake: Eisenbrauns, 1994): 172.

9   Line 226 "Nintu Mixed clay", Line 256"she nipped off fourteen pieces of clay"

10 Isaac M. Kikawada, "The Double Creation of Mankind in *Enki and Ninmah, Atrahasis I 1–351,* and *Genesis* 1–2." in Hess, Richard S., and David Toshio Tsumura ed.. *"I Studied Inscriptions from before the Flood." Ancient Near Eastern, Literary and Linguistic Approaches to Genesis 1 11* (Winona Lake: Eisenbrauns, 1994): 170..

11 A.R. Millard, "a New Babylonian 'Genesis' Story", in Hess, Richard S., and David Toshio Tsumura ed.. *"I Studied Inscriptions from before the Flood." Ancient Near Eastern, Literary and Linguistic Approaches to Genesis 1 11* (Winona Lake: Eisenbrauns, 1994): 119..

12 Helge S. Kvanvig, *Primeval History: Babylonian, Biblical, and Enochic: an Intertextual Reading* (Leiden; Brill, 2011.), 29.

13 Lambert and Millard also comments that "to this traditional concept the author of Atrahasis has added one item, which occurs in a passage (I.208-30) full of perplexing phrases. It was a common Mesopotamian view that man had a spirit that survived death, which could, if not properly buried and supplied with offerings, trouble the living. It is this spirit (Bab. etemmu) that the author is explaining in addition to the usual material aspects of life. No other surviving creation account from Sumerians or Babylonians attempts to explain this." see W.G. Lambert and Alan Millard, *Atra-Ḫasīs: The Babylonian Story of the Flood* (Winona Lake: Esienbrauns, 1999), 22..

14 lines 215, 217, 228, 230.

take a closer look at the first creation account in order to understand the different elements involved in the creation process of human beings.

3 Spirit in Creation Account One

In the first creation account, the main section is in lines-192-148, which constitute a thematic and structural unit, they are concerned with the first stage of the creation of humanity. They begin with the request that the gods give birth to a goddess to form man, and they end with the gods renaming her as the "mistress of all the gods" in gratitude to what she had done.[15] It is helpful to refer to Moran's diagram of this section:

A gods	narrative	192-193
	speech	194-197
B birth-goddess	narrative	198-199
	speech	200-203
	narrative	204-205
C Enki	speech	206-217
	narrative	218-230
	narrative	231-236
B' birth-goddess	speech	237-243
	narrative	244-245
A' gods	speech	246-248[16]

Importantly from the above structure, the creation account of human beings displays the literary feature of the intermingling of narrative and speech. The process of the creation of human beings is carried out with the narrative and the speeches of gods. The narrative of lines 192-193: they summoned and asked the goddess, the midwife of the gods, wise Mami. This narrative of the scene is a one of divine council, in which the gods make the decision to creating human beings.[17] In so doing, the stage is set for the creation of human beings in the following lines.

---

15 William L. Moran, Ronald S. Hendel (ed.), *The Most Magic Word: Essays on Babylonian and Biblical Literature* (Washington, DC: Catholic Biblical Association of America, 2002), 75.
16 William L. Moran, Ronald S. Hendel (ed.), *The Most Magic Word: Essays on Babylonian and Biblical Literature* (Washington, DC: Catholic Biblical Association of America, 2002), 76.
17 The idea of "divine council" is a common concept in the Ancient Near Eastern world. see Mark J. Boda, J. Gordon McConville, *Dictionary of the Old Testament Prophets* (Downers Grove, Illinois: IVP Academic, 2012), 162.

It is easy to identify the main emphasis of this unit. Also, the concentric structure gives formal expression to the pivotal importance of Enki's speech (lines 206-217) on the nature of human beings.[18] In this creation account, continued is the Sumerian tradition of forming man from clay, adding to the material the blood and spirit or "ghost" (*eṭemmu*) of a god.[19] It is this "spirit" that the author is explaining in addition to the usual material aspects of life.[20]

The question is what is the "spirit" (*eṭemmu*)? What does it mean in the creation account of human beings? In order to answer these questions, one needs to go to the texts and contexts to understand the meaning and usage of this word.

In order to gain a good understanding of the whole creation account, it is better to examine the portion of lines 206-217[21].

206 On the first, seventh, and fifteenth day of the month
207 I will make a purifying bath
208 Let one god be slaughtered
209 so that al the gods may be cleansed in a dipping
210 From his flesh and blood
211 Let Nintu mix clay
212 That god and man
213 May be thoroughly mixed in the clay
214 So that we may hear the drum for the rest of time
215 Let there be a spirit (*eṭemmu*) from the god's flesh.
216 Let it proclaim living as its sign
217 So that this be not forgotten let there be a spirit(*eṭemmu*).

This is Enki's speech addressed to the divine council, with the detailed procedure for creating human beings. Lines 221-234 in the narrative form a depiction of the actual creation procedure, echoing the creating command by Enki.[22] This literary feature of speech and narrative is a remarkable mark of creating human beings. The narrative is the actual forming of the human beings, almost

---

18   William L. Moran, Ronald S. Hendel (ed.), *The Most Magic Word: Essays on Babylonian and Biblical Literature* (Washington, DC: Catholic Biblical Association of America, 2002), 76.
19   Richard J. Clifford, *Creation Accounts in the Ancient Near East and in the Bible* (Washington, DC: Catholic Biblical Association of America, 1994), 79
20   W.G. Lambert and Alan Millard, *Atra-Ḥasīs: The Babylonian Story of the Flood* (Winona Lake: Esienbrauns, 1999), 22..
21   the text is from Lambert and Millard, 58-59.
22   lines 206-207 is in parallel with line lines 221-222, lines 208-209 is in parallel with lines 223-224, lines 210-211 is in parallel with lines 225-226, lines 214-215 is in parallel with lines 227-228, 216-217 is in parallel with 229-230.

in the same parallel with the command of Enki. In the creation account, "spirit" (*eṭemmu*) occurs at lines 215, 217, 228, and 230. The usage of "spirit" (*eṭemmu*) occurs in lines 215 and 217 in Enki''s speech and the rest two usages occurs in lines 228 and 230 in the form of the narrative of the actual process of creating human beings.

This text states that mthe an is created from the mixing of clay, the blood and flesh of a slain god,[23] with the third element of spirit (*eṭemmu*). The spirit, is it from god or from man? Lambert suggests that the spirit is man's, he remarks that "it was a common Mesopotamian view that man had a spirit that survived death, which could, if not properly buried and supplied with offerings, trouble the living"[24] However, in reference to the context, both in lines 215 and 228, all claim that "spirit from the god's flesh," and the fact that dead gods in Mesopotamia survived as ghosts is attested to.[25] Thus, the spirit is this account is not from man, but from the slain god.[26]

It is also of great significance to notice that after the god is slaughtered, the first step in creating man is to mix the clay with the flesh and blood from god (lines 210, 225), and the second step is to let there be a spirit from the god's flesh (line 215-228). After these two steps, the man is proclaimed living and this signifies with emphasis of the role of the spirit, "so that there be not forgotten let there be a spirit" (lines 217 and230).

Having argued that the spirit is from god, then it is necessary to examine what kind of god it is. In line 208, "Let one god (*ilam isten*) be slaughtered," the key term is "one god"(*ilam isten*), which is a difficult phrase.[27] Moran suggests that it should be boldly translated as "the leader-god".[28] Kvanvig remarks that "he god slaughtered, out of whose flesh and blood human was created is the leading god in the rebellion of the Igigu".[29] However he does not give an explanation of why this one god is identified as the leading god in the rebellion. In

---

23   Tzvi Abusch, "Ghost and god: Some Observations on a Babylonian Understanding of Human Nature", 366.

24   Lambert, 22.

25   kvanvig points out that "we notice in KAR 4, Atrahasis, and Enuma Elish that the gods are slaughtered. They are not killed in the sense that their existence is ended. The gods will continue to live on in the body and mind of the new human being", see Helge S. Kvanvig, *Primeval History: Babylonian, Biblical, and Enochic: an Intertextual Reading*, 49.

26   William L. Moran, Ronald S. Hendel (ed.), *The Most Magic Word: Essays on Babylonian and Biblical Literature*, 82-83.

27   William L. Moran, Ronald S. Hendel (ed.), *The Most Magic Word: Essays on Babylonian and Biblical Literature*, 80.

28   Ibid., 80

29   Helge S. Kvanvig, *Primeval History: Babylonian, Biblical, and Enochic: an Intertextual Reading*, 45.

constrast, Moran gives a convincing reason that the one god whom at Enki's advice puts the gods put to death is the leader god, for this explains why he is characterized as "who had personality" (*sa isu tema*), and later have been slaughtered "together with his personality" (*qadu temisu*), it could fit the rebel leader for his characteristic of having *temu*, which is most easily understood of the part he played in the rebellion. *Temu* carries the meaning of having schemed to overthrow Enlil, and it is this scheme that this god comes to his death.[30] Oden also supports the idea that this *etemmu* belonged originally to the slain rebel god, and that is placed within humans to remind them of their status and of the dangers of rebelling against the senior gods.[31] The spirit (*etemmu*) is from the flesh of the rebel god, and is of great significance in our understanding of the creation account of human beings in *Atrahasis*.

Furthermore, there are also some word plays in this creation account that express the deep thought of the author in regards to the composition of this epic. The slaughtered god is identified as the god who had "personality" (*temu*) (line 223). For the *temu*, Kvanvig translates it as "planning capacity,"[32] Jacobsen suggests it as "idea,"[33] and Kensky renders it as "sense".[34] This author agrees with Oden that given the term's use in other literature it indicates "intelligence" or "plan", and the fact that the rebel god, who clearly led the rebellion and who presumably plotted its course, is identified by his possession of this attribute suggest as translation of ability/capacity to plan/scheme.[35]

The *temu* is a word play with *etemmu*, Abusch recognizes a word play here that the god who possess *temu* is on the one hand, and the Babylonian word *etemmu* "spirit" on the other. This word play implicitly treats *etemmu* as having been formed from the slaughtered god that humankind possesses the spirit of and survives after death in the form of that spirit.[36] Oden is more accurately arguing that with the very creation of humans in this Epic comes an indication of the tension, which inevitably leads to rebellion. Humans are created with the "spirit" (*etemmu*) of the leader god, which is a reminder to them of the consequences of rebellion. Although, they are also created with that god's

---

30 William L. Moran, Ronald S. Hendel (ed.), *The Most Magic Word: Essays on Babylonian and Biblical Literature*, 81.

31 Robert A. Oden, Jr., "Divine Aspirations in Atrahasis and in Genesis 1–11", *Zeitschrift für die alttestamentliche Wissenschaft* 93.2 (1981): 202.

32 Helge S. Kvanvig, 44.

33 Thorkild Jacobsen, *The Treasures of Darkness: A History of Mesopotamian Religion* (New Haven: Yale University Press, 1976.), 118.

34 ||Tikva Frymer-Kensky,."The Atrahasis Epic and Its Significance for Our Understanding of Genesis 1-9." *The Biblical Archaeologist* (1977): 149.

35 Robert A. Oden, Jr, 202.

36 Tzvi Abusch, 369.

"scheming"(*tëmu*) nature. It is difficult not to see in the play between *etemmu* and *tëmu* a pun, and it is equally not difficult to see in this pun a presage of the remainder of the Epic.[37] In the creation account, the created human beings inherit the characteristics of *temu* and *etemmu* the slaughtered god.

This author argues that it is because of the element of *etemmu* in creation of human beings that envisages the flood narrative in the Epic. In lines 217 and 230, both emphasizes that with the help of the "spirit" (*etemmu*), there will be no forgetting, the spirit is to keep refreshing the memory of the dead god.[38] We go back to the rebel scene, one line reads "[The lamentation was] heavy, [we could] hear the 'noise' (*rigmu*)"(line 179). Their rebelling and complaining is described as "noise"(*rigmu*). Rigmu is transferred from the Igigu to humankind in the creation[39]after the creation of the human beings, Mami address the gods that "you raised a cry (*rigmu*) for mankind" (line 242),[40] It is not surprising that after the creation of human beings and letting them do the work, Enlil heard their "noise"(*rigmu*) (lines 356) could not sleep because of "noise"(*rigmu*) (line 358), and eventually he sent the flood to wipe out the human beings. Kvanvig points out that *Rimgu* occurs 23 times in the text and appears in all sections of the poem:

> The initial assignment of the responsibilities for the universe.
> The rebellion of the Igigu
> The divine assembly and the creation of humans
> The disasters sent by the gods
> Deliberations in the divine assembly before the flood
> The flood itself
> Divine reactions during the flood.[41]

The variety of *rigmu* is intened and contributes to the narative's ironic quality.[42] In one sense *rigmu* is the thematic word running throughout the whole epic.

It is because of the "spirit" (*etemmu*) that keeps the memory of the past and presages the flood narrative, and which bridges the two "noise" (*rigmu*), namely the rebellion and the flood narrative. Potentially, there may be even be a world play of in the creation of human beings with the two elements of

---

37   Robert A. Oden, Jr, 203.
38   Moran, 83,
39   Helge S. Kvanvig, 77.
40   This is Lambert's translation, see Lambert, 69, perhaps a better rendering is by Kvanvig, "you have cast off(?) the noise upon humankind" see, Kvanvig, 45.
41   Helge S. Kvanvig, 76.
42   Ibid., 77.

"blood"(*damu*) and "spirit" (*etemmu*)[43] with "noise" (*rigmu*), With this word play, it would strengthen the connection to this rebel-creation-flood meta narrative.

4 Conclusion

Atrahasis adopts the literary device of double creation accounts of human beings. In the first creation account, the "spirit" (*etemmu*) from god is a vital element in the creation of human beings. This account features the speech of Enki, it follows the pattern of speech and narrative in the process of creation of human beings (lines 206-217).

The "spirit" (*etemmu*) occurs four times in the first creation account. "Spirit" (*etemmu*) signifies the importance and reality of passing the planning schemes from the dead god to the created human beings. This emphasizes that created human beings carry on the character of the rebellious leader god. Also, noted is the "noise" that they made in the rebellion. This is also passed on to human beings as the function of the spirit is to refresh of the past and envisages the flood narrative that the "noise" that the created human beings make.

In summation, "spirit" (*etemmu*) functions as the bridging point in the overarching narrative of rebellion, creation and the flood narrative.

---

43 Abusch notices the word play of "blood"(*damu*) and "spirit" (*etemmu*) see, Abusch, 368.

PART 5

Comparative Religious and Cultural Studies

∴

CHAPTER 9

A Comparative Perspective on Two Yelikewen Official Families in the Yuan Dynasty*

Xiaoping Yin

1   Introduction

Yelikewen 也里可溫, or Arkehum, or ärgägün, is a term for Christians in the Yuan Dynasty who mainly came from western lands and lived in China during the 12th to 14th centuries.[1] Saeki pointed out that *Jingjiao* 景教 (Luminous Religion) was a foreign religion just spreading among the foreigners in China.[2] Pelliot also stated that the Christianity in East Asia during the 13th and 14th centuries was a religion being held by non-Chinese such as Alains, Turks and some believing Mongols.[3]

Instead of the term "foreigners", a contemporary word "*semu*" 色目 (literally color-eyed), initially referring to people with a rare and unusual surname and from western lands in the Yuan Dynasty,[4] should be more proper for "*Yelikewen*". *Semu* reveals the non-Chinese background of *Yelikewen*, however, unlike the Nestorians in Tang China who were mainly Iranian Persians, Sogdians and their descendants living in China, the *Yelikewen* were mostly Turkic people.

---

*   It is a result of the project supported by Philosophy and Science Foundation for the Twelfth Five-Year Plan in Guangdong 廣東省哲學社科 "一二五" 規劃項目 "比較視野下的唐元景教研究" (GD15CLS03) and Philosophy and Science Foundation for the Twelfth Five-Year Plan in Guangzhou 廣州市哲學社科 "一二五" 規劃項目 "嶺南學者與景教研究" (15Y23).

1   Cf. Yin Xiaoping 殷小平, "Yuandai dianji zhong Yelikewen hanyi shi shi 元代典籍中也里可溫涵义試釋" [On the interpretations of "Yelikewen" in the Yuan Dynasty in Chinese contexts], in *Ouya Yanjiu* 歐亞研究 [*Euroasian Studies*], No. 9, ed. Yu Taishan 余太山 and Li Jinxiu 李錦繡 (Beijing: Zhonghuashuju 北京：中華書局, 2009): 66-80; Chen Yuan 陳垣, *Chenyuan Xueshu Lunwenji* 陳垣學術論文集 [*Collected articles of Chen Yuan*], (Beijing: Zhonghuashuju, 1988), 1-56.

2   P.Y. Saeki 佐伯好郎, *Chugoku ni Okeru Keikyo Suibo no Rekishi* 中國に於ける景教衰亡の歴史 [*The History of the Decline and Fall of Jingjiao in China*], (Kyoto: Doshisha 同志社, 1955), 54-55.

3   P. Pelliot, "Chrétiens d'Asie Centrale et d'extrême-Orient", *T'oung Pao*, 15(5) 1914, 643.

4   Meng Siming 蒙思明, *Yuandai Shehui Jieji Zhidu* 元代社會階級制度 [*The Social Class System in the Yuan Dynasty*], (Shanghai: Shanghai renmin chubanshe 上海：上海人民出版社, 2006), 41-43.

"*Semu*" is also a key word relating to the special social hierarchy in the Yuan Dynasty. According to this hierarchic system, the population were strictly divided into four classes: the first one being Mongols; the second, *Semu*, including the western Central Asians and some northern nationalities such as Tangut 唐兀, Naiman 乃蠻 and Qanqlis 康里; Han 漢人, including Khitan 契丹 and Jurchen 女直, and Mangi 南人 being classified into the lower two classes.[5] Among the peoples with the *Yelikewen* background, Ongut 汪古, Uighur 畏兀兒, Qipchaq 欽察 and Alain 阿速 are classified as *Semu*, and Kerait is classified as Mongol. Since the Mongols and *Semu* people undoubtedly enjoyed the most privileges financially and politically at that time, accordingly, *Yelikewen* met its development summit in China. Not only did the government establish a bureau *Chongfu Si* 崇福司 specifically to administrate Christian affairs, but also exempted the *Yelikewen* people from the land, trade taxes or other labor obligations. A vital fact should be stressed that this hierarchic system made *Yelikewen* attain official positions more easily. For example, there were nearly two hundred "*Yelikewen*" recorded in Chinese documents and archeological findings, most of them were officials occupying various posts from the highest authorities to the local governments.[6]

I believe the official background is one of the most striking characteristics of *Yelikewen,* which distinguishes them from the Christians in Tang China. As known to all, the latter were mainly monks and missionaries from Daqin 大秦 and Persia 波斯.[7] The official background is also of significance when evaluating the contributions and the historical role of *Yelikewen*. Rather than highlighting the missionizing aspect, the performance of these official Christians reflected in various fields may offer a broader perspective; in other words, the official Christians played quite different roles under different circumstances. In this article, it discusses *Yelikewen* people's diverse contributions in the Yuan Dynasty, through exploring two *Yelikewen* families, one being the Ma family, and the other Aixue's family.

---

5   Tao Zongyi 陶宗儀, *Nancun Chuogeng lu* 南村輟耕錄, (Beijing: Zhonghuashuju, 1997), 12-14.
6   Yin Xiaoping, *Yuandai Yelikewen Kaoshu* 元代也里可溫考述 [*Studies on the Christians in the Yuan Dynasty*], (Lanzhou 蘭州: Lanzhou University Press, 2012). Zhang Jiajia 張佳佳, "Yuan Jininglu Jingjiao shijia kaolun: yi Antanbuhua jiazu beike cailiao wei zhongxin 元濟寧路景教世家考論 —— 以按檀不花家族碑刻材料為中心" [A study and commentary on a Nestorian Family in Jining Circuit in the Yuan Dynasty: Based on materials on the Stele Inscriptions of the Antanbuhua Family], *Lishi Yanjiu* 歷史研究 [*Historical Research*] (5) 2010: 39-59.
7   Lin Wushu 林悟殊 and Yin Xiaoping, "Tangdai Jingseng Shiyi 唐代景僧釋義" [On Interpretations of *Jingseng* (the Nestorian Monks) in the Tang Dynasty], *Wenshi* 文史 1(2009): 181-204.

2 The Same Religious Background: The Nestorian Families from the Western Lands

The Ma family was from Ongut, the well-known-Nestorian and *semu* tribe in Jin and Yuan dynasties. Ongut was located in Tiande Circuit 天德路, Xijing Circuit 西京路 and the extensive areas at the north-eastern corners of the great bend of Yellow River. Since it was on the crossroads and border areas between Song, Jin and Liao countries, it had formed intercultural communities and enjoyed a significant military position from 10th to 13th centuries.[8] It was verified by abundant resources that Christianity prevailed in the territory of Ongut. For example, a famous Nestorian monk named Marcus, later known as Mar Yabalaha III in the East Church, was born in a hereditary Nestorian family in Ongut;[9] Marco Polo also recorded that many Nestorians living in the city of Tenduc.[10] Three families of Ongut, including the kingly family, the Zhao 趙 and the Ma 馬, were noted for their superior position in Yuan China, and all of them held the Nestorian faith.

*Mashi Shipu*馬氏世譜 [*the Ma Family Genealogy*], composed by a Chinese scholar Huang Jin 黃溍 (1277-1357), stated that the ancestors of the Ma family were the noble "*Niesituoli*" 聶斯脫里 (or Nestorian) from western lands, in Chinese being 馬氏之先出西域貴族聶斯脫里.[11] It is the only explicit record referring to "Nestorian" directly in Chinese sources, differentiating itself from the usage of "*Jing Jiao*景教" in the Tang Dynasty or "*Yelikewen*" in the Yuan Dynasty. It is a crucial proof of the Nestorian faith of this family. Another

---

8   Zhou Liangxiao 周良宵, "*Jin Yuan shidai de Jingjiao* 金元時代的景教" [*Jingjiao* in the Jin and Yuan dynasties], in *Jingjiao, the Church of the East in China and Central Asia*, ed. R. Malek (Sankt Augustin: Institut Monumenta Serica, 2006), 197-208. M. Sakurai 櫻井益雄, "Oko Buzokuko 汪古部族考", *Journal of Oriental Studies (Tokyo)* 東方學報 (東京) 6(1936): 1-22; Gai Shanlin 蓋山林, "Yuandai Wanggubu diqu de Jingjiao yiji yu Jingjiao zai dongxifang wenhuajiaoliu zhong de zuoyong 元代汪古部地區的景教遺跡與景教在東西方文化交流中的作用" [The *Jingjiao* relics in the region of Ongut in the Yuan Dynasty and the role *Jingjiao* played in the intercultural relations between China and western world], *Yazhou Wenming Luncong* 亞洲文明論叢, (Chengdu: Sichuan renmin chubanshe 成都：四川人民出版社, 1986), 143-155.
9   P. Pelliot, "Chrétiens d'Asie Centrale et d'extrême-Orient", *Toung Pao*, 15(1914): 632.
10 A.C. Moule and P. Pelliot, *Marco Polo: the Description of the World*, (New York: AMS Press INC, 1976), 181-184.
11 Huang Jin 黃溍, *Mashi Shipu* 馬氏世譜 [*The Ma Family Genealogy*], in *Quan Yuan Wen* 全元文, (Nanjing: Jiangsu renmin chubanshe 南京：江蘇古籍出版社, 1999), (vol. 967), 36.

proof relating to their Christian belief is that many family members were recorded as "*Yelikewen*".[12]

From the middle 11th century to the early 14th century, there had been eight generations of the family residing in China.

The first generation moved to northwest China and settled down the fertile grasslands in Didao 狄道, and therefore, Pelliot and Yule titled this tribal group "Ganzhou Uighur".[13] The patriarch of the family was named Helumisi 和祿采思, which might be translated from a Christian name "Horam Mishael" or "Waggis", or "Gewagis". The second generation Timur Yuege 帖穆爾越歌 (or Täm ürügä) obtained the post of Commander of horse and foot soldiery 馬步軍指揮使 for his military achievements. The third generation, led by Ba Saoma Yelichu 把騷馬也里黜 (might be Bar Sauma Elišo), moved to Tianshan 天山, Jingzhou 淨州, a place near the territorial boundaries between Jin 金 and Mongol and was predictably convenient for the trading activities. Since then, the family had lived there for about four generations. As was recorded, Ba Saoma Yelichu was devoted to the agricultural cultivation and stock farming. Moreover he expanded his social circle by making acquaintance with some Chinese intellectuals, and his name was consequently forwarded to the front of Emperor Xizong 金熙宗 (1119-1149).[14]

Ma Qingxiang 馬慶祥, the leader of the fourth generation, had a scholarly name Ruining 瑞寧 [means auspiciousness and peace], whose lesser style was "*Xilijisi*" 習禮吉思 or Sargis. He primarily served the Jin government as staff supervisor of horse and foot soldiery 兵馬判官 at Fengxiang 鳳翔, and then he moved to Jundu 浚都 (Kaifeng 開封). He excelled in six western languages besides his outstanding horse archery. It was recorded that Genghis Khan appreciated his talent and summoned him several times, but Ma Qingxiang, as a loyal officer of the Jin Dynasty, never considered the offer from Genghis Khan, and he died in a battle between Mongol and Jin.[15]

Ma Yuehenai 馬月合乃 (or Johanna, 1216-1263), the grand-grand-father of Ma Zuchang, was the head of the fifth generation. He was authorized the Minister of Board of Rites in 1261. Among eleven sons of Ma Yuehenai, Ma Shizhong 馬世忠 was the eldest one whose final official post was Transport Commissioner of *Changping Cang* 常平倉 (Ever Normal Granary); and Ma

---

12   Chen Yuan 陳垣, *Yuan Xiyuren Huahua Kao* 元西域人華化考, (Shanghai: Shanghai guji chubanshe 上海: 上海古籍出版社, 2000), 18-23.
13   Sakurai, "Oko Buzokuko", 1-22.
14   Pelliot, "Chrétiens d'Asie Centrale et d'extrême-Orient", 630.
15   Huang, *Mashi Shipu*, 36.

Shichang 馬世昌 was the second eldest son, who served in *Li Bu* 吏部 (Board of Civil Appointments).[16]

Ma Run 馬潤 (1255-1313), the son of Ma Shichang, was known as a poet and Confucian in his time.[17] His noted son Ma Zuchang 馬祖常 (1279-1338), who might be the most acknowledged figure of the family, eventually held *Yushi Zhongcheng* 御史中丞（President of the Censorate）. Being a noted scholar, his collected poems *Shi Tian Ji* 石田集 was highly evaluated by the contemporary intellectuals. As is remarked by Su Tianjue 蘇天爵 in the preface, the poetry of Ma Zuchang followed the poetic tradition of Sui 隋 and Tang 唐 and those of Han 漢 and Wei 魏 dynasties.[18] To some extent, the family was well known around the country because of Ma Zuchang's outstanding academic achievements. Xu Youren 許有壬 claimed that Ma Zuchang was the first scholar in his tribe and his success exerted a positive influence on the family members to embrace the Chinese culture. Besides the literary achievements and political performance, little was mentioned about his Nestorian background in the contemporary documents.

A few Nestorian names have been listed as above. If we search further, more Christian names could be uncovered, such as Johanna (two), Denha (two), Sarghis (three), Joseph, Paulus, Abraham, Jacob, and so on.[19] In contrast, more family members chose the Chinese name, which I will discuss later in the transformation of the family.

Another famous *Kelikewen* family is Aixue's family. Aixue (1227-1308), or Isa, was an eminent Nestorian in Yuan China, and he was believed to be from Fulin 拂菻, or Phurom, the Eastern Roman Empire in Tang China called by Syrian in the 12th and 14th centuries. Pelliot believed that Aixue was an Arabic-speaking Syrian.[20] In 1246 CE Aixue was recommended to Guyuk by Rabbanata 列班 •

---

16 Ibid, 38.
17 Yuan Jue 袁桷, "漳州路同知朝列大夫贈汴梁路同知騎都尉開封郡伯馬公神道碑銘 *Zhangzhoulu Tongzhi Chaoliedafu zeng Bianlianglu Tongzhi Jiduwei Kaifeng Junbo Magong Shendao Beiming*", *Qingrong Jushi Ji* 清容居士集, (Shanghai: The Commercial Press, 1936), 395-397.
18 Chen Yuan 陳垣, *Western and Central Asians in China Under the Mongols,* transl. Ch'ien Hsing-hai, 錢星海, L.C. Goodrich (Los Angeles: Monumenta Serica at the University of California, 1966), 41-46, 143-145.
19 Huang, *Mashi Shipu, 38-40*; Yuan Haowen 元好問, "Hengzhou Cishi Majun Shendaobei 恒州刺史馬君神道碑", in *Yishan Xiansheng Wenji* 遺山先生文集 (Shanghai: The Commercial Press, 1936), 272-274.
20 Pelliot, "Chrétiens d'Asie Centrale et d'extrême-Orient", 639.

阿答, a famous Nestorian missionary of the East Church,[21] since then he had been serving in the Mongol court until he died in 1308 CE.

Before being sent to Ilkhan Empire in the diplomatic mission to have an audience with Arghun in 1283 CE, Aixue had served in court as an interpreter for his proficiency in western languages for over thirty years, and the director of the Offices of Western Astronomy and Islamic Medicine for about twenty years.[22] The Ambassador of the mission, Bolod 孛羅, stayed in Iran while Aixue insisted returning to China in 1285 CE.[23] After a two-year adventurous journey from western lands back to China, Aixue was immediately appointed a series of vital posts, firstly President of Palace Library 秘書監 (*Mishu Jian*) in 1287 CE, two years later *Chongfu shi* 崇福使 (Director of *Chongfu Si* 崇福司), then in 1297 CE *Pingzhang Zhengshi* (Minister of State 平章政事) and *Qinguo Gong* 秦國公 (Duke of Qin Kingdom) in 1298 CE.[24]

Kublai awarded Aixue for his loyalty. Bolod, being the former Prime Minister of the Yuan government, was born in China but betrayed his mother country, while Aixue, a foreigner from western lands, pledged loyalty to the Yuan Dynasty and risked his life in returning China, whose dedication to the country overweighed that of Bolod.[25]

Aixue got married with Sala 撒剌, a Kerait woman, who was a maid serving the wife of Guyuk in the court.[26] The name Sala might come from a typical Christian name "Sarah".

The eldest son of Aixue, Yeliya 也里牙 or Elijah, inherited the rank and posts from his father, which included *Qin guo gong* (Duke of Qin Kingdom), *Chongfu Shi,*, *Taiyi Yuan Shi* 太醫院使 (the head of the Royal Hospital and Academy of Medicine) and the officer of *Si tian tai* 司天臺 (the Imperial Astronomical Observatory).[27] He married the daughter of Chancellor Timor. As the head of

---

21   P. Pelliot, *Les Mongols et ía Papauté,* transl. Feng Chengjun 馮承鈞 (Beijing: Zhonghuashuju, 2008), 28-62. Cheng Jufu 程鉅夫, "Fulin Zhongxianwang Shendaobei 拂菻忠獻王神道碑", in *Quan Yuan Wen* (vol. 535), 324.

22   Xiao Qiqing 蕭啟慶, "Yuandai de Tongshi he Yishi: Duoyuan minzu guojia zhong de goutong renwu 元代的通事和譯史: 多元民族國家中的溝通人物" [*The translators and the interpreters in the Yuan Dynasty: the communicating figures in a multi-ethnic Nation*], in *Yuanchaoshi Xinlun* 元朝史新論, (Taipei: Asian Culture Ind. Co. Ltd. 台北: 允晨文化實業有限公司, 1999), 348.

23   Pelliot, "Chrétiens d'Asie Centrale et d'extrême-Orient", 640.

24   *Yuan Shi* 元史, (Beijing: Zhonghuashuju, 1978), (vol. 134), 3248-3249; Pelliot, "Chrétiens d'Asie Centrale et d'extrême-Orient"; Cheng Jufu, "Fulin Zhongxianwang Shendaobei", 324-326; Han Rulin 韓儒林, "Aixue zhi zai tantao 愛薛之再探討" [Restudy on Aixue], in *Qiong Lu Ji* 穹廬集, (Shanghai: Shanghai renmin chubanshe, 1982), 93-108.

25   Cheng, "Fulin Zhongxianwang Shendaobei", 325.

26   Ibid.

27   *Yuan Shi*, (vol. 134) 3248-3249; Cheng, "Fulin Zhongxianwang Shendaobei", 325-326.

the Royal Hospital and Academy of Medicine, he was in charge of all affairs of making and delivering medicine in the court and administrating the physicians in the empire.[28] Elijah was executed in 1330 CE (the first year of *Zhishun* 至順 Period) under the charge of sorcery activities of using Taoist *Fulu* 符籙 (talismanic registers) in the court.[29] The family declined thereafter. However, this record was still suspected. Tu Ji 屠寄 considers that the real reason for the execution was that Yeliya got involved in the political struggle of the throne, with no clues for Elijah's conversion to Taoism traced in the extant materials.[30]

Tianha 腆合 (or Denha) was the second son of Aixue. He served as *Hanlin Xueshi Chengzhi* 翰林學士承旨 (Hanlin Academician Recipient of Edicts) and was given an honorable title *Zishan Dafu* 資善大夫 (Grandee Admonisher of the Fifth Order). Heisi 黑廝 was the third son. He was an official serving in the Department of *Xuanhui* 宣徽院 and his responsibility was to manage the court diet including meals, drinks, and other things relating to foods and feasts.[31] Kuolijisi 闊里吉思, also recorded as Kefujisu 克呼濟蘇, was the fourth son of Aixue and enjoyed a bureaucratic honor of *Taizhong Dafu* 太中大夫 (Superior Grand Master of the Palace). Luhe 魯合 (possibly Luke) inherited Aixue's third-court-grade post in *Guanghui Si* 廣惠司 (the Bureau of Islamic Medicine).[32] As the Director of the Bureau, he was in charge of making Arabic medicines and medical syrup, healing *Kesig* 怯薛 (the imperial guards), the poor and the lonely in the capital.[33] Yueni 約尼, probably being the Christian name Johnny, was the youngest son of Aixue. His name was only recorded in *Fulin Zhongxianwang Shendao Bei* 拂菻忠獻王神道碑 [*the Tombstone of Loyal King of Fulin*] and he himself was a *Kesig* of Royal Palace *Xingsheng* 興聖宮宿衛.[34] Aixue had a daughter named Onesimus 阿納昔木思.[35]

Besides the above-mentioned sons and daughter of Aixue, there was another figure, whose name was Ashikedai 阿實克岱 but was never mentioned in *Yuan Shi* 元史 and *the Tombstone of Loyal King of Fulin*. Chen Yuan pointed out that it was Aixue himself, while Han Rulin considered that it was the eldest son of Aixue, who might accompany the latter to Ilkan Empire as an inter-

---

28 *Yuan Shi*, (vol. 88) 2220-2221.
29 Ibid, (vol. 34) 761.
30 Tu Ji 屠寄, *Mengwuer shiji* 蒙兀兒史記, (Shanghai: Shanghai guji chubanshe, 2012), 714.
31 *Yuan Shi*, (vol. 134) 3249; Cheng Jufu, "Fulin Zhongxianwang Shendaobei" 326.
32 Ibid.
33 *Yuan Shi*, (vol. 88) 2221.
34 Cheng, "Fulin Zhongxianwang Shendaobei", 326.
35 *Yuan Shi*, (vol. 34) 761.

preter. Han speculated further that Ashikedai might hold Director of *Chongfu Si* after Aixue.³⁶

3   The Varied Paths to the Officialdom

3.1   *The Ma Family: From Trading to Confucianism*

The Ma Family had served Jin and Liao governments for a long time due to their economic and military talent. In the early Yuan Dynasty, Ma Yuehenai was appointed a high official position for his financial contribution. The close relation between Yuehenai and Kublai was emphasized greatly in *Yuan Shi* 元史 [*The Official History of Yuan Dynasty*]. It was said that in 1259 when Kublai conquered the Southern Song Dynasty, his army stationed in Kaifeng, where he received the aid from Yuehenai who was in charge of local financial affairs at that time. As recorded, Yuehenai transported millions of *chin* 斤 of salt from Jinan 濟南 to Kaifeng, and he additionally made a huge donation to Kublai in the following year (1260 CE) when the latter was involved in political struggle with Arigh Bukha (died in 1266 CE). Kublai promised he would award him in return for his generosity and loyalty. As expected, Yuehenai was appointed the Minister of Board of Rites and was presented a golden military seal.³⁷

The astonishing fortune of Yuehenai was a key to his entering the upper class. As was recorded in *Yuan Shi,* he donated five hundred warhorses to Kublai personally. In fact, the commercial tradition could be traced back to the third generation of the family. Since Ba Saoma Yelichu (Bar Sauma Elišo) moved to Tianshan of Jingzhou, a place close to the border trading market, he became wealthy through farming and cultivation.³⁸ Ma Zuchang confessed that both his grand-grandfather and grandfather were eminently rich around the border region.³⁹ The case of Yuehenai was not exceptional. On the whole, there were many merchants, especially the Uyghur ones, who had established their official career and had associated with the golden family for their possessions and economical talent.⁴⁰

---

36   Yao Sui 姚遂, "Zhongyigong zhi 考崇福使阿實克岱追封秦國公忠翊公制", *in Quan Yuan Wen,* (vol. 300) 360-361. Han, "Aixue zhi zai tantao", 114-115.
37   *Yuan Shi,* (vol. 134) 3245.
38   Yuan, "Hengzhou Cishi Majun Shendaobei", 606.
39   Ma Zuchang 馬祖常, "Gu Libu Shangshu Magong Shendao Beiming 故禮部尚書馬公神道碑銘" [*The Inscription of Deceased Duke Ma, Minister of Board of Rites*], in *Quan Yuan Wen,* (vol, 1042) 499.
40   Cf. Meng, *Yuandai Jieji Zhidu,* 125-130. Xiao Qiqing, *Xiyuren yu Yuanchu Zhengzhi* 西域人與元初政治 [*Westerners with politics in the early Yuan Dynasty*], (Taipei: National Taiwan University 台北：台灣大學, 1966), 10-15.

After Ma Yuehenai died, the Ma family declined suddenly. Two relevant reasons were elaborated in the inscription memorizing the deceased mother of Ma Zuchang. For one, the family was dispossessed by the treacherous Prime Minister Ahmad 阿合馬, and for another, their descendants were unfamiliar with the financial managements. As narrated by Ma Zuchang himself, the grown sons never stepped into the family lands, and thus the family property was run by the household servants.[41] The first reason indicated the conflict between Christians and Muslims in Yuan China,[42] as Ahmad was a Uyghur Islamic merchant and was in charge of finances of the government. The second reason revealed that the Ma family had lost their commercial tradition, resulting in their dependence on their household servants to run their farms and business on their behalf.[43]

Yuan Jue 袁桷 (1266-1327) put forward the third reason. He held that Ma Shichang was so absorbed in associating with elites that he spent out all his property, which led the family to a situation of poverty 傾眥粟結俊彥家日困落.[44] Whatever reason it might be, due to the family's impoverished situation, the descendants were compelled to revitalize the family in other ways. Yuan Jue proposed that the method was the Confucianism[45]. For instance, Ma Run, the son of Ma Shichang, found himself homeless and deprived at the age of ten. Fortunately, he was familiar with Confucian classics and he finally passed the imperial examination at the capital city. Since then he was appointed some public posts and raised his social position.[46] In fact, it has been a quite long tradition before Ma Run's success that the youngsters of the family had been trained in Confucianism.[47] As was mentioned above, among eleven sons of Ma Yuehenai, most were given Chinese names instead of Nestorian ones. The family succeeded in reviving through the imperial examination in the Mid-Yuan Dynasty.

41 Ma Zuchang, "Gu Xianbi Liangjun Furen Yangshi Muzhimin 故顯妣梁郡夫人楊氏墓誌銘" [The Epitaph of My Deceased Mother, Madame of Liang County], in *Quan Yuan Wen*, (vol, 1042) 519.
42 Zhou, "Jin Yuan shidai de Jingjiao".
43 Meng, *Yuandai Jieji Zhidu*.
44 Yuan, "Kaifeng Junbo Magong Shendao Beiming", 396.
45 Ibid.
46 Ma,"Gu Libu Shangshu Magong Shendao Beiming", 499.
47 It was recorded that Ma Yuehenai had the children trained with *Shi* 詩, *Shu* 書 and *Li* 禮 (Chinese: 以詩書禮儀訓其子孫), *Shi*, *Shu* and *Li*, literally meant *Shi Jing* 詩經 [The Classic of Poetry], *Shu Jing* 尚書 [The Classic of History or Book of Documents] and *Zhou Li* 周禮 [The Rites of Zhou], referred to the Confucian classics and rituals. Cf. Su Tianjue, "Ti Mashi lanhui tu 題馬氏蘭蕙圖" [Inscription on the Orchid Painting by Ma], in *Zixi Wengao* 滋溪文稿 (Beijing: Zhonghuashuju, 1997), (vol, 29): 499.

Ma Run encouraged the revival of Confucianism in *Guangzhou* 光州. For example, in order to improve the local customs, he built a temple for the distinguished Confucian scholar Sima Guang 司馬光 (1019-1086) during his official service there.[48] He was thus considered a Confucian and was recorded in *Songyuan Xue'an Buyi* 宋元學案補遺 [*Additional Intellectual Cases of Song and Yuan*]. Besides, Ma Run excelled in literature and had published the collected works titled as "*Qiao Yin Ji* 樵隐集" [*The Collected Works of the Hermitic Woodcutter*].

Among the offspring who passed the imperial examinations, Ma Zuchang was the most notable one, and therefore, Su Tianjue 蘇天爵 (1294-1352) considered Ma Zuchang as the first Confucian scholar of the family.[49] Ma Zuchang won the first scholarship both in the Provincial and the Metropolitan Examinations (in 1315 CE), and the second scholarship in the Palace Examination, since then he went into a successful public life and established himself President of the Censorate and Vice Military Affairs Commissioner eventually.[50]

Many family members followed the same regular official path as Ma Zuchang did, and they were: Ma Zuyi 馬祖義, who succeeded in *Xiangshi* 鄉試 (the provincial examination) and was granted *Hanlin guoshiyuan bianxiu* 翰林國史院編修 (the Compiler in *Hanlin* Historiography Academy); Ma Zuxiao 馬祖孝, *Jinshi* 進士 (the advanced scholar who passed the Palace Examination) in 1315 CE; Ma Zuqian 馬祖謙, *Guozi jinshi* 國子進士 (the advanced scholar through the imperial examination as a student of the Imperial Academy), Associate Administer in *Baode* County 保德州同知, *Darughachi* 達魯花赤 of Shulu District 束鹿 and Archivist of Zhaogong Brigade 昭功萬戶府知事; Ma Shide 馬世德, *Jinshi, Xingbu Shangshu* 刑部尚書 (Minister of Board of Punishment); Ma Zugong 馬祖恭, *Guozisheng* 國子生 (the student of Imperial Academy); Ma Zushan 馬祖善, *Jinshi*; Ma Zuxian 馬祖憲 and Ma Xianzi 馬獻子, both were *Guozi jinshi*; Ma Zuyuan 馬祖元, Ma Zuzhou 馬祖周, Timur 帖木爾 and Ma Youyi 馬猶子 were all *Xianggong Jinshi* 鄉貢進士 (the presented scholar who succeeded in the provincial examination but failed in the metropolitan examination at Board of Rites).[51] To sum up, it seemed

---

48   Wang Zicai 王梓材, Feng Yunhao 馮雲濠, *Songyuan Xue'an Buyi* 宋元學案補遺 [*Additional Intellectual Cases of Song and Yuan*], (Shanghai: The Commercial Press, 1994), (vol. 82) 215.

49   Su, *Zixi Wengao*, 138.

50   Chen, *Yuan Xiyuren Huahua Kao*, 18-23.

51   Cf. Huang, *Mashi Shipu*, 36-40; Qian Daxin 錢大昕, *Yuan Jinshi Biao* 元進士表, (Nanjing: Jiangsu Guji chubanshe, 1998), 42, 131; Su, *Zixiwengao*, 138; Qian Daxin, *Yuanshi shizu biao* 元史氏族表, (Nanjing: Jiangsu guji chubanshe, 1998), 279; Wang and Feng, *Song Yuan*

that the Ma family had lost the commercial tradition by the Mid-Yuan Dynasty, and meanwhile, the Nestorian faith of the family became too vague to be recognized in the 14th century.

3.2   Aixue's Family: Prominence in Western Scientific Knowledge

In contrast to the success of the Ma Family, Aixue started his official career quite differently. As mentioned above, Aixue had served in *Guanghui Si* 廣惠司 (Bureau of Islamic Medical) and *Huihui Sitian Tai* 回回司天臺 (Islamic Astronomical Bureau) for a long time, and his offspring thus inherited the posts in these bureaus. Similarly, the Director of *Chongfu Si* also became the hereditary post of the family since this office was founded by Aixue.[52]

Aixue and his family were esteemed for their talent of western linguistics, western science and technology, and the familiarity with Nestorianism as well. Naturally, Aixue was put to some relevant posts.

Firstly, he was responsible for the interpreting affairs in the court as a *kelemechi* 怯里馬赤 for his linguistic talent. When the Mongols entered the central plains while conquering the Jin Dynasty, the linguistic issue in the empire became diversified and complicated. The Mongol rulers and the courtiers, speaking different languages, needed to communicate with each other. In consequence, the Mongol emperors were always accompanied by reliable interpreters. Aixue was an interpreter, who played a significant role both in government affairs and diplomatic affairs. When Aixue arrived in Mongolia in 1240s, the Mongol Empire was becoming a multicultural nation and was in great need of multilingual talents. Since then, Aixue had been serving in the court as a *kelemechi* until 1270s. *Kelemechi* was considered belonging to *Kesig*. Although not given any official rank, it was still a highly rewarded post. The interpreters were much trusted by the emperors due to the long-term accompany, and, as a result, many interpreters got vital official posts accordingly in Yuan China.[53] Aixue was a typical example. As an interpreter and an envoy, he visited the western lands several times, and eventually grasped the opportunity to get the promotion. In 1283 CE, Aixue attended the mission to Persia as the *kelemachi*. When he came back from Iran, he was appointed a series of much

---

Xue'an Buyi, 215; Gan Wenchuan 干文傳, "*Chongxiu Xueji* 重修學記" [The Inscription of the re-constructing the school], in *Wudu Wencui Xuji* 吳都文萃續集(vol, 4).

52   Yin Xiaoping, "Chongfu Si and Zhangjiao Si: On the Christian Administration in Yuan China", in *Sanyijiao Yanjiu---Lin Wushu.Xiansheng Guxi Jinian Lunwenji* 三夷教研究——林悟殊先生古稀紀念論文集, ed. Zhang Xiaogui 張小貴 (Lanzhou: Lanzhou University Press, 2014), 381-404

53   Xiao, "Yuandai de Tongshi he Yishi", 323-384.

more important official posts. Even when Aixue was promoted to Director of the Palace Library in 1287 CE,[54] he still served Kublai as an interpreter.[55]

Secondly, Aixue was involved in the foundation of *Huihui Sitian Tai,* or Islamic Astronomical Bureau, due to his learning in western astronomy. In the early 1260s, Kublai nominated Aixue to administer two offices associated with the western astronomic and medical affairs.[56] In terms of western astronomy, it seemed that the government had not established a specific institution for it in the beginning. The related office was attached to *Kesig*. Aixue managed this office until *Huihui Sitian Tai* was founded in 1271 CE.[57] The first Directorate of the Bureau was the distinguished Arabic astronomer Jamal al-Din 札馬剌丁, who was also appointed the Directorate of the Palace Library two years later.[58] In comparison with Jamal al-Din, Aixue served a shorter period in *Huihui Sitian Tai,* and played a less important role. In 1273 CE, even though Aixue had held the Directorate of the Islamic Medical Bureau, he still served as the interpreter in the meeting of Kublai and Jamal al-Din due to his excellence in both Arabic and western astronomy.[59] Nevertheless, the initial establishment of Islamic Astronomical Bureau should be attributed to the participation of Aixue. Possibly, being one of the founding members, his son Elijah was appointed a post of this Bureau by inheritance.[60]

Thirdly, Aixue was involved in the preparation of *Guanghui Si,* or the Islamic Medical Bureau, for his medical talent. More specifically, the establishment of *Guanghui Si* was largely relevant to Aixue.[61] In 1260s, Aixue was asked to administer the western medical affairs, and in 1273 CE, as was recorded in *Yuan Shi,* "[the emperor] transformed the Capital Medical Institution founded by Aixue to the Bureau, and [the emperor] named it *Guanghui Si* 改回回愛薛所立京師醫藥院名廣惠司".[62] He was undoubtedly the first Directorate of this newly built bureau.[63] The primary official rank of *Guanghui Si*, with reference to the Directorate of *Tai Yiyuan* 太醫院 (the Imperial Medical Bureau) established in 1272 CE, was supposed to enjoy the lower rank of fifth court degree 次

---

54 *Yuan Mishujian Zhi* 元秘書監志, ed. Gao Rongsheng 高榮盛 (Hangzhou: Zhejiang guji chubanshe 杭州: 浙江古籍出版社, 1992), (vol, 9) 165.
55 Ibid, (vol, 1) 32.
56 *Yuan Shi,* (vol. 134) 3249.
57 Ibid, (vol. 90) 2297.
58 *Yuan Shi,* (vol. 7) 136. *Yuan Mishujian Zhi,* (vol. 9) 165.
59 *Yuan Mishujian Zhi,* (vol, 1) 31. Xiao Qiqing believed that the *kelemachi* was the in-turns duty of Aixue in *Kesig*. Cf. Xiao, "Tongshi he Yishi", 434.
60 Cheng, "Fulin Zhongxianwang Shendaobei", 326.
61 Ibid, 325,
62 *Yuan Shi,* (vol. 8) 147.
63 Ibid, (vol 88) 2222.

五品; in 1319 CE its rank reached the upper third court degree 正三品.⁶⁴ Considering the deepest relationship between Aixue and *Guanghui Si*, his son Luke inherited the post of Director of it.⁶⁵

In summary, Aixue served as *kelemachi* for the longest time. When the Yuan Dynasty constructed the new nation that combined systems and institutions of the Jin, the Mongol and the Song, Aixue was appointed the directors of those newly-built bureaus relating to western astronomy and medical science. Due to the western scientific knowledge passed down in the family, his offspring occupied the posts in these bureaus through official inheritance.

4 The Reasons of the Different Paths

As is discussed above, the Aixue family excelled in the scientific area, while the Ma family performed better in Chinese literature, Confucianism and local administration.

As for the religious achievements, although the Ma family originated from "the western Nestorian nobility 西域聶斯脫里貴族", they had not devoted themselves to Christian affairs. Conversely, Aixue and his family obviously made more contributions to the prosperity of Christianity in China. Unlike the Ma family, Aixue kept a close relationship with both the upper Mongol Nestorian women and the missionaries of East Church. One contribution that Aixue made was that he founded the first administrating office *Chongfu Si* for Christian affairs in China. It was the advocacy made by Aixue that *Chongfu Si* could be founded in the central authorities in 1289 CE.⁶⁶ Therefore, Aixue was the first officer to be appointed the Directorate to the bureau. During his official service in *Chongfu Si*, he successfully promoted the official position of Christianity to be equal to the Buddhism and Taoism. With Aixue's strong support, the Samarkandian Nestorian Ma Xuelijisi 馬薛里吉思 (Mar Sarghis) accomplished building seven churches in Zhenjiang 鎮江 and Hangzhou 杭州.⁶⁷

What leads to the dissimilar performance of two families? I think the duration of settlement might be of significant relevance. From Aixue's arrival in 1240s to the execution of Elijah in 1330 CE, it was just eighty years that witnessed the flourishing and fall of this family. However, as for the Ma family, it

---

64 Ibid.
65 Cheng, "Fulin Zhongxianwang Shendaobei", 326; *Yuan Shi*, (vol. 134) 3250.
66 Yin Xiaoping, "*Yuandai Chongfushi Aixue shishi bushuo* 元代崇福使愛薛史事補說" [*Supplements to the historical events of director Aixue of Chongfu Si in the Yuan Dynasty*], *Xiyuyanjiu* 西域研究 [*Western Regions Studies*], (3) 2014: 95-103.
67 Yin, "The Christians in Jiangnan".

had been almost two hundred years since they moved to and settled down in China. The Ma family were more easily influenced and attracted by Chinese culture, thus they have the characteristics of being indigenized, in other words, being sinicized. Four causes should be taken into consideration when discussing the indigenization in Yuan China.

The first reason is the restart of the imperial examination in the Mid-Yuan Dynasty, which promoted the recovery of Confucianism.

The scholarly performance in Yuan China was usually disregarded. As is criticized, under the racial-based system of Tatars, the Confucians were despised and under-classified to the ninth class in the society. Therefore, the restart of the Imperial Examination in 1315 CE (the 2nd year in the Yanyou Period 延祐) was considered a turning point in the revival of Confucianism in Yuan China.[68] Not only the youngsters of Mongol, *Semu* and *Han* could be provided with a regular path to the officialdom besides the inheritance, but also the descendants from the scholarly families of the Southern Song or other lower classes could enter the public life through the imperial examination.[69] As a case in point, Ma Zuchang was such an scholarly-official who succeeded in the Palace Examination in 1315 CE. Together with him were some Chinese scholars such as Xu Youren 許有壬 and Huang Jin 黃溍. Both Xu and Huang were born in a Confucian family of the Southern Song Dynasty and thusly had a close relationship with Ma Zuchang. The imperial examination produced a group of multicultural scholar-officials for the government. Moreover, it lowered the existed barrier between the classes and ethnic groups, which accelerated the social mobility in China. The Ma family chose the Imperial Examination as a regular path to the public life as most of Chinese Confucian families did, which was considered a strong proof that it had been transformed to a Confucian family, and this could be fulfilled only in the middle of the Yuan times when the Imperial Examination was restarted.

The second is the unrestrained mobility of Mongol and *Semu* people in Yuan China.[70] Generally, the migrating routes of the Ma family was from western lands outside of China to the nomadic Northwest China, then the region in

---

68 Meng, *Yuandai Jieji Zhidu*, 46-64.
69 Xiao Qiqing, "*Yuandai keju yu jingying liudong: Yi Yuantong* yuannian jinshi wei zhongxin 元代科舉與菁英流動 ——以元統元年進士為中心" [The Imperial Examination and the social mobility of elites: on the successful candidates in the first year of *Yuantong* Period], *Hanxueyanjiu* 漢學研究 [*Chinese Studies*], 5(1) 1987: 129-160; Su, *Zixi Wengao*, 65-66; Chen, *Yuan Xiyuren Huahua Kao*, 113.
70 As pointed out by Zhao Yi 趙翼, the Mongol and *semu* people could dwell and move freely according to the institution of the Yuan Dynasty 元制，蒙古色目人隨便居住. Cf Zhao Yi, *Haiyucongkao* 陔餘叢考, (Beijing: Zhonghuashuju, 2006), 355.

Liaodong 遼東 (Jurchen Jin), and then in *Jingzhou* 淨州, the junction region between Mongol and Jin. It was until the early Yuan period that the family entered the central China. In the time of Ma Yuehenai, the family settled in Kaifeng, the capital of the Northern Song Dynasty. In the generation of Ma Run, the family moved to Guangzhou 光州, the hometown of famous scholar Sima Guang. Ma Run recognized Guangzhou as his birthplace instead of Jingzhou or western lands, and during his official service in Guangzhou he led the ceremony in memory of Sima Guang to educate the local people and uphold the local customs. I hold that such behavior was under the influence of the dominant culture in Guangzhou. After Ma Run, the young generations became officials by passing the imperial examination. Due to their official services in the governments at all levels, they were sent to all parts of China, such as Songjiang 松江, Chengdu 成都, Nanjing 南京 and other academic centers of China, to participate in the local administration. Luo Xianglin 羅香林 claimed that the Christian officials like the Ma family members spread the Christianity when travelling around the country.[71] However, I hold that it just led to the opposite consequence. Many Ma members who got official posts were already Sinicized, and moreover, they would be more easily attracted and influenced by the local Chinese culture. Comparing the Ma family inhabiting the hinterland of China with those living in the plains of Ongut tribe, it would be more convinced. Many Nestorian relics uncovered in Inner Mongolia reveal that the Ongut tribal people maintained the Christian faith for a long time, with little changed in their spiritual life.[72]

The third one is the intermarriage. In a multi-ethnic and multi-cultural society, the intermarriage between different ethnic groups is a key to the group acculturation. Xiao Qiqing 蕭啟慶 noticed that it was very common for those Mongol and *Semu* advanced scholars 進士 [*Jinshi*] to get married with Chinese women.[73] According to the studies by Hong Jinfu 洪金富, about 279 inter-marital cases in Yuan China were Chinese women marring non-Chinese men, and the number of inverse cases being 160.[74] As to the Ma family, they initially got married with Chinese women in the late Jin times[75] and more frequently in the

---

71 Luo Xianglin 羅香林, *Tang Yuan erdai zhi Jingjiao* 唐元二代之景教, (Hongkong: Zhongguo xueshe 香港: 中國學社, 1966), 167.

72 Gai, "Yuandai Wanggubu diqu de Jingjiao yiji".

73 Xiao, "Yuandai Keju yu jingying liudong", 182-187; Xiao Qiqing, "Yuandai menggu semu jinshi beijing de fenxi 元代蒙古色目進士背景的分析" [On the background of the Mongol and *semu* scholars in the Yuan Dynasty], *Hanxueyanjiu*, 18(1) 1990: 101-137.

74 Hong Jinfu 洪金富, "*Yuandai hanren yu feihanren tonghun wenti chutan* 元代漢人與非漢人通婚問題初探", (resume publication) *Shi Huo* 食貨, 6 (12) 1977: 652.

75 Ibid, 655.

Yuan times. For example, the daughter of Ma Qingxiang married a Chinese named Yang 楊;[76] Ma Yuehenai married Bai 白氏 (wife) and Zhang 張氏 (concubine);[77] The wife of Ma Run was Lady Yang 楊, who was the daughter of Chinese official Yang Yan 楊琰, furthermore, two concubines of Ma Run were Chinese, respectively Li 李氏 and Liang 梁氏.[78] Ma Zuchang married a Kerait 克烈 woman named Suo 索氏,[79] and his sister married Dulietu 篤列圖 (1312-1348), who was *Zhuang Yuan* 狀元 (Number One Scholar) in 1330 CE and the follower of Ma Zuchang.[80] The granddaughter of Ma Zuchang was a noted female, who married Feng Wenju 馮文舉, a *Jinshi* and the local administrator in Chengdu. As a descendant of a scholar-official of the Yuan Dynasty, Ma committed suicide for the country together with her husband when the rebel army captured the city. The intermarriage with Chinese or Mongol scholar-officials could be regarded as the cause as well as the embodiment of the acculturation of the Ma family.

The fourth one is the social circle. The social circle of Ma Zuchang mainly consisted of the intellectuals and literati, including not only the Chinese scholars but also the Mongol and *Semu* elites, such as Yu Ji 虞集, Chen Lü 陳旅, Sa Tianci 薩天賜, Wang Shixi 王士熙, Wang Jie 王結, Wang Jiwen 王繼忞, Fu Ruojin 傅若金, Xue Han 薛漢, Yang Zhonghong 楊載 and etc.[81] As was described by Su Tianjue 蘇天爵, the social circle of Ma Zuchang consisted of two typical groups, one being the elites in the South Yangtze River region 江左賢達, the other the scholars of the State Academy 館閣之士.[82] Chen Lü (1288-1343), being one of the portages of Ma Zuchang, was born in a Confucian family in Fujian Province. He was discovered by his Bole 伯樂 Ma Zuchang when the latter was in his official service in Fujian as the Provincial Judge of the Censorate. Chen Lü went to the capital with Ma Zuchang and was recommended by Zhao Shiyan 趙世延, who was another outstanding scholar from Ongut tribe, to the State Academy later.[83] Among the disciples of Ma Zuchang were many advanced scholars, such as Yuan Jue 袁桷, Yu Ji and etc. Just as con-

---

76   Yuan, "*Hengzhou Cishi*", 606.
77   Yuan, "Kaifeng Junbo Magong Shendao Beiming", 396.
78   It should be pointed out that the mother of Yang Yan was the sister of Ma Yuehenai. See Ma, "Gu Libu Shangshu Magong Shendao Beiming", 518.
79   Su, *Zixi Wengao*, 143.
80   Xiao Qiqing, "*Yuanchao duozu shiren quan de xingcheng chutan* 元朝多族士人圈的形成初探" [A preliminary study on the formation of a multi-ethnic scholars circle in the Yuan Dynasty], in *Yuanchaoshi Xinlun*, 216.
81   Yin, *Yuan Yelikewen Kaoshu*, 175-177.
82   Su, *Zixi Wengao*, 499.
83   *Yuan Shi*, (vol. 190) 4347-4348; Chen Lü 陳旅, *Anyatang Ji* 安雅堂集, "Preface".

cluded in an elegiac poem *"Wan Ma Boyong Zhongcheng"* 挽馬伯庸中丞 by Hu Zhu 胡助:

> His eminent writings set an ideal model for the state academy; the rituals he established were eulogized in the government; for his dedication to enforcing the law [in the Censorate], his hair turned grey; being favored by him many talents were uncovered and collected. 文章宗館閣，禮樂著朝廷。執法頭先白，掄才眼更青。

The Ma family could not have converted to Confucianism all of a sudden. Conversely, they had experienced a very slow transition in two hundred years---from the Liao to the Jin and finally to the Yuan Dynasty, in a long run and step-by-step process of sinicization. It looked more like a Confucian family rather than a Christian one in the middle of Yuan times. Their achievements in both literature and Confucianism indicated their active embrace of Chinese culture instead of passive reception. Otherwise, they could not have performed so well in the scholarly circles in Yuan China.

5   Conclusion

There were many *Yelikewen* (Christians) in Yuan China, but regarding to their historical positions and contributions, they still lacked the due influence. In contrast to the Christians in the Tang Dynasty, the religious activities of *Yelikewen* were relatively less attractive and less recorded. The account of their missionary work was quite incomplete. Only in *Zhishun Zhenjiang zhi* 至順鎮江志 [*the Gazzetter of Zhenjiang in the Zhishun Period*] could we find some scattered information relating to the religious aspects, such as the facts of building seven churches by Ma Xuelijisi,[84] and the settlement of some *Yelikewen* elites, a local residence registration of nearly 350 *Yelikewen in* Zhenjiang.[85] However, the lives of these 350 *Yelikewen* people still remain unknown.

In Chinese history-writing tradition, only officials and elites could be recorded in the official documents. Consequently, most of known *Yelikewen* were officials. The Ma family and the Aixue's family were cases in point and the relevant account was more detailed. Based on these materials, I delineate the two families' Nestorian faith, discuss their different official paths, professional

---

84   *Zhishun Zhenjiang zhi* 至順鎮江志 [*the Gazzetter of Zhenjiang in the Zhishun Period*], ed. Tuotuo 脫脫, YuXilu 俞希魯，(Nanjing: Jiangsu guji chubanshe, 1999), 365-366.
85   Ibid, 90-93.

performances and roles in the society. From the perspective of the spreading Christianity, Aixue played a more significant role in the Christian history in China by successfully founding *Chongfu Si*. This first bureau for administrating Christian affairs in China proved that Christianity had reached a higher official position, which could compete with Taoism and Buddhism. Besides, it sustained the local Christian development to some extent. Additionally, Aixue and his family helped spread the western scientific knowledge in China, including Islamic medical knowledge and Islamic astronomical knowledge. Aixue had himself an outstanding multi-linguistic talent and held the post of *kelemechi* for a long time.

The Ma family represented another type of official Christians. This Uighur family moved from Central Asia to China long before the Yuan Dynasty was founded. They excelled in the commercial and military affairs, and represented the *Semu* merchants, on whom Kublai Khan relied heavily in the early Yuan times. However, the family declined before long because of their political conflict with Muslim officials and the later economical failure. The later generations returned to the public life through the Imperial Examination. In the middle of the Yuan Dynasty, there emerged lots of advanced scholars in the family. They associated with Chinese or non-Chinese scholars by marriage and social ties, and they performed eminently well in literature, Confucianism and politics, just as those Chinese scholars did.

Whether being sinicized or still believing in Christian, both families made great contributions to Chinese society. The Aixue's family eventually declined and faded away in Chinese history because of their involvement in the political struggle relating to the throne, while the sinicized Ma family gradually integrated with Chinese culture and became a part of Chinese after the Yuan Dynasty.

CHAPTER 10

From "Shiyuan 十願" (Ten Vows) to "Shijie 十誡" (Ten Commandments): Importance of Absent Elements in Translation as Case Study of Inculturation of Christianity during the Early Tang Dynasty (7th Century)

Zhu Li-Layec

In recent studies on Sino-Christian dialogues the concept of inculturation is constantly mentioned and applied as a methodical framework. It highlights the impact of the local culture which gives new form to the Christian texts and thus describes a process of re-making or re-formation of the content using expressions and ideas proper to the local culture.[1] While the most studies concentrate on Chinese elements that are added into the Christian literature to show how much the Christians were influenced by the local culture, it should be pointed out that on the other hand, the absence of certain Jewish-Christian elements is just as important for the analysis on the inculturation. This aspect has not yet been sufficiently investigated.

I would like to make a case study on the mentioned points of Jingjiao Christian based on "The book of Jesus" (Xuting mishisuo jing 序聽迷詩所經).[2] The

---

1 Nicolas Standaert S. J., "Inculturation and Catholic-Chinese Relations in Late Ming and Early Qing," in *Contacts between cultures. Eastern Asia: History and Social Sciences, Volume 4*, ed. Bernard Hung-Kay Luk (Lampeter: Edwin Mellen Pr, 1993) 329-334.

2 Book of Jesus, passages on the so called Ten Vows: 但事天尊之人，為說經義並作此經，一切事由大有歎處，多有事節由緒少。但事天尊人，及說天義，有人怕天尊法，自行善心及自作好，并諫人好，此人即是受天尊教，受天尊戒。人常作惡及教他人惡，此人不受天尊教，突墮惡道，命屬閻羅王。有人受天尊教，常道我受戒，教人受戒。人合怕天尊，每日諫悞，一切眾生皆各怕天尊，並綰攝諸眾生死活，管帶綰攝渾神。[…] 如有人受戒及不怕天尊，此人及一依佛法，不成受戒之所，即是返逆之人。[…] 以若人先事天尊及 聖上，即事父母不闕，此人拎天尊得福不多 。此三事，一種先事天尊。[…] 眾生有智計，合怕天尊及 聖上，並怕父母。好受天尊法教，不合破戒，天尊所受，及尊教，先遣眾生礼諸天佛，為佛受苦置立天地，只為清淨威力因緣。眾生若怕天尊，亦合怕懼 聖上。聖上前身福私，天尊補任，亦無自乃天尊耶，属自做聖上，一切眾生皆取聖上進心。如有人不取 聖上駆使，不伏其人，在拎眾生即是返逆。償若有人受 聖上進心，即成人中解事，並伏駆使，及好之人并諫他人做好，及不自作惡，此人即成受戒之所。[…] 第二事 聖上，[…] 據此， 聖上皆是神生，今世雖有父母見存，眾

focus is put on the passage of "Shiyuan 十願" (or more exactly "sanshi qiyuan 三事七願") – especially the commandments considering the monolatry – and the subsequent transition passage with which the narrative part begins. The following point is particularly remarkable: the elimination of the historical background of Israel that should be essential to justify the establishment of God's law and to introduce the narrative of Jesus' story. Such textual changes considering the absent elements in the Chinese texts makes it clear that the Jingjiao Christians have consciously tried to adapt themselves to the dominant Chinese cultural environment and to "translate" Christian doctrine to the local culture.

First of all, it should be pointed out that in this version of the Ten Vows, a shift of narrative perspectives can be observed: Whilst the subject of the Ten Commandments is God, the men are the ones to take the initiative in the Ten Vows. The Ten Commandments are given and perceived as a direct speech of God to the Israelis as it begins with the phrase "And God spake all these words, saying".³ So, we can find the following description in Exodus:

"Moses went up unto God, and the LORD called unto him out of the mountain, saying, Thus shalt thou say to the house of Jacob, and tell the children of Israel; Ye have seen what I did unto the Egyptians, and how I bare you on eagles' wings, and brought you unto myself. Now therefore, if ye will obey my voice indeed, and keep my covenant, then ye shall be a peculiar treasure unto me above all people: for all the earth is mine: And ye shall be unto me a kingdom of priests, and an holy nation. These are the words which thou shalt speak unto the children of Israel."⁴

生有智計，合怕天尊及 聖上，並怕父母。 […] 聖上維須勤伽習俊， 聖上宮殿於諸佛求得， 聖上身总是自由。第三須怕父母，祇承父母，將比天尊及 聖帝。以若人先事天尊及 聖上，即事父母不闕，此人於天尊得福不多。此三事， […] 第三事父母。為此普天在地並是父母行， […] 眾生有智計，合怕天尊及 聖上，並怕父母。 […] 天尊说云，所有眾生返諸惡等，返逆於尊，亦不是孝。第二願者，若孝父母并恭給所有。眾生孝養父母，恭承不闕，臨命終之時乃得天道為舍宅，為事父母，如眾生無父母，何人處生？第四願者，如有受戒人向一切眾生皆發善心，莫懷睢惡。第五願者，眾生自莫煞生，亦莫諫他煞，所以眾生命共人命不殊。第六願者，莫姦他人妻子，自莫宛。第七願者，莫作賊。第八，眾生錢財，見他富贵並有田宅奴婢，天睢妬。第九願者，有好妻子並好金屋，作文證加謀他人。第十願者，受他寄物，并將費用天尊，并處分事極多。 The text used in this paper is quoted from the edition of Wu Changxing 吴昶興 (ed.), *Daqin Jingjiao liuxing zhongguo bei. Daqin Jingiao wenxian shiyi* 大秦景教流行中國碑。大秦景教文獻釋義 [*Da Qin Jingjiao Liuxing Zhongguo Bei: The Xian Stele: Text Analyses with Commenteries on Documents of Da Qin Jingjiao*], (Xinbei Shi: Ganlan Huayi, 2015).

3   The Bible text, as in the following, is quoted from the online version of the King James Bible <https://www.kingjamesbibleonline.org/>. Here Exodus 20,1.

4   Ex., 19, 3-6.

Therefore, the subject is God who established the laws, while the Israelis as subordinated objects had to accept those laws. In contrast, the Chinese word "yuan 願" underlines the motivation of those who fear and follow the teaching of the Venerable in Heaven (or the heavenly Lord, as Li Tang translated it). The "yuan" signifies a solemn vow or oath before a deity to whom one prays with promises of a thanks offering, if his prayer were heard and fulfilled. In doing so, the individual is put to the foreground.[5] Thus, by translating "commandment" into "vow", a change of perspective takes place. We should remember here, that in the history of Israel it was God, not the people, who initiated the conclusion of the covenant. Such active role of God scarcely existed in the Chinese tradition. On the contrary, people in China had to ask for the mercy and benevolence of supernatural forces. Therefore, the change of the narrative perspective is understandable.

Now we turn to the two versions of the Decalogue which differ from each other on many points.

A substantial difference between the Ten Vows and Ten Commandments concerns the history of Israel: In the "Book of Jesus", the history of Israel was not mentioned at all. Consequently, the announcement of the Ten Commandments is removed from their religious-cultic context; this includes the commandments of monolatry, the observance of the Sabbath day, the prohibition of abuse of God's name, in short, the specific commandments and prohibitions for religious experiences which can be attributed to the God-led history of Israel, the chosen people. In Exodus we can read the following sentences:

> I am the LORD thy God, which have brought thee out of the land of Egypt, out of the house of bondage. (20,2); [...] Remember the sabbath day, to keep it holy. Six days shalt thou labour, and do all thy work: But the seventh day is the sabbath of the LORD thy God: in it thou shalt not do any work, thou, nor thy son, nor thy daughter, thy manservant, nor thy maidservant, nor thy cattle, nor thy stranger that is within thy gates: For in six days the LORD made heaven and earth, the sea, and all that in them is, and rested the seventh day: wherefore the LORD blessed the sabbath day, and hallowed it.[6]

Also in Deuteronomy the same (self-) assertion of God is to be found, though with different words:

---

5 *Gudai hanyu cidian* 古代漢語詞典 [*Lexicon of Classic Chinese*], (Beijing: Shangwu Yinshu guan, 2014).

6 Ex., 20, 2, 8-11.

> I am the LORD thy God, which brought thee out of the land of Egypt, from the house of bondage. Thou shalt have none other gods before me. Thou shalt not make thee any graven image, or any likeness of any thing that is in heaven above, or that is in the earth beneath, or that is in the waters beneath the earth: Thou shalt not bow down thyself unto them, nor serve them: for I the LORD thy God am a jealous God, visiting the iniquity of the fathers upon the children unto the third and fourth generation of them that hate me, And shewing mercy unto thousands of them that love me and keep my commandments. Thou shalt not take the name of the LORD thy God in vain: for the LORD will not hold him guiltless that taketh his name in vain. Keep the sabbath day to sanctify it, as the LORD thy God hath commanded thee. Six days thou shalt labour, and do all thy work: But the seventh day is the sabbath of the LORD thy God: in it thou shalt not do any work, thou, nor thy son, nor thy daughter, nor thy manservant, nor thy maidservant, nor thine ox, nor thine ass, nor any of thy cattle, nor thy stranger that is within thy gates; that thy manservant and thy maidservant may rest as well as thou. And remember that thou wast a servant in the land of Egypt, and that the LORD thy God brought thee out thence through a mighty hand and by a stretched out arm: therefore the LORD thy God commanded thee to keep the sabbath day.[7]

We can see clearly that in these passages the leadership of God who chose the Israelis as His people and intervened actively in men's history. Especially the liberation from Egypt plays a central role in the constitution and the establishment of the Ten Commandments. The Exodus story as a narrative element comes together with the patriarchal history of Genesis as a unique unity.[8] For this reason, they are treated extensively in the original version(s). However, in "Book of Jesus", the first commandments concerning the God-man-relationship were compressed into one single command: "All human beings have fear for the heavenly Lord … first, serve the heavenly Lord."[9] The accentuation of monotheism / monolatry is largely reduced. This can probably be explained by the fact that the "Book of Jesus" is not a complete translation of the Bible, and there is no mention of the history of Israel which builds the main part of the Old Testament. Therefore, it had to be difficult to explain or to justify the first commandments *en détail*.

---

7 Deuteronomy 5, 6-15.
8 Jan Assmann, *Exodus. Die Revolution der Alten Welt* (München: C.H. Beck, 2015), 80f.
9 English translation from Li Tang, *A Study of the History of Nestorian Christianity in China and its Literature in Chinese. Together with a New English Translation of the Dunhuang Nestorian Documents*. 2nd revised edition. (Frankfurt / Main: Peter Lang, 2004), 149-150.

We then encounter the decisive distinction between the Jewish religion and others: For the Israelis, faith in God is inextricably connected to their own history since they had personally experienced God and His guidance. Basically speaking, the presence of God and the experience of individuals with God represent the core of the faith that begins with the covenant between God and Abraham and goes through the history of Israel. In particular, God's guidance is considered the basic for the promulgation of his laws as he spoke to Moses:

> Ye have seen what I did unto the Egyptians, and how I bare you on eagles' wings, and brought you unto myself. Now therefore, if ye will obey my voice indeed, and keep my covenant, then ye shall be a peculiar treasure unto me above all people: for all the earth is mine: And ye shall be unto me a kingdom of priests, and an holy nation. These are the words which thou shalt speak unto the children of Israel.[10]

The covenant between God and the Israelis was affirmed and strengthened through his repetitive self-assertion.

The monolatric or the monotheistic tradition of the people of Abraham is therefore inseparable from the historical event of the liberation from Egypt. This is also clearly to be seen in the initial verses of the Decalogue. In both Exodus and Deuteronomy, as quoted above, the act of God to guide His people out of Egypt is stated as the justification why Israelis should only worship Him as God, rather than worshiping several gods, idols, or figures from other creatures. In other books of the Old Testament, too, God's guidance from Egypt appears as an often-recurring theme which has always been connected with the statement that the Israelis should have no other gods besides Him, that they should not be afraid of the other peoples with whom they were to fight and that they should listen to His words. This is connected in particular with the prohibition of idolatry – more precisely formulated, the prohibition of making images of other creatures and offering them, whose interpretation and justification are found in Deuteronomy:

> Take ye therefore good heed unto yourselves; for ye saw no manner of similitude on the day that the LORD spake unto you in Horeb out of the midst of the fire: Lest ye corrupt yourselves, and make you a graven image, the similitude of any figure, the likeness of male or female, The likeness of any beast that is on the earth, the likeness of any winged fowl that flieth in the air, The likeness of any thing that creepeth on the ground, the

---

10 Ex., 19, 4-6.

likeness of any fish that is in the waters beneath the earth: And lest thou lift up thine eyes unto heaven, and when thou seest the sun, and the moon, and the stars, even all the host of heaven, shouldest be driven to worship them, and serve them, which the LORD thy God hath divided unto all nations under the whole heaven. But the LORD hath taken you, and brought you forth out of the iron furnace, even out of Egypt, to be unto him a people of inheritance, as ye are this day. Furthermore, the LORD was angry with me for your sakes, and sware that I should not go over Jordan, and that I should not go in unto that good land, which the LORD thy God giveth thee for an inheritance: But I must die in this land, I must not go over Jordan: but ye shall go over, and possess that good land. Take heed unto yourselves, lest ye forget the covenant of the LORD your God, which he made with you, and make you a graven image, or the likeness of any thing, which the LORD thy God hath forbidden thee.[11]

In addition to the first two commandments, there is also the commandment to commemorate the Sabbath day. It is interesting to note the explanation in the Deuteronomy why the Israelis should observe the Sabbath day: They should remember that "thou wast a servant in the land of Egypt, and that the LORD thy God brought thee out thence through a mighty hand and by a stretched out arm: therefore the LORD thy God commanded thee to keep the sabbath day."[12] God created not only the world and the people, but also liberated his people from oppression and slavery. Thus, the act of salvation was placed in the relation to those commandments by which the Israelite religious-cultic practices should be distinguished from that of the neighbouring peoples. Considering this, we may ask whether Christians could succeed in conveying the Ten Commandments, wrested from the Old Testament textual framework, to the Chinese-speaking public who had no idea about the historical context. The prohibition of making images of created things and offering them is not only a main theme of the Ten Commandments, but this is mentioned again and again throughout the Old Testament and its significance is repeatedly underlined by the prophets. In Isaiah 44: 13-17, for example, we can find the following description:

The carpenter stretcheth out his rule; he marketh it out with a line; he fitteth it with planes, and he marketh it out with the compass, and maketh it after the figure of a man, according to the beauty of a man; that it may

---

11   Deut., 4, 15-23.
12   Deut., 5, 15.

remain in the house. He heweth him down cedars, and taketh the cypress and the oak, which he strengtheneth for himself among the trees of the forest: he planteth an ash, and the rain doth nourish it. Then shall it be for a man to burn: for he will take thereof, and warm himself; yea, he kindleth it, and baketh bread; yea, he maketh a god, and worshippeth it; he maketh it a graven image, and falleth down thereto. He burneth part thereof in the fire; with part thereof he eateth flesh; he roasteth roast, and is satisfied: yea, he warmeth himself, and saith, Aha, I am warm, I have seen the fire: And the residue thereof he maketh a god, even his graven image: he falleth down unto it, and worshippeth it, and prayeth unto it, and saith, Deliver me; for thou art my god.[13]

Also in Psalm 115, 2-8 we can find a call not to make images:

> Wherefore should the heathen say, Where is now their God? But our God is in the heavens: he hath done whatsoever he hath pleased. Their idols are silver and gold, the work of men's hands. They have mouths, but they speak not: eyes have they, but they see not: They have ears, but they hear not: noses have they, but they smell not: They have hands, but they handle not: feet have they, but they walk not: neither speak they through their throat. They that make them are like unto them; so is every one that trusteth in them.[14]

In the "Book of Jesus" there is a similar description that explains why people should not have an image or why they should not worship images of creatures:

> The heavenly Lord worked laboriously to create all beings. All beings were not far from the knowledge of Fo. They made human figures to be devoted to (worship). The good have good luck, the evil have evil cause. Ignorant beings used clay and wood to made camels, cows and horses, many creatures, river deer and deer. They made these figures with faces, but they could not give them life.[15]

Furthermore, man should consider that:

---

13   Isaiah 44: 13-17.
14   Psalm 115, 2-8.
15   Book of Jesus, C. 41-44: 天尊受許辛苦，始立眾生。眾生理佛不遠，立人身自專，善有善福，惡有惡緣。無知眾生遂泥木馳象牛驢馬等眾生及麋鹿；雖造形容，不能与命。English translation see Tang, "Nestorian Christianity in China and its literature," 148.

> Then human beings were confused. They started to make gold images, silver god-like figures and bronze statues. They also made images out of clay and wood. What is more, they made many domestic animal statues. The persons they made look like human beings; the horses made look like horses; the cows made look like cows; and the donkeys made look like donkeys, but they cannot move, nor can they talk, or eat. They have no breath and flesh; no skin, no organs, and no bones.[16]

An extremely similar, if not literally consistent, description is to be found in Deuteronomy 4, 28: "And there ye shall serve gods, the work of men's hands, wood and stone, which neither see, nor hear, nor eat, nor smell."[17]

In contrast to the Old Testament tradition, in which the collective experiences with God form the basis of faith, the above-mentioned historical context cannot be found in the two Alopen documents. Instead, in the Book of Jesus, the first vow "to fear and serve the lord in heaven", immediately follows the paragraph about the prohibition of idolatry. Thus, the two first commandments are interchanged in their textual positions, whilst the latter is not explicitly treated as part of the divine laws, but as a separate theme. Without reference to the history of Israel the prohibition of worshiping images is justified as following: "The heavenly Lord worked laboriously to create all beings." The Creation is therefore unique and is reserved for God only, since He can make the created alive; when human beings build statues or idols, they could look so real, but they could never get the real life. Because of this, people should obey the Venerable in Heaven (tianzun 天尊). In this passage it is explained *en détail* that the life-giving creation, which must have meant a laborious work even for God, was regarded as the sole cause for the prohibition of idolatry. This indirectly pointed to the commandment of the worship of a single God, but is not explicitly formulated in the "Book of Jesus".

That all creatures should fear the venerable in heaven, follow his laws, and serve him with reverence, is not explicitly defined as the first one in the catalogue of the Ten Vows, while the others are listed with a clear numbering and an imperative expression. In the absence of the self-presentation of God who stated that he was the God of Abraham, the God of Isaac, and the God of Jacob, in short, that he was God of the patriarchs of Israel, the Venerable in Heaven is presented exclusively as the Creator in the Book of Jesus. Thus, the corresponding (first) vow is described as following:

---

16   Ibid, C. 47-51: 眾生自被誑惑，乃將金造像，銀神像及銅像，并泥神像及木神像；更作眾眾諸畜產。造人似人，造馬似馬，造牛似牛，造驢似驢，維不能行動，亦不語話，亦不喫食息，無肉無皮，無器無骨。 English translation see Tang, "Nestorian Christianity in China and its literature," 148-149.

17   Deut., 4, 28.

However, the one who serves the heavenly Lord explains fully the doctrines of Heaven. Some people, due to fear for the law of the heavenly Lord, exercise a heart of kindness, do good and persuade others to do good. Such a person has received the teaching of the heavenly Lord and obeyed His law. One who always does evil things and teaches others to do evil is the one who has not received the teaching of the heavenly Lord. He falls into the evil way immediately. His life belongs to the Yanluowang. There are others who obey the teachings of the heavenly Lord. They always say: I obey the law and teach others to do the same. All human beings have fear for the heavenly Lord. Every day, one should correct one's fault. All beings have fear of the heavenly Lord who controls the life and death of all beings, guides and controls stupid gods.[18]

To sum up: As a result of the above discussion, we can draw a preliminary conclusion that in "Book of Jesus", the special position of the Jingjiao God is revealed by the repeated exhortation of the unique, life-giving and universal creation. Such narrative differs in its content from the Old Testament doctrine according to which not only the creation, but above all the direct intervention of God in the history of Israel was decisive for the establishment of the monotheistic tradition. The result, however, remains the same despite this different argumentation: People are bound to worship and offer the one Creator God, while idolatry is forbidden.

Last of all: In contrary to the first three vows which attract the attention of historians and theologians due to their peculiarity resulting from the particular cultural environment, the other seven commandments, especially those concerning the social order, are usually generally perceived as a general ethical prescription which should be regarded as natural law independent from the special cultural and regional background. In such a generalized view, the concordance between the biblical texts and the translation versions in Chinese or other languages is usually emphasized, while some minor changes in concrete expression which are relevant to the interpretation of cultural adaptation are neglected.

---

18   Book of Jesus, C. 55-61: 但事天尊人，及說天義，有人怕天尊法，自行善心及自作好，并諫人好，此人即是受天尊教，受天尊戒。人常作惡，及教他人惡，此人不受天尊教，突墮惡道，命屬閻羅王。有人受天尊教，常道我受戒，教人受戒，人合怕天尊，每日諫愄。一切眾生皆各怕天尊，并灣摄諸眾生死活，管带綰摄渾神。English translation see Tang, "Nestorian Christianity in China and its literature," 149.

PART 6

A Review and Academic Report

∴

CHAPTER 11

Review of the Studies on the Research History of Authenticity of *The Discourse on Monotheism* and *The Jesus Messiah Sutra* in Kyou-shooku

Lanping Wang and Qiaosui Zhang

The Discourse on Monotheism (*Yishen lun* 一神论) (Yu 羽 460) collected by Tomioka Kenzô (福冈谦藏) in 1916, and *The Jesus Messiah Sutra* (*Xuting mishi suojing* 序听迷诗所经) (Yu 羽 459) collected by Takakusu Junjirô (高楠顺次郎) in 1922 or 1923, have for a long time thought to have been authentic Dunhuang manuscripts, ever since their release. They have also been used as the original historical materials of early Christianity in China for the research on *Jingjiao* (景教) in the Tang Dynasty.[1] In 1951, Peter Yoshiro Saeki(佐伯好郎) wrote,

As far as we know, no scholars at home or abroad have ever expressed their opinions against the genuineness of these documents, whilst those who made a special study on the subject are all convinced of the genuineness of these Nestorian manuscripts from both external and internal evidences.[2]

However, in recent decades, the authenticity of the above-mentioned manuscripts has been questioned by Lin Wushu (林悟殊) and Rong Xinjiang (荣新江), who are academic authorities in Dunhuang studies and *Jingjiao* (景教) studies. According to Lin, the first one to question the authenticity of the

---

1 The first complete photocopies of *The Discourse on Monotheism* and *The Jesus Messiah Sutra* were published in 1931. Cf. Toru Haneda 羽田亨 ed., *On the One-God Part III* 一神论卷第三, *Sutra of Jesus, the Messiah* 序听迷诗所经一卷 (Kyoto: The Academy of Oriental Culture Kyoto Institute, 1931). The complete color photocopies of the manuscripts were published in Japan in 2012. Cf. Kyou-shooku 杏雨书屋 ed., *Dunhuang miji* 敦煌秘笈 [*The Secret Dunhuang Documents (Vol.VI)*] (Osaka: Takeda Science Foundation, 2012), 84-87, 89-96. For more information on the two photocopies, transcriptions and research history, one may refer to Lin Wushu, *Tangdai Jingjiao zai yanjiu* 唐代景教再研究 [*New Reflections on Jingjiao of the Tang Dynasty*] (Beijing: Zhongguo shehui kexue chubanshe, 2003), 186-193, 208-216. The photocopies of these two manuscripts are also clearly released on pages 387-402, 350-386 in Lin's appendix, with line numbers assigned for easy reference. The line numbers referred in this article are same as those in Lin's book. Also Cf. Wang Lanping 王兰平, *Tangdai Dunhuang hanwen Jingjiao xiejing yanjiu* 唐代敦煌汉文景教写经研究 [*Study on Dunhuang Jingjiao Manuscripts of the Tang Dynasty*] (Beijing: Minzu chubanshe, 2016), 301-321.

2 Peter Yoshiro Saeki, *The Nestorian Documents and Relics in China* (Tokyo: The Academy of Oriental Culture Tokyo Institute, 1951), 114.

above-mentioned manuscripts is Wu Qiyu (吴其昱). Back in the early 1990s, Wu told Lin that *The Jesus Messiah Sutra* and *The Discourse on Monotheism* (hereinafter referred to as "the two manuscripts") are not authentic Dunhuang manuscripts but it is very difficult to prove.³ In 2000, Lin pointed out that the origin of *The Discourse on Monotheism* was unknown, and there were enormous contrasts between the handwriting and connotation. The handwriting was neat and beautiful while its contents were full of errors and out of order. Therefore, it was not an authentic original Dunhuang manuscript but a forgery made by a modern scribe in the early twentieth century. Lin further conjectured that this manuscript was based on an ancient manuscript. This manuscript could have been the work of the Jesuits between the late Ming Dynasty and early Qing Dynasty, or more likely, this manuscript was *Jingjiao* manuscript, the content of which was similar to *The Discourse on Monotheism* in remaining Dunhuang manuscripts. Then it fell into the hands of some antiquary, however, it was too tattered to be sold at a good price, so a fraud master was asked to re-write and re-make it and it became a refined hand-copied forgery.⁴

A year later, Lin also pointed out that the origin of *The Jesus Messiah Sutra* was unknown, and there was a big contrast between the handwriting and the connotation of this manuscript. Compared to *The Discourse on Monotheism*, there were more errors in this manuscript. Therefore, Lin questioned that *The Jesus Messiah Sutra* was just like *The Discourse on Monotheism*, a refined hand-copied forgery from the same modern scribe. Lin also held the view that we should take a serious attitude towards the use of those two manuscripts before a reasonable explanation on the doubts could be given by academia.⁵ Whether

3   Lin Wushu, "Fugangqiancangshi cang *Jingjiao yishenlun* zhenwei cunyi 富冈谦藏氏藏景教《一神论》真伪存疑 [Doubts Concerning the Authenticity of The Discourse on Monotheism from the Tomioka Collection]," *Tang yanjiu* 6 (2000): 72; Lin, *Tangdai Jingjiao zai yanjiu*, 193-194; Lin Wushu, "*Jingjiao* fugang gaonan wenshu bianwei bushuo 景教富冈高楠文书辨伪补说 [Additional Notes on the Authenticity of Tomioka and Takakusu's *Jingjiao* Manuscripts]," *Dunhuang Tulufan yanjiu* 8 (2005): 35; Lin Wushu, *Zhonggu sanyijiao bianzheng* 中古三夷教辨证 [*Debate and Research on the Three Persian Religions: Manichaeism, Jingjiao and Zoroastrianism in Mediaeval Times*] (Beijing: Zhonghua shuju, 2005), 215; Lin Wushu, *Lin Wushu Dunhuang wenshu yu yijiao yanjiu* 林悟殊敦煌文书与夷教研究 [*Study on Dunhuang Manuscripts and the Three Persian Religions*] (Shanghai: Shanghai guji chubanshe, 2011), 369.

4   Lin, "Fugangqiancangshi cang *Jingjiao yishenlun* zhenwei cunyi," 67-86; Lin, *Tangdai Jingjiao zai yanjiu*, 186-207; Lin, *Lin Wushu Dunhuang wenshu yu yijiao yanjiu*, 324-346; Lin Wushu, "Dunhuang hanwen *Jingjiao* xieben yanjiu shuping 敦煌汉文景教写本研究述评 [Review on the research of Dunhuang *Jingjiao* manuscripts], " *Ouya xuekan* 3 (2002): 266-269; Lin, *Zhonggu sanyijiao bianzheng*, 183-188.

5   Lin Wushu, "Gaonanshi cang *Jingjiao xutingmishisuojing* zhenwei cunyi 高楠氏藏景教《序听迷诗所经》真伪存疑 [Doubts Concerning the Authenticity of The Jesus Messiah Sutra from the Takakusu Collection]," *Wenshi* 55 (2001): 141-154; Lin, *Tangdai Jingjiao zai yanjiu*,

for the study of *Jingjiao* in the Tang Dynasty or for Dunhuang Studies, the above-mentioned statements of Lin are ground-breaking. Although Rong xinjiang did not make a clear statement about Lin's opinion, he also began to question the two manuscripts and believed that further investigation on different aspects should be conducted.[6]

In 2005, Lin slightly revised his original opinion on the two manuscripts after a more comprehensive investigation, stating that they were refined hand-copied forgeries. He believed that the two manuscripts were forgeries made on the basis of scrabbling up the Chinese version of theological works of Jesuits in the Ming and Qing Dynasties.[7] After the above-mentioned articles of Lin were published, Zhao Heping (赵和平) and Matteo Nicolini-Zani also briefly responded that further research on the authenticity of the two manuscripts needed to be done, particularly on the original manuscripts. However, they did not scrutinize the doubts in the manuscripts put forward by Lin.[8] In 2005, Zeng Yanqing (曾阳晴) in Taiwan held an ambiguous view on the above-mentioned viewpoints of Lin. On one hand, Zeng believed that Lin's hypothesis seemed impossible, on the other hand, he also agreed that *The Jesus Messiah Sutra* might be a re-written forgery.[9]

In 2006, the author of this article analyzed Lin's above-mentioned viewpoints in his doctoral dissertation and drew the conclusion that the contents of the two manuscripts were genuine. Although the argumentation was not sophisticated enough, it was the first time a different opinion was raised among

---

208-228; Lin, *Lin Wushu Dunhuang wenshu yu yijiao yanjiu*, 347-368; Lin, "Dunhuang hanwen *Jingjiao* xieben yanjiu shuping," 269-277; Lin, *Zhonggu sanyijiao bianzheng*, 188-201.

6 Rong Xinjiang 荣新江, *Dunhuangxue shiba jiang* 敦煌学十八讲 [*Eighteen Lectures on Dunhuangology*] (Beijing: Beijing daxue chubanshe, 2001), 244.

7 Lin, "*Jingjiao* fugang gaonan wenshu bianwei bushuo," 35-43; Lin, *Zhonggu sanyijiao bianzheng*, 215-226; Lin, *Lin Wushu Dunhuang wenshu yu yijiao yanjiu*, 369-380; Lin Wushu, "Additional Notes on the Authenticity of Tomioka's and Takakusu's Manuscripts," in *Jingjiao: The Church of the East in China and Central Asia*, ed. Roman Malek & Peter Hofrichter (Nettetal: Steyler Verlag, 2006), 133-142; Lin Wushu, "汉文マニ教经典と汉文景教经典の巨视的比较 A Comparison of Chinese Buddhist Classics and *Jingjiao* Classics," in *Zhongguo zongjiao wenxian yanjiu* 中国宗教文献研究 [*Study of Chinese Religious Literature*], ed. Institute for Human Sciences of Kyoto University (Kyoto: Linchuan shudian, 2007), 377-409. Until 2014, the treatises of Lin proposed the two manuscripts are forgries, Cf. Lin Wushu, "*Jingjiao* 'jingfen' kao 景教 '净风' 考 [Research on Pure Wind of *Jingjiao*]," *Xiyu yanjiu* 3 (2014): 60.

8 Matteo Nicolini-Zani, "Past and Current Research on Tang *Jingjiao* Documents: A Survey," in *Jingjiao: The Church of the East in China and Central Asia*, 29; Zhao Heping 赵和平, "Lin Wushu *Tangdai Jingjiao zai yanjiu* 林悟殊《唐代景教再研究》 [Review of *New Reflections on Jingjiao of the Tang Dynasty by Lin Wushu*]," *Dunhuang Tulufan yanjiu* 8 (2005): 381.

9 Zeng Yangqing 曾阳晴, *Tangchao hanyu Jingjiao wenxian yanjiu* 唐朝汉语景教文献研究 [*Study on the Chinese Jingjiao Literature in the Tang Dynasty*] (Taibei: Huamulan wenhua gongzuofang, 2005), 202-205.

academia.[10] Since 2010, Wu Changxing (吴昶兴) in Taiwan has published several articles, in which he reanalyzed the meaning of the title of *The Jesus Messiah Sutra*. Wu thought that it unconvincing that Lin considered *The Jesus Messiah Sutra* a forgery simply based on the so-called errors of hierarch's name in this scripture. In particular, through the analysis of the contents of *The Jesus Messiah Sutra*, Wu believed that this scripture was not "worthless" as Lin said. And he has always used the two manuscripts as authentic texts for the study of *Jingjiao* in the Tang Dynasty.[11]

In 2011, Xiang Bingguang (项秉光) tried to explain the contradiction between the beautiful handwriting and the errors in the two manuscripts put forward by Lin, from the perspective of preachment writing and also through the investigation on the internal evidence and wording in the two manuscripts.[12] Since 2013, Zhang Xuesong (张雪松) indicated that although there is a possibility the two manuscripts could be refined hand-copied forgeries as Lin said, it is still too early to conclude based on current evidence.[13] In 2013, Huang

---

10 Wang Lanping, *Tangdai Dunhuang hanwen Jingjiao xiejing yanjiu* 唐代敦煌汉文景教写经研究 [*Study on Dunhuang Jingjiao Manuscripts of the Tang Dynasty*], Doctoral Dissertation of Lanzhou University, 2006.

11 Wu Changxing 吴昶兴, "Lun *Jingjiao xutingmishisuojing* zhong zhi shangdi, jidu yu jiushi sixiang 论景教《序听迷诗所经》中之上帝、基督与救世思想 [The Thought of God, Christ and the Salvation of *The Jesus Messiah Sutra*]," *Jidujiao Taiwan jinhui shenxueyuan jinshen xuekan* (2010), 3-46; Wu Changxing, "*Jingjiao xutingmishisuojing* jingming wenti zaiyi 景教《序听迷诗所经》经名问题再议 [Re-discussion About the Title of *The Jesus Messiah Sutra*]," *Zhongtai shenxue lunji* 1(2010): 230-242; Wu Changxing, *Zhen chang zhi dao: Tangdai Jidujiao lishi yu wenxian yanjiu* 真常之道：唐代基督教历史与文献研究 [*The True and Eternal Way: Bibliographic Research of Assyrian Church of the East in Tang Dynasty*] (Xinbei: Taiwan *Jidujiao* wenyi chubanshe, 2015), 169-210; Wu Changxing ed., *Daqin Jingjiao liuxing zhongguo bei: daqin Jingjiao wenxian shiyi* 大秦景教流行中国碑：大秦景教文献释义 [*Study on the Jingjiao Monument in Xi'an and other Literature*] (Xinbei: Ganlan chuban youxian gongsi, 2015), 49-128.

12 Xiang Bingguang 项秉光, *Sanzhong Jingjiao Dunhuang xiejuan kaoshi* 三种景教敦煌写卷考释 [*Textual Research on Three Kinds of Dunhuang Jingjiao Manuscript*], Master Dissertation of Shanghai Normal University, 2011, 11-33.

13 Zhang Xuesong 张雪松, "Shilun Lishengduo jiucang Dunhuang xieben zhong de *Jingjiao* wenxian – jiantan Dunhuang Tangdai hanwen *Jingjiao* wenxian de zhenwei wenti 试论李盛铎旧藏敦煌写本中的景教文献 —— 兼谈敦煌唐代汉文景教文献的真伪问题 [Comment on *Jingjiao* Manuscripts from Li Shengduo's Collection and Disscussion about the Authenticity of *Jingjiao* Manuscripts from Dunhuang]," *Hanyu wenxian yu zhongguo Jidujiao yanjiu guoji xueshu yantaohui* 汉语文献与中国基督教研究国际学术研讨会 [International Symposium on Chinese Literature and Christian Research], Shanghai: Shanghai University, 2013; Zhang Xuesong, "Chuyi xiancun Dunhuang Tangdai *Jingjiao* wenxian de zhenwei wenti 刍议现存敦煌唐代景教文献的真伪问题 [Comment on the Authenticity of *Jingjiao* Manuscripts of the Tang Dynasty from Dunhuang]," *Shangrao shifan xueyuan xuebao* 1 (2016): 48, 51-52.

Changyuan also pointed out that more evidence is needed to support the "refined hand-copied forgeries" hypothesis and he himself still uses the two manuscripts as authentic ones for research.¹⁴

In 2014, Rong xinjiang, who had been studying this issue for over ten years, was perhaps inspired by the transliteration of "Messiah" into "Mi shihe (弥施河/弥师诃)" in the Dunhuang manuscripts *Sutra of Laozi converting the Tartars* (*Laozi huahu jing* 老子化胡经) and *Records of the Treasure of the Law* (*Dharmaratna*) *in successive ages* (*Lidai fabao ji* 历代法宝记), he then further demonstrated the so-called doubts on the basis of Lin's relevant works, and began to explicitly agree with Lin's viewpoint. Rong believed that the two manuscripts were more likely to be copied from Chinese versions of Christian literature from the Ming and Qing Dynasties. However, the transcriber might not have been familiar with Christian religious doctrines, and in order not to give himself away, he invented words to replace corresponding proper nouns. Rong believed that the existing doubts are solid enough to question the authenticity of the two manuscripts, therefore, they should not be used as *Jingjiao* texts in the Tang Dynasty until those doubts are satisfactorily explained. Rong also criticized those scholars who still regarded the two manuscripts as authentic ones and used them for research, saying "as for the attitude toward Lin's above-mentioned viewpoints, some *Jingjiao* researchers are hesitant, some are unwilling to accept, and others ignore". Rong stated that the two manuscripts should be excluded from the authentic Dunhuang manuscripts, he said, "This could be an awful blow to religious historians. However, if a religious history is expected to be convincing and sacred, it must be based on real historical materials. Therefore, no matter how painful it is to accept, the history of *Jingjiao* in the Tang Dynasty needs 'retrogressing' and rewriting".¹⁵

In 2015, the author of this article analyzed the evidence that Lin had used for the "refined hand-copied forgery" hypothesis and believed this evidence was not solid enough to draw that conclusion, because the evidence of different writings for the same character in *The Discourse on Monotheism* also exists in other recognized authentic Dunhuang manuscripts. Therefore, the author be-

---

14 Huang Changyuan 黄昌渊, *Zhongguo gudai Jidujiao yanjiu – yi 7 zhi 14 shiji Jingjiao wei zhongxin* 中国古代基督教研究 —— 以 7 至 14 世纪景教为中心 [*The Study of Christianity in Ancient China Centering in Jingjiao from 7th to 14th Century*], Doctoral Dissertation of Shaanxi Normal University, 2013, 36, 38.

15 Rong Xinjiang, "Dunhuang *Jingjiao* wenxian xieben de zhen yu wei 敦煌景教文献写本的真与伪 [Research on the Authenticity of *Jingjiao* Manuscripts from Dunhuang]," in *Sanyijiao yanjiu – Lin Wushu xiansheng guxi jinian lunwenji* 三夷教研究 —— 林悟殊先生古稀纪念论文集 [*Research on the Three Persian Religions: Memorable Essays of Lin Wushu 70th Anniversary*], ed. Zhang Xiaogui 张小贵 (Lanzhou: Lanzhou daxue chubanshe, 2014), 280-289.

lieved that the doubts raised by Lin are inexistent.¹⁶ In 2016, the author continued to analyze the authenticity of the two manuscripts from the perspective of character pattern and drew the conclusion that the two manuscripts did not show any traces of forgery.¹⁷

In Lin's three articles and Rong's one article mentioned above, the main viewpoint is that the two manuscripts may be refined hand-copied forgeries based on ancient Dunhuang manuscripts, but more likely, they were transcripts made on the basis of the Chinese version of theological works of Jesuits in the Ming and Qing Dynasties. Anyway, they are absolutely not authentic manuscripts, but forgeries made by a modern scribe. Both Lin and Rong are scholars who have global influence in this field. Their viewpoints are worthy of academic attention. However, we should also point out that except for Wu Qiyu, Lin and Rong, many other scholars including the author still tend to regard the two manuscripts as authentic. In fact, no final conclusion has yet been drawn.

Compared to the existing and recognized *Jingjiao* manuscripts in the Tang Dynasty, *The Discourse on Monotheism* and *The Jesus Messiah Sutra* are the longest. Over the past one hundred years, they have also been used as authentic manuscripts by scholars. The importance of their authenticity is as Lin said, "if the manuscripts were not written in the Tang Dynasty, but were forged by some modern people, then the various statements made in the area of Ancient Christianity in China in the past century or so based on the two manuscripts have to be reconsidered".¹⁸ Considering the importance of this issue, the identification of the authenticity of the two manuscripts is particularly urgent and also needs to be approached with caution, because it relates to another major issue that whether or not the two manuscripts can still be used as the original historical materials of *Jingjiao* in the Tang Dynasty. As previously mentioned, although the authenticity of the two manuscripts has been strongly questioned, further debate is still necessary. The author of this article has been con-

---

16 Wang Lanping, "A Textual Analysis of Chinese Characters with their Variants in two Dunhuang *Jingjiao* Manuscripts," *Ching Feng* 1-2 (2015): 23-31. In 2016, Zhang Xuesong also pointed out that it is not uncommon to find that the same Chinese character written in differernt forms in Dunhuang manuscripts, referring to Zhang, "Chuyi xiancun Dunhuang Tangdai *Jingjiao* wenxian de zhenwei wenti," 51.

17 Wang Lanping, "Riben xingyu shuwu cang fugang wenshu gaonan wenshu zhenwei zai yanjiu 日本杏雨书屋藏富冈文书高楠文书真伪再研究 [Re-criticism on the Authenticity of Two Manuscripts from Takakusu and Tomeoka's Collections Possessed by Kyoushooku in Japan]," *Dunhuangxue jikan* 1 (2016): 10-33; Wang, *Tangdai Dunhuang hanwen Jingjiao xiejing yanjiu*, 98-121.

18 Lin, "*Jingjiao* fugang gaonan wenshu bianwei bushuo," 36; Lin, *Zhonggu sanyijiao bianzheng*, 217; Lin, *Lin Wushu Dunhuang wenshu yu yijiao yanjiu*, 371.

cerned about this issue since 2006, and proposed a viewpoint different from Lin and Rong, which was not to attract attention by being novel but to follow Lin and Rong's rigorous attitude toward research. The author hoped that his humble opinion could be used as a "minnow" to catch a "whale" and he also believed that the truth would become clearer through further discussion.

Despite the fact that the origin of the two manuscripts is not yet known, Wu Changxing and the author have made a detailed explanation of other doubts proposed by Lin and Rong.[19] Whether or not the relevant analysis was objective or reasonable, the author believed that readers had their own judgement. Lin's conjecture that the two manuscripts were refined forgeries hand-copied by a modern scribe based on ancient Dunhuang manuscripts, might not be possible. It is also unlikely that they were transcripts made on the basis of the Chinese version of theological works of Jesuits in the Ming and Qing Dynasties. In fact, Lin also pointed out in his above-mentioned articles that, in terms of contents and ways of expression, it is hard to believe the two manuscripts were fabricated by any modern scribe. Lin took *The Discourse on Monotheism*, lines 249-279 as an example, stating that using the word "hanging high (悬高)" to convey the meaning of crucifixion was obviously something learnt from the early missionaries in China. That makes it difficult for modern scribes to forge this from imagination.[20] The two manuscripts contain many examples of expressions similar to those in ancient texts, though not to repeat them here. The two long and magnificent manuscripts include much Christian religious knowledge, especially in transliterations and the Pingque (平阙) format,[21] which cannot be accomplished by modern random work. More importantly, if we treat the two manuscripts as modern counterfeits, how do we explain that no modern character pattern is found in all of ten thousand words? Even if the forger imitated verbatim according to the ancient version, it is still hard to imagine that modern counterfeits of original Dunhuang manuscripts had reached such a high level. Moreover, Zhang Yongquan (张涌泉)'s analysis of suspicious character patterns in original Dunhuang manuscripts has clearly

---

19   Wang, *Tangdai Dunhuang hanwen Jingjiao xiejing yanjiu*, 57-123; Wang Lanping, *Lishi wenxian yanjiu conggao (jiaji)* 历史文献研究丛稿（甲集）[*Study Series of Historical Documents (Vol. 1)*] (Shanghai: Fudan daxue chubanshe, 2017), 1-103; Wu, "Lun *Jingjiao xutingmishisuojing* zhong zhi shangdi, jidu yu jiushi sixiang," 3-46; Wu, "*Jingjiao xutingmishisuojing* jingming wenti zaiyi," 230-242; Wu, *Zhen chang zhi dao: Tangdai Jidujiao lishi yu wenxian yanjiu*, 169-210.

20   Lin, "Fugangqiancangshi cang *Jingjiao yishenlun* zhenwei cunyi," 73-74; Lin, *New Reflections on Jingjiao of the Tang Dynasty*, 195-196; Lin, *Lin Wushu Dunhuang wenshu yu yijiao yanjiu*, 331-332.

21   Pingque (平阙) format is something that people will write in a new line or leave a space when they meet some special words in writing.

demonstrated that this is nearly impossible.[22] In recent years, Wu Changxing's comments on the authenticity of *The Jesus Messiah Sutra* are quite reasonable. They are cited here as a conclusion. Wu said, "Lin believed that the possibility of *The Jesus Messiah Sutra* being authentic is extremely low because of the contradiction between the exterior and contents of the manuscript, and it should be a 'refined hand-copied forgery', which may be re-written according to a certain ancient Chinese *Jingjiao* manuscript. If looking at the handwriting of *The Jesus Messiah Sutra*, Lin's statement is quite acceptable. However, if judging by the contents, then it is necessary to carefully consider the research value of using this manuscript to study the spread of *Jingjiao* doctrines in China. Moreover, *The Jesus Messiah Sutra* is a manuscript with over two or three thousand characters in length, forging the whole contents was against economic value. Besides, there is material of Christian theology as well and many traces of Syrian transliterations into Chinese which requires counterfeiters not only to be familiar with the writings of the Tang Dynasty, but also to be familiar with Christian doctrines and Syrian. This counterfeiting technique involved was too difficult to be "a piece of cake" like Lin said.[23] So did *The Discourse on Monotheism*.

---

22 Zhang Yongquan 张涌泉, "Dunhuang juanzi bianwei yanjiu – jiyu zixing fenxi jiaodu de kaocha 敦煌卷子辨伪研究 —— 基于字形分析角度的考察 [Studies on the Authenticity of Dunhuang Manuscripts from the use of both standard and vulgar forms of Chinese Characters]," *Wenshi* 65 (2003): 222-239.

23 Wu, "Lun *Jingjiao xutingmishisuojing* zhong zhi shangdi, jidu yu jiushi sixiang," 12. Wu, *Zhen chang zhi dao: Tangdai Jidujiao lishi yu wenxian yanjiu*, 180.

Index

Allaha   4, 12-18, 77
Alopen   37-49, 71, 74, 75, 79-81, 101, 150
anthropology   XX, 87
Augustine   VIII-IX, 63
authenticity   4, 6, 8, 9, 84, 87, 88, 155-162

Barth, Karl   XX
Bible   4, 5, 12-18, 24-29, 40, 80, 99, 108, 117, 144, 146
body   XII, XIII, 6, 9-11, 15, 29, 33, 61, 75, 105, 118
Buddhism   17, 25, 27, 31, 33, 66, 76, 77, 82, 86, 88-91, 110, 111, 137, 142

Chanting   22-34
Chen Yuan 陈垣   87, 125, 128, 129, 131, 134, 138
Christianity   XVII, 3, 4, 7-9, 20-24, 26, 27, 30, 31, 33, 38-41, 43, 49, 60, 66, 71, 72, 74-81, 82-93, 99-102, 104, 108, 110, 111, 125, 127, 137, 139, 141, 146, 149, 151, 155, 159, 160
Christians   X, XII, XV, 9, 24-26, 31, 39-43, 52, 66, 71, 74-81, 83-93, 125, 126, 133, 137-142, 143-148
Chrysostom   VIII
church of the East   VII, XVIII, 7-9, 19, 22-24, 26, 27, 34, 38-41, 48, 67, 71, 77-81, 92, 127, 157, 158
Communatio Idiomatum   XIV, XVIII, XIX, XX
Confucianism   132-134, 137, 138, 140-142
Confucius   XXI, 56, 64, 79, 129
Council of Ephesus   XII-XVI, 41
Council of Nicaea   X

Dunhuang   24, 28, 29, 32, 33, 97-101, 103, 105, 109, 111, 146, 155-162

Ethic   14, 15, 50, 53-60, 63, 66, 151

faith   VII, XI, XVI-XIV, XXI, 7, 11, 14, 22-25, 27, 28, 30, 33, 34, 50, 55, 56, 62, 63, 65-67, 74, 90, 127, 135, 139, 141, 147, 150

God   VII-XIX, 1, 4, 5, 7, 9-19, 24, 27, 29, 31, 34, 48, 50-68, 71, 75, 84, 87, 89, 90, 91, 98, 102, 104, 106-108, 110-121, 144-151, 158
Holy Spirit 净风   XVII, 11, 60, 61, 98, 103, 107, 108, 111,

Jesus   VII, IX-XX, 6, 9, 11, 17, 18, 31, 57, 67, 71, 73, 98-112, 143-151, 155-162
Jingjiao 景教   VII, XXI, 3-9, 16, 18, 20, 22, 24, 27-29, 33, 34, 37, 40, 50, 66, 67, 71, 89, 93, 101, 125-127, 133, 139, 143, 151, 155-162
Jingjing 景净   16, 66, 67, 100, 101

Klimkeit, Hans-Joachim   23, 24, 33, 71, 106

life   VIII, IX, XXI, 13, 14, 17, 24, 26-28, 31, 33, 38, 50, 51, 56, 59, 61, 63, 64, 67, 75, 79, 99, 115, 117, 130, 134, 138, 142, 149, 150, 151
Lin Wushu   3, 4, 8, 24, 28, 33, 98, 102, 111, 126, 135, 155-161
liturgy   14, 22-34
love   23, 44, 50-68, 146
Luther   VII-XXI

Manichaeism   27, 33, 79, 97, 101-112, 156
Monotheism (Yishen Lun 一神论)   3-21, 56, 60, 146, 155, 156, 159-162

Nestorianism   XVIII, 39, 42, 48, 66, 76, 77, 80, 86, 88-93, 101, 102, 135
Nestorian Stele   4, 7, 37, 38, 66, 74, 89, 101, 102, 126, 144
Nestorius   VII-VIII, IX-XXI
New Testament   12, 23, 52-59, 63, 108

Old Testament   23, 50, 53-55, 58, 67, 103, 116, 146-151

Psalms   23-27, 52, 83, 149

religion   7, 20, 23, 25, 29-34, 38, 39, 42, 45, 63, 66, 75-79, 90, 101, 102, 113, 119, 125, 147, 157, 159

Saeki, P. Y.   3-7, 20, 83, 86, 87, 89, 125
Shijie (Ten Commandments 十诫)   XIII, 52, 54, 55, 57, 63, 64, 67, 143-151
Shiyuan (Ten Vows 十愿)   143-151
Sims-Williams, Nicholas   24, 26
soul   XIII, 9, 10, 15, 27, 29, 34, 67, 76, 103, 104
spirit   10, 28, 75, 87, 100, 113-121, 139
St. Thomas the Apostle   43, 71-74, 79-81

Tang dynasty   VII, 4, 20, 27, 28, 30, 32, 37-39, 42-49, 66, 71, 74, 76, 78, 89, 90, 100-102, 110-112, 126, 127, 141, 143, 155, 157-162

theology   VII, VIV, XIX, XX, 9, 13, 19, 24, 38, 40, 55, 58, 106, 162
Tianzun 天尊   4, 5, 9-18, 150
Trinity   XII, 37, 60-62, 66, 111
Turfan   22-29, 33, 34, 97, 103, 104, 111

Wu Changxing 吴昶兴   37, 144, 158
Wu Qiyu 吴其昱   156, 160

Yelikewen 也里可温   85, 125-142
Yuan dynasty   77, 80, 82, 87, 88, 91-93, 101, 125-127, 130, 132, 133, 135, 137-142

Printed in the United States
By Bookmasters